A
Strategy
of
Decision

A
Strategy
of
Decision

Policy Evaluation as a Social Process

DAVID BRAYBROOKE
and
CHARLES E. LINDBLOM

THE FREE PRESS
A Division of Macmillan Publishing Co., Inc.
New York

Social science and philosophy meet in this book. One way of explaining the purposes of the meeting is to indicate how it came about.

The stimulus that first led Lindblom to pursue this line of study—in several articles for the professional journals and subsequently in this book—was his difficulty in satisfying a skeptical Swiss economist that our economists and policy analysts have any firm ground on which to build a case for American-style anti-trust legislation. Coming from a country whose policies toward monopoly are strikingly different from ours, the Swiss economist could find no more substantial rationale for American policy than mere agreement—the concurrence of the highly subjective judgments of many economists. He could make the point—and quite conclusively—that, for all the deference shown by American economists to the theory of pure competition, neither that theory, nor any other theory, nor any form of comprehensive analysis so far suggested made a more convincing case for American policy than for Swiss cartel policy.

Responding to this challenge, Lindblom set about looking for some explanation of the prevailing consensus on American public policy that seemed more illuminating than "this is our considered judgment." In doing so, he picked up from his earlier work with R. A. Dahl (in Dahl and Lindblom, *Politics, Economics and Welfare* [New York: Harper, 1953]) the concept, relatively undeveloped there, of incrementalism. It seemed plausible to suggest that what economists, other social scientists, policy analysts, and decision-makers generally do in the face of a complex problem, even when they try to be rational, does not at all approximate rational decision-making as it is conventionally described in the literature of decision-making. The clue to how they normally do achieve defensible analyses of their policy problems seemed to lie in further development of the incremental concept—leading to an account of analytic practices that focus on alternatives differing only incrementally, in a political system that normally offers only that range of alternatives.

Looking further into actual practices in evaluating and deciding on alternative public policies, Lindblom found that they succeed, where conventionally conceived decision-making does not, in taking intelligent account of the costliness—in time, energy, and other resources—of analysis, as well as of the impossibility, for sufficiently complex problems, of bringing analysis to an end. He concluded that in the actual practices of policy analysts and decision-makers one can find an interlocked set of adaptations to these and other difficulties in choice that are not taken into account in conventional theories of choice; and that these adaptations, discussed in this book under the name of "disjointed incrementalism," explain how considered evaluations of policy can be reached when the rationales suggested by conventional theories of choice cannot be provided.

When Lindblom asked Braybrooke to read and comment on an early short manuscript in which some of these adaptations were discussed, Braybrooke found that the discussion had significant implications for certain topics in ethical theory. When Braybrooke in turn showed Lindblom the outlines of some ideas that he was developing in social and political ethics, Lindblom found them directly useful and complementary to his own thinking about policy evaluation and decision-making. He suggested that a joint book might be planned.

Braybrooke had for some time been thinking about the intelligibility of utilitarianism. There are at least three objections to accepting it as intelligible: the want (in spite of Bentham's proposals) of a definite interpersonal calculus; the want of a rule for bringing accounts of consequences to an end; the want of a rule for specifying the reference group for which consequences are to be considered. In his doctoral thesis (Cornell, 1953), Braybrooke had explicated the notion of a felicific census, which, he argued, serves as an effective substitute for Bentham's unrealized project of a felicific calculus. It was offered as a model, closer to practice than any calculus, of how utilitarian considerations are actually brought to bear on disputes about policy.

Since that time, Braybrooke had been exploring the problem of consequences, so far inconclusively. It was at this point that the convergence with Lindblom's thinking seemed most illuminating; certainly the convergence transformed the problem in Braybrooke's eyes. A start was made, in the light of Lindblom's thinking, toward explaining how the census notion functioned in the actual context of policy discussion, in which policy proposals, like policies themselves, are continually being superseded or reshaped.

It was only when collaboration on this book was very far advanced that Braybrooke saw that the problem of reference groups called for treatment parallel to that given the problem of consequences and inspired by the same sort of thinking. Most of his discussion of ethical theory, moreover, was developed especially for the book, once the book was underway. The general approach to ethical theory offered here, however, reflects ideas that Braybrooke had been developing earlier; the treatment of the emotive theory was foreshadowed in several of Braybrooke's previously published writings. Perhaps most significant of all in establishing a common point of departure was the convergence between Lindblom's thinking about adaptations ignored by conventional models for evaluation and Braybrooke's belief that, while political circumstances make it impossible to make straightforward deductive application of moral principles in decision-making, philosophers have not explained how principles are to be applied otherwise.

We decided to collaborate on a book, in which we would combine both approaches and topics. The result is this work, Chapters 2 through 6 of which are primarily Lindblom's, Chapters 7 through 10 primarily Braybrooke's. Each of us has, however, taken responsibility for criticizing and amending the other's chapters, and we have spent many hours jointly working out the relationships between the two sets of chapters. Exploring these relationships has led us into many additional topics, whose relevance we have jointly discovered and jointly investigated. Each of us concedes to the other considerable, though not unlimited, authority over the content of his own chapters; and, in Braybrooke's case, this has led in the end to a wide sweep through the whole field of ethical theory (although many detailed findings have been omitted because of considerations of proportion). No reader can miss the difference between our styles of thought and expression. It is a congenial difference, we add, that was not an obstacle to our collaboration, but rather continually excited efforts to put our thoughts together.

We have collaborated not only with one another, but we have also enlisted the collaboration of many friends, both social scientists and philosophers, who read and criticized earlier drafts: Alan R. Anderson, Brian Barry, Ralph S. Brown, Jr., J. P. Corbett, James W. Fesler, H. L. A. Hart, Robert E. Lane, Omar K. Moore, Arthur Okun, John Rawls, Thomas C. Schelling, Marcus G. Singer, and Aaron Wildavsky. We thank all of them for their attention; in several cases, it was extraordinarily close attention, for which we are particularly thankful.

We also wish to thank Barbara D'Onofrio, Corrine Glass, and Anne Granger, secretaries to the Departments of Philosophy and Economics at Yale University, for skillful typing and mimeographing; and Joseph C. Glass, Carleton Jones, and Peter Gran, student assistants assigned to us by the Yale bursary program, for their help in preparing the manuscript for publication. During part of the time that we were working on the manuscript, Braybrooke was supported by a grant from the Rockefeller Foundation and

Lindblom by the Ford Foundation and the Social Science Research Council. We wish to thank each of these foundations. Our statements and opinions are, of course, our own and not those of the foundations.

D. B.
C. E. L.

New Haven
October, 1962

CONTENTS

PART ONE

CURRENT CONCEPTIONS OF POLICY ANALYSIS AND EVALUATION

CHAPTER 1

RECEIVED IDEALS: DEDUCTIVE SYSTEMS AND WELFARE FUNCTIONS

A curious paradox bedevils social scientists and others involved in the evaluation and choice of policies. They habitually resort to certain practices that enable them to cope with the task of organizing information in ways relevant to making policy decisions. Yet their conceptions of evaluation and decision-making typically imply contempt for these practices. For the most part, this discrepancy goes unnoticed and unexplained. It is reflected, however, in the uneasiness which people, especially social scientists, often display while they are engaged in evaluation.

We hold that there is no ground for being uneasy about the discrepancy, so long as the practices used in evaluation and decision-making are appropriate to the circumstances in which policies have to be chosen. This they commonly are; it is the professed conceptions of evaluation and decision-making that commonly are not. To explore these actual practices and to see how they are adapted to fill gaps left by the inadequacies of professed methods is the task of this book.

Consider the troubled mien with which the economist often leaves a Congressional committee-room, however ably he has testified there. He may have spoken as pertinently and pointedly on behalf of a certain proposal for closing loopholes in the income tax laws as anyone could. Yet he wonders, on leaving, whether he has not, under the pressure of time and circumstance, sacrificed professional ideals. Has he not perhaps swept beyond the bounds of his professional competence to give expert advice? Has he not mixed the empirical and evaluative aspects of the question too freely? Has he failed to give the committee due notice that his criteria for policy are criteria that the committee might repudiate? Has he failed to clarify the hypotheses and qualifications required to make his testimony sound?

The same uneasiness, which we take to be a symptom of the discrepancy between practice and ideal, may be illustrated in sophisticated second thoughts by both the author and the scientific public about (say) a journal article proposing a special curriculum for bright students in the public schools. The argument in the article may be cogent and perceptive. Its author may, by all ordinary, nonprofessional standards of analysis, appear to have gone to the heart of the matter. Yet what if the article is tested against the standards of thoroughness that social science and philosophy have established for evaluation and decision-making? The author has not exhausted all the considerations relevant to choosing a new curriculum. He has not traced all the important consequences of adopting this curriculum in preference to others that might be designed to serve the same ends. He has not, for that matter, fully described what his ends are or worked out a scheme for coordinating them in all the circumstances that may arise. If his argument is convincing, it is convincing without his having gone through the standard operations generally prescribed for rational decision-making.

By no means all the people making intelligent efforts at evaluating social policies are social scientists or, indeed, experts of any kind, nor are all social scientists concerned with giving advice about policies. In this book, however, social scientists will be taken as representative of the whole class of people concerned with evaluating social policies. All such people share the problem of mustering information and applying it in making decisions; none of them can escape the necessity of trying to make sense of evaluation. For social scientists, the problem is a professional burden, since if they do engage in evaluation, it is a matter of professional responsibility to make the most effective possible use of the information at their disposal while still observing the scruples of professional disinterestedness. Moreover, social scientists, by definition, command better-organized knowledge than nonscientists. It is part of their job to understand the scope and application of this knowledge.

The more resourceful, extensive, and self-critical social science is, the more likely it is to engender sound policy advice—indeed, if it is properly weighted, the best advice available. Given some means of discounting and overcoming the professional tendency to give disproportionate weight to one's own specialty and one's own special theories, it is difficult to see how, if the social scientist cannot do a good job of relating information to policy decisions, anyone else can be expected to. Moreover, for all its remaining uncertainties, social science today prepares its initiates to do the work of evaluation and decision-making better than ever before. There is more and better social science on hand. There is also greater use of it.

What has experience taught social scientists and other policy analysts about practices of evaluation and decision-making? How do they actually proceed with the work of evaluating and choosing among policies? Their actual practices as distinct from what they say they do or ought to do—have never been systematically described. Whether or not what they do adds up to a tolerably reasonable set of practices is a question that has been choked off by their preoccupations. Whenever they have reflected on evaluation and decision-making, social scientists—and not social scientists alone—have been preoccupied with certain formal conceptions of these processes, conceptions that have been so much honored and so little criticized that it is difficult to imagine that they are not in fact appropriate ideals. In this book, we want to describe what evaluators and decision-makers actually do in the face of policy problems.

We shall begin, however, by specifying what they believe they do and ought to do. How do they interpret or conceive of their own activities in evaluation, especially as regards their use of value concepts? How do they commonly propose to improve their methods to bring about maximum rationality and the most effective evaluative use of information?

1—Conceptions and Ideals of Evaluative Method

Social scientists, of course, differ in their conceptions of suitable methods of evaluation. We can quickly dismiss some obviously defective ideas.

Naïve conceptions. For example, one primitive approach that might be called "the naïve criteria method" holds that merely announcing a few general values—"security," "employment," and "price stability," perhaps—supplies enough evaluative machinery to propel descriptive knowledge toward definite recommendations. There are perhaps circumstances in which evaluators can get away with this approach—but only when the discussion is very loose or when there is in fact more machinery in play than they have cared to unmask.

Even if the values are expressed as postulates—"Unemployment shall not be allowed to exceed 5 per cent of the labor force," "The cost-of-living index shall not be allowed to rise more than one per cent per annum"—the naïve criteria method is sure to break down in any serious test. Other criteria press for attention. Should they be treated as if they were irrelevant? Unexpected conflicts develop among the criteria postulated. Are these conflicts to be disregarded? The postulates make no provision for conflicts or for other values. They do not even rank the values they express.

Besides being an inadequate method in practice, the naïve criteria method is, of course, defective in conception, for it gives no clue as to the source, history, or relevance of the values postulated. They may, for all the method has to say, be invented on the spot. A satisfactory conception of method would have to do more. It would have to anticipate obvious difficulties involving other values, and conflicting values, and the ways in which both these difficulties are aggravated by differences of opinion. The naïve criteria method may claim the virtues of simplification, but it would be unwise to grant this claim without some show of proof, which the method does not offer, that the sort of simplification it offers is justified.

A common gesture toward improving the naïve criteria method —but one that is itself clearly defective—takes the form of "the naive priorities method." This method takes the difficulty about conflicting values into account. Its defect is that it goes no further than merely ranking all the values considered in order of priority. It may put "freedom" ahead of "economic growth" and "economic growth" ahead of "equality"; or "combatting unemployment" ahead of "combatting inflation" and both of them ahead of "restoring competition."

Declarations of this kind no doubt supply some information about the evaluator's general attitudes—but how much use are they in settling on specific policies? Suppose that the provisions for "freedom" are already very extensive and that there is a question of making a considerable improvement in material welfare at the cost of some apparently minor modifications in these provisions. Does the list of priorities show what should be done in such a case? Is it even clear that the modifications would reduce freedom in all senses? How does one balance some people's freedom in one respect against other people's in another?

Again, suppose that in a specific case a community has to choose between substantially extending "equality" at relatively little cost in other values and extending "freedom" in a relatively minor way, but at a high cost in the same other values. What recommendations are to be inferred from the list of priorities? The answer is any recommendations one likes; the list neither helps nor restricts drawing inferences among them.

Merely announcing that one is putting "freedom" ahead of

"equality" does not explain in what sense it is being "put ahead" or how far. In general, if the list of priorities runs V_1, V_2, V_3, V_4, V_5, V_6, V_7, V_8, etc., the list itself gives no indication of which policy to choose when the choice lies between policies offering different combinations of benefits. For example, the list does not indicate whether or not a policy offering V_1, V_5, V_7 is preferable to a policy offering V_2, V_4, and V_6. It does not even indicate whether or not a policy that offers more V_1 alone is to be preferred to a policy that offers more V_2 alone. If V_1 is assumed to be preferred, absurd consequences follow: Is any amount of V_1, no matter how small, to be preferred to any amount of V_2, no matter how large?

Apart from its insufficiency for dealing with conflicting values, the naïve priorities method is liable to the same objections that were brought against the naïve criteria method. In conception, it ignores questions of source or relevance, and it ignores differences of opinion and the need for justifying the simplifications that it claims to effect. One would expect sophisticated evaluators to abandon it along with the naïve criteria method, unless they could find (alas!) no better method or unless they could obtain a better method by keeping the priorities notion and filling in the gaps in its first formulation. In the latter case, the naïve priorities method itself would be discarded, to be sure, but it might deserve modest honors as a rough approximation of more satisfactory methods.

Along these lines, one might readily think that the defect of the priority list is simply that the values have not been sufficiently clarified. If one made clear exactly in what senses and under what circumstances "freedom" was to be sought and exactly what one meant by "equality," there would be no special problem in understanding what one meant by putting "freedom" ahead of "equality." And so with all the other values listed. No doubt a great deal of work—too much, perhaps, for such a procedure to be more than an ideal—would be required to get all the possible interrelations of these values out into the open; but these interrelations are just the aspects of the concepts involved that would become explicit in the course of defining each of them with ideal precision.

The rational-deductive ideal. These more sophisticated lines of thought, which many social scientists have followed—and philosophers before them—find their fullest expression in what we shall call "the rational-deductive ideal," one of the two ideals of evaluative method to which we propose to give extended attention in this book. Many people, social scientists among them, are inclined to think that the most rational and satisfactory procedure for evaluating policies would be something like that described in the following instructions, assuming that they could be carried out:

Let ultimate values be expressed in general principles satisfactory to everybody who is ready to attend to the arguments identifying them—or, if there is no hope of that, satisfactory at least to those who are now undertaking a specific job of evaluation. Let these principles, which may embody notions of happiness, welfare, justice, or intuitive notions of goodness, be stated so exactly that they may be arranged intelligibly in an order of priority that indicates precisely which principles govern the application of others and when. Then derive within the limits of such a system intermediate principles that are suitable for application in particular cases, and that—allowing for rare cases of equality in net benefits —will indicate unambiguously which of alternative policies is to be chosen, according to the values they would promote.

The intermediate principles of such a system would specify the sort of information that would be decisive for rating any policy above or below its alternatives. If these principles are formulated as hypothetical propositions (which is the most convenient way to formulate them), they take something like the following form:

In conditions C, D, E, etc. (themselves derived from the ultimate principles), if such-and-such are the facts about Policy P and such-and-such are the facts about Policy Q, then P is better than Q.

For example, given that due process is observed and compensation is paid and (perhaps certain other conditions), if Policy P would remove certain dangers to the health and safety of the community caused by an existing use of private property, while Policy Q, although it would improve certain recreational facilities, would leave those dangers (and the existing use of private property) untouched, then P is better than Q. Once we substitute, in this intermediate principle, "compelling the dye-works in the town center to shut down," for "Policy P" and explain that the dangers consist of fumes and excessive traffic, the way is open for us to move directly from these facts to recommending the policy of shutting down the dye-works rather than Policy Q ("spending the money on a new playground").

Ideally, the system would be complete, not necessarily in the sense that it mentioned every contingency but in the sense that its ultimate principles were rich enough to supply the intermediate principles or the sequence of intermediate principles that one would need to decide any case that might come up. With such a system, the uncertainties of evaluation would have been mastered on the values side. For, on the values side, determination of policy becomes simply a matter of calculation, a question of feeding in the observed facts and thinking consistently through a sequence of logical transformations. One discovers the facts, looks up (or derives) the relevant hypotheticals, and deduces by strict logic which policy is to be selected. Nowadays, the work does not even seem impossibly tedious; one imagines that a suitably programed computer could do it.

The rational-deductive ideal, so conceived, represents an ideal of science transferred to the field of values. For on the facts side too, the traditional ideal of science, going back to Plato and Aristotle, is the ideal of a complete deductive system—as a way of organizing knowledge (not, of course, for empirical scientists, as the sole way of obtaining it). If it is fantastic to imagine having such a system for all phenomena, it has not necessarily been thought fantastic to have it for a specific range of phenomena. The triumph that men attributed to Newton was a triumph of this kind —invested with fantasy by Laplace's boast of being able to calculate the positions and velocities of all the particles in the universe at any time if he knew their positions and velocities at any other.

In ethics, all manner of philosophers have subscribed to this ideal, beginning with the man who first conceived it, Plato. Both Aristotle and St. Thomas had reservations about the precision with which what can be known of values determines what is to be done in particular cases. In Aristotle's case, at least, if these reservations are explored, they lead away from the rational-deductive ideal. But it is fair to say that the historical effect of both men's writings has been to promote the view that, insofar as there is genuine knowledge in ethics, it can be elaborated in the form of a deductive system. John Locke also held this ideal; in ethics, furthermore, he was no more of an empiricist than Plato, for he believed that the content of ethics could be established with absolute certainty by *a priori* reasoning. Kant thought that we can discover *a priori* a universally effective method of testing decisively every moral judgment. If it is made an axiom that one ought to do whatever the test of the Categorical Imperative requires, then this universal method furnishes a system containing every judgment that passes the test.

The ethical discussions of most philosophers, from the Middle Ages through modern times, have concentrated on ethics in the narrow sense, which is concerned with the actions that it is our duty to do, the policies that it is our duty to choose.[1] One has to guess from this what they would say of ethics in the larger sense, which involves choices among actions and policies all of which are morally permissible, although they differ in benefits. In the case of one major philosopher—the doggedly fact-minded Bentham—we do not have to guess. Bentham thought that the way to discover moral principles was to consider what could be consistently and effectively recommended to people, taking people as they are. His manifold lexicographical investigations aside, the system that he championed was meant to be fundamentally very simple. At the same time, it was meant to be a complete system, which applied to every choice of policy; it not only went beyond ethics in the "duty" sense, but it subordinated "duty" to the criteria laid down for the larger sphere. The principle of utility, accompanied by the felicific calculus, is offered as a way of determining every conceivable policy question.

The example of Bentham—and, in another way, the example of Kant—shows that the ethical system offered to satisfy the rational-deductive ideal need not be a complicated one. If the right key can be found, the whole plan of the system will open up immediately —or so it may seem before getting down to cases. Whether the complications appear in the basic formulation of the system or only in its applications, however, people who subscribe to the rational-deductive ideal are ready to confront them bravely. In an intrepid statement of the ideal, the sociologist Florian Znaniecki writes,

You cannot isolate . . . arbitrarily one practical cultural problem and its solution from the rest of the human cultural world; you must take into consideration all the other practical cultural problems which are connected with it now and may become connected with it as an actual consequence of your activity—your own problems, those of the individuals and groups whose cooperation you must enlist, and those of the wider society whom you wish to influence through those individuals or groups. Otherwise, divergent, perhaps conflicting, standards of valuation and norms of conduct will continually interfere with the planful realization of your cultural "end." This "end" as a value and the activity pursuing it must be incorporated into an axiological and normative system organizing conceptually all the values and activities which are or will be connected with it in the active experience of all the people who are or will be involved in the realization of your plan.[2]

Znaniecki will not allow anything relevant to be excluded from consideration. He will not spare himself or other evaluators even the difficulties involved in obtaining agreement on the system from all the people who will be affected by its determinations.

The welfare function. Other social scientists—particularly economists—have sought to reduce the complications of the rational-deductive ideal by treating them quantitatively. They have championed the technical notion of a general social welfare function. This method is the second ideal to be considered at length in this book. In one form it was introduced originally under the explicit auspices of the rational-deductive ideal; its acknowledged inventor, Abram Bergson, writes of

a welfare function, W, the value of which is understood to depend on all the variables that might be considered as affecting welfare: the amounts of each and every kind of good consumed by and service performed by each and every household, the amount of each and every kind of capital investment undertaken, and so on. The welfare function is understood initially to be entirely general in character; its shape is determined by the specific *decisions on ends* that are introduced into the analysis. Given the decisions on ends, the welfare function is transformed into a scale of values for the evaluation of alternative uses of resources.[3]

Specific decisions on the ends that are to determine the shape of the function may presumably be identified with the primary decisions that the rational-deductive ideal calls for; they fix the ultimate principles from which every other value judgment necessary for evaluating policies is to be derived. In this view, the innovation represented by the social welfare function consists at most in substituting rules for manipulating numerical variables for the more general techniques of deduction that are envisaged in the rational-deductive ideal.[4]

There is another way of conceiving the social welfare function. It involves so great an innovation that the function is best treated as a substitute for the rational-deductive ideal, rather than as a way of applying it. According to this conception, one need not require that the ends be formulated or specified at any time. If one can get away with it, of course, an enormous simplification will have been brought about and the intricacies of ethical controversy will have been by-passed in one bold move. Instead of formulating ends, which may awaken controversy about which ends to formulate and certainly will make difficulties about how the formulations are to be connected, one expresses direct preferences among various possible states of affairs in society (social states). Such preferences are not deductions from formulated principles but consist instead of reactions to all the features of each state of society that might be subject to preference—whether or not these features are noted separately in the course of forming the total impressions that establish preferences among states.

This conception of the social welfare function can be illustrated from the writings of Kenneth J. Arrow. It differs from Bergson's conception, in its reduced requirements for the information of values. Because Arrow, like Bergson and other writers on welfare economics, is especially interested in the problem of how welfare is distributed among the individuals or households within the society for which the function is to be constructed, he defines a social welfare function as "a process or rule which, for each set of individual [preference] orderings $R_1, \ldots, R_n$ for alternative social states (one ordering for each individual), states a corresponding social ordering of alternative social states, R." [5] This definition, however, can be taken perfectly generally. Any rule for "passing" from individual orderings to a social ordering would satisfy it, even perverse and arbitrary rules that entirely disregard the individual orderings; otherwise Arrow would not need to go on to state axioms excluding such rules. The point that interests us is that no matter how many or how few people play an effective part in the process of arriving at the social ordering, none is required to formulate the principles on which he is acting. Ends may be left unformulated; so may any or all of the features of alternative social states that attract attention—and so, for that matter, may the *raison d'être* of the rule that gives the social ordering of possible states of affairs in society.

In the case of some writers, it is difficult to tell which conception of the welfare function they have in mind. Jan Tinbergen, for example, writes,

Economic policy is directed toward the maximalisation of the ordinary ophelimity functions. In a narrower sense we may restrict the meaning of the term "economic policy" to the behaviour of organised groups, such as trade unions, agricultural or industrial organisations, etc. Here some *collective ophelimity function* will be the object to be maximized. In its most specific and most relevant sense the notion of economic policy will, however, refer to governments. . . . Whereas in the nineteenth century governmental behaviour was perhaps almost restricted to a fiscal activity, since then the development has ever been more into the direction of an attempt at looking after the "*general interest*," in whatever sense that may be taken. We shall indicate this entity by the symbol Ω. It is a function of a certain number of variables which we will call "target variables" and throughout this book indicate by y_k or in vector form by y. A certain numerical value of some y_k will be called "*a target*." These targets will be chosen so as to make $\Omega(y)$ a maximum. Acts meant to attain this maximum may also be referred to as the optimum policy, as far as it makes sense to conceive of other policies as well. [6]

Tinbergen is certainly endorsing the notion of a social welfare function in this passage; but while his use of "ophelimity" (a concept of preferences taken as they are, without restriction by ethical formulas) points to the more radical conception of the welfare function, his use of the phrase "the general interest"—which, like "the public interest," might seem to invite being defined by formulating ultimate principles of value—points to the less radical conception.

Because it is a more distinct alternative to the rational-deductive ideal, we shall, for purposes of discussion, adopt the more radical conception of the social welfare function, which dispenses with the need to formulate the ends to be achieved by proposed policies. The less radical conception, which can be assimilated to the rational-deductive ideal, will be treated incidentally in our discussion of that ideal itself.

There is, of course, a catch in the simplification that the radical conception offers for the value problem. If one is pursuing the question of what is the best and fairest way of distributing welfare among individuals or households, one has to consider that the rule for passing from individual preferences to ranking social states may be ethically objectionable. It certainly cannot be passed without question as ethically neutral; one may legitimately ask, for example, *whose* ends does the rule serve, if anybody's?

Nevertheless, the radical conception of the social welfare function retains many attractions that may be acknowledged without pursuing such questions. If it does not eliminate controversy about values, it does shift the field of controversy from questions about formulating ends to technical questions about adopting procedures, questions that seem relatively unvexed by emotive confusions and that may represent a promising new start toward working agreement on methods of introducing values into evaluation. More important, it suggests a way of achieving a complete ranking of social policies that economizes formulations for both those who express preferences among social states and those who apply the rule for reaching the social ordering. This characteristic, which makes the radical conception of the social welfare function a distinctive method of analysis and evaluation, is the one that especially interests us. The problem of finding a satisfactory rule for passing from individual orderings to a social one, which this method presents to moralists, we shall not take up directly.[7]

It is worth noting that the four conceptions of evaluative method that we have distinguished—the naïve criteria method, the naïve priorities method, the rational-deductive ideal, and the welfare function in its radical version—may be regarded as attempts to define ways of determining "social welfare" or "the public interest." Although we shall probably not have occasion to treat the two expressions again in this book, preferring as we do different language, the book may be regarded as a contribution to the literature on "social welfare" and "public interest."

2—The Undertaking of This Book

Dismissing the naïve criteria and the naïve priorities methods as too primitive to deserve more attention, we undertake to show that both the rational-deductive ideal and the welfare function are not merely incapable of being fully realized (which everyone admits) but are, in most circumstances and most connections, fruitless and unhelpful as ideals. They—and the general approach to problem-solving and decision-making from which they derive— do not take into account the manifold difficulties, which we shall treat at some length, that beset social analysts and evaluators in the real world. They do not offer to those who conscientiously desire to approximate them any clues as to how to cope with these difficulties.

Yet the difficulties are being coped with all along—by practices that the ideals, far from accommodating, lead people to doubt and scorn. These practices are quite different from such developing specialties as operations research, systems analysis, and electronic computation that do not call the ideals into question.[8] We undertake to describe these practices systematically: by observing the practices of social scientists, a number of recurrent features of their procedures in evaluation can be collected. These features do not always appear in combination. When they are combined, the effect given to each differs from evaluator to evaluator and from topic to topic. Nevertheless, we shall treat them as features of a combined social *strategy* of evaluation, and we shall give each feature maximum weight in order to show how much it can contribute to overcoming the difficulties of evaluation that the received ideals of method ignore. Since the features we have collected are to a large extent mutually reinforcing, they have a combined effect in reducing these difficulties.

The account we shall give of this strategy or technique will pass through several stages of complication. We shall begin with an account of the difficulties of evaluation that the rational-deductive ideal and the welfare function fail to meet, and we shall trace this failure to a mistaken application of a certain conception of problem-solving, a general intellectual ideal from which both these special ideals of evaluative method derive. Then, after considering the sort of political climate in which evaluators in our society typically operate, we shall lay out a plain description of the features of a strategy of evaluation that is adapted to coping with the difficulties that must be faced in that climate. The description will be illustrated from contemporary writings in social science. But it will abstract as far as possible from the content of the specific values that people using the strategy may be seeking to promote.

We intend to show that the strategy is an effective way of using information even when the evaluators who use it differ greatly over the values they wish to promote. Indeed, one of our main points about the advantages of the strategy is that it is adapted to situations in which multiple conflicting values are championed by different participants.

This discussion, constituting Parts One and Two of the book, does not require from the reader the least interest (or confidence) in philosophical ethics. If any philosophical questions do arise, they are not questions about what values people ought to promote in choosing policies. Rather, they are questions of logic in a broad sense or of epistemology, questions about effective and ineffective ways of collecting and using information (although we shall not be concerned with technical questions about statistical procedures). Not until the third part of the book does the argument move close to ethical topics; even there, the main lesson, like the main lesson of the first two parts, is descriptive and value-neutral.

We shall move definitely into ethics in the fourth part of the book. However, our argument never logically requires us to abandon neutrality with respect to specific values—although our sympathy with certain familiar values and with the rationales offered for them by writers like Hume will no doubt be clear. We shall show how the strategy can be reconciled with some leading notions of ethics. That does not require endorsing those notions. We shall show that the strategy rehabilitates the intelligibility of utilitarianism and that, joined with the strategy instead of with Bentham's sketch of a calculus, utilitarianism can meet the standard objections to the intelligibility of its procedures. These objections are worth treating because of their general significance for understanding practices of evaluation, regardless of one's opinion of utilitarianism or of ethical systems in general. However, no one who practices the strategy is obliged to subscribe to utilitarianism or to have a theory of ethics of any sort, nor do we insinuate that everyone's practice will betray conformity to one or another such theory.

This book is by no means the first to attack the received ideals of evaluative method and the relevance of the notion of problem-solving on which these ideals depend. Other philosophers and social scientists have shared our suspicions of these ideals. Karl Popper [9] and Gunnar Myrdal [10] have led our contemporaries in recognizing some of the most prominent features of the strategy that we mean to exhibit, and they have discussed the significance of these features in terms to which we for the most part assent. Earlier writers, especially David Hume, perceived the importance of the same points, and the spirit that attends to them is, in broad outlines at least, very much like the spirit that animated John Dewey's notions of evaluation and choice. Since the points of correspondence between Dewey's notions and our own are not points on which we sought to emulate him, they may perhaps be taken as helping to corroborate Dewey's theses with complementary but independent results. Yet can the results be independent, when Dewey has done so much to affect the climate of the social sciences, at least in America? So many of us who have grown up in that climate have come to hold similar views, after reflecting seriously on the difficulties of evaluation and on observable evaluative practices, that we can make at most only incremental claims to saying something new.[11]

CHAPTER 2

A CRITIQUE OF THE CLASSICAL IDEALS

1—Feasibility and Conceivability

Difficulties with the rational-deductive ideal and the social welfare function begin with specific failures to meet identifiable practical problems of policy evaluation. The naïve priorities proposal for handling values, already dismissed in the preceding chapter, cannot be consistently formulated and still remain rich enough to deal with choices that can easily be imagined between conflicting values. The two remaining received ideals can be consistently formulated, but it is a long road from operability in principle, which is all that is guaranteed by their consistency, to operability in practice.

To be sure, the rational-deductive ideal and the welfare function are useful for purposes other than policy analysis. That these two concepts are operational in principle is in itself, of course, evidence that those who use either of them have tested whether one can know what he means when he speaks of a coherent value system—no small accomplishment. Moreover, the two concepts or systems are useful in theoretical work. When restricted to a very small and special world, a world in which all values are marketable goods and services and the distribution of income is fixed, a limited social welfare function, for example, can be constructed by formula in such a way as to be helpful in the process of evaluating alternative hypothetical patterns of resource allocation. In all but the most meticulous uses of these concepts, however, their genuine virtues can be mistaken for their relevance for evaluating alternative public policies.

The fundamental reason why analysts do not employ a rational-deductive system or a welfare function in policy analysis is simply that no one has ever been able actually to construct either. As for rational-deductive systems, the most plausible examples hardly amount to more than preliminary proposals. As for the welfare function, social scientists have been rather quick, when challenged on the point, to concede the actual impossibility (without necessarily, however, recognizing the implications of the admission).*

Some policy analysts, however, are not discouraged. Conceding the impossibility of construction now or ever, they believe one ought nevertheless to continue to aspire to the methods as ideals. That one should regard the two evaluative schemes as ideals raises the question, In what sense do these systems represent worthy aspirations? Analysts typically do not hold the proposed methods

* Because Kenneth Arrow's distinguished contribution to the literature of the social welfare function (*Social Choice and Individual Values,* John Wiley & Sons: New York, 1951) has often been misunderstood, it seems desirable at this point to indicate that the line of discussion on the social welfare function taken here is distant from his. In the first place, we are considering such a function as a practicable guide to policy analysis; he considered it primarily as an analytic aid to theorists. Second, his particular point was not that the construction of any social welfare function was impossible, as some readers have taken it to be, for if that were the case, nothing more need be said here or elsewhere about such a function. Instead, he argued that if one wishes to incorporate into a social welfare function a reconciliation of the diverse or conflicting preferences of different individuals in any group (a significant but quite special problem that we do not single out for particular attention until a later chapter), no welfare function could be constructed that would meet certain plausible criteria. In language closer to his, the aggregation of diverse individual preferences into a preference function for a group is impossible if one specifies certain elementary conditions that, he argued and we concur, most thoughtful people would believe such a function should meet. Third, with many other problems of constructing a welfare function—for example, the

to be worthy aspirations on grounds that within a few generations it will be possible to construct a rational-deductive system or a welfare function. Rather, they aspire to them in the belief that to be closer to achieving their construction is better than being farther away. They assume, first, that part of such a system is better than no part of the same system and, second, that part of such a system is better than any alternative realizable system.

But, as we shall see, much of the attraction of these systems lies in their promise of comprehensiveness; and one can doubt the usefulness of quite incomplete rational-deductive systems or welfare functions.[1] Even more important is the principal thesis of this book —that social analysts have in fact hit upon a mutually reinforcing and defensible set of evaluative practices that, if clearly understood, would raise great doubts in their own minds as to whether the received ideals are worth aspiring to even as ideals.

Thus it is by no means to be taken for granted that the two systems represent useful ideals. Analysts' frustrations in trying to put them into practice and their failure to construct either a rational-deductive system or a welfare function sufficient for policy analysis represent fundamental rather than secondary objections to the systems. The ensuing summary of complexities familiar to people engaged in the evaluative process will throw light on the analyst's difficulties in approximating either of the two ideals in useful ways. What would his problems be if he tried?

2—Multiplicity of Values

As many of us know from our own experience, the mere multiplicity of values relevant to typical public-policy decisions is

---

question of human capacities to undertake such a construction or the possibility of constructing a function on some basis other than the aggregation of individual preferences—he was not concerned except in passing.

Every difficulty in the construction of a welfare function reduces somewhat its appeal as a guide to policy evaluation, but, strictly speaking, the problem Arrow identified is not at all a conclusive objection to the use of a welfare function for either analytical purposes in theory or for policy evaluation. Conversely, solving his problem would not solve those that analysts meet in trying to apply a welfare function to actual policy analysis.

a first stumbling block to constructing a rational-deductive system or a welfare function.

Suppose traffic congestion requires either a greatly improved or a new highway between two cities. As policy objectives go, it is not an especially complicated one to specify, yet even the specification of this simple objective begins to awaken multiple ideas of goal values that must be taken into account by a decision-maker. In a recent case in Connecticut, the appropriate choice of location for a new highway between Hartford and New Haven clearly depended on the type of traffic for which the new facility was to be built; hence deciding upon the type of traffic became an inescapable value problem. Should the highway be built primarily for trucks, for inter-city passenger automobiles, or for commuters? Defend any one class of traffic or combination, and one is driven back onto a bewildering variety of relevant values. Should the highway be for commuters? Is it good for New Haven and Hartford to encourage commutation? What about urban congestion, tax inequalities between central and subsidiary towns, the number of traffic deaths, the amenities of life at the center or the periphery? Why does anyone believe a highway is good in the first place? Because citizens should get what they want? Or because social mobility is a good thing? Or because progress demands it? Or because more transportation is good for business? And so forth.

Even for a detail—whether the highway should run through this or that neighborhood—another large group of side values emerges as relevant: those pertaining, on the one hand, to the preservation of settled neighborhoods, and, on the other hand, to equity in the distribution of losses. Moreover, as all of us sometimes pause to observe, our difficulties are augmented because policy-making is not simply a pursuit of objectives but is rather an expenditure of some values in order to achieve others. Quite aside from the probability that goal values themselves are multiple, costs or input values are also multiple.

Values are multiple, we might point out, not merely because people have many different interests. Multiplicity also results from the manifold ways in which these interests or values may be expressed. There is no way of getting to the end of the list because there are so many ways of formulating any part of its contents. One way of formulating a list of values would be to set up a list of rules, which might take in each case the form, "Any policy with the feature F is prescribed" (or "any policy with the feature G is prohibited"). Even if the rules on the list were reduced to such a standard form, there would still be many possible variations. The themes that might figure in substitutions for F (or G) could vary in important ways even when they belonged under roughly the same heading. Compare, for example, "improving living conditions" with "raising the standard of living" and either one with "promoting prosperity." Again, rules on roughly the same subject might vary greatly in the sorts of qualifications and exceptions they allowed, either by implicit assumption or by explicit mention in the substitutions for F (or G). Liberal Democrats might be willing to subscribe to a rule about encouraging private enterprise; but one suspects that it would be a rule with a different scope, as regards qualifications and exceptions, from the rule that conservative Republicans might propose on the same subject.

In fact, people do not normally formulate rules when they are discussing values. One has to deal instead with multiple sets of themes, none of which may be offered in a rule-like embodiment and all of which are capable of generating a great variety of rules. Instead of offering rules, people express concern—"Surely there must be some way of reducing the opportunity of the bureaucracy to exercise arbitrary power." They launch proposals—"There are reasons for thinking that our foreign policy would be more effectively supported by other nations if we had a consistent long-term plan for economic aid." They display inclinations toward compromise—"If we have to put up with some inflation to restore employment, can't we make sure it creeps?" These are all ways—among innumerable others, varying immensely in form and susceptible of very diverse systems of classification—of introducing conceptions of values into discussion.

In the face of multiplicity of values, many analysts simply stop trying to organize it into a rational-deductive system or welfare function. They feel that they do not have time to try, and many would question whether any human mind has the capacity. Some would go so far as simply to declare that an attempt to organize into a rational-deductive system such specific values as are involved in the highway-location problem would be ridiculous, especially since most attempts to construct such a system remain at the level of moral rules and do not descend to the kind of value affected by highway location. As for the welfare function, the number of possible combinations of input and output values—that is the number of possible social states—that could be expected to result from any decision on highway location staggers the imagination. Short of ranking them, merely to list them runs beyond what many analysts would think it worthwhile to attempt.

3—Instability or Fluidity of Values

These familiar difficulties would plague analysts even if they never changed their minds about values. But, as everyone knows, analysts do change their minds, and they must cope with instability of values in addition to multiplicity. To a degree, the two difficulties are inseparable. One of the reasons why values are unstable is that people shift from one way of formulating them to another. Even if we supposed that people could be brought to agree to definite rules for applying evaluative themes to the ranking of policies, it would be difficult to deduce from among the multiple possibilities precisely which rules would suit their intentions—and their intentions are liable to shift as they compare one formulation with another. Since they normally do not have any intention of being bound by a rule, how much more unstable must be the conceptions and commitments they introduce when they mention themes of value! They do not mean to bind themselves to any one formulation or even to any one theme.

The difficulty of instability goes beyond shifts in formulation, however. It undermines the established convictions that keep those shifts within limits and dominates the regions where such convictions have never been formed. Values change with time and experience. Experience with social security, war, and inflation alters evaluations of them, just as experience with automobiles, mechanical dishwashing, and esoteric music alters evaluations. Evaluations change not simply as a result of experience with the thing valued, as in the above examples, but also as a result of new information and other experience. One's evaluation of unemployment compensation, of a limited term of office for the President of the United States, or of nationalization of industry in Great Britain may alter as a result of new information, an intellectual reorientation deriving from study and reflection, or some subjective political experience that may be proximate to the political phenomena evaluated or quite remote from it.

Changes as complicated as these may occur even if one's concepts, both of things to be valued and of reasons for valuing them, remain the same. In general, however, it is to be expected that changes of taste will reach beyond changes in information and attitude and will involve changes of concept as well. Fluidity of values goes hand in hand with fluidity of language. New things to value and new reasons for valuing them emerge, and old ones drop out. Modern advertising seeks constantly to create new wants and makes a strenuous business of dealing in conceptual novelties, but the process generating them would pervade human life and language anyway, on both the personal and the cultural levels. A boy learns to value the practice of pure mathematics as he acquires the concept of pure mathematics; originally, he neither knew such a subject existed nor any reasons for valuing it. Sea-bathing has a high value in our culture today, and all sorts of policies affecting the sea-coast must heed it. The reasons for valuing it are (as in many other cases) partly intrinsic to the concept. The concept of sea-bathing was from the start the concept of something worth doing, first for medical reasons, later for pleasure. Before the eighteenth century, there was no such concept. People who found themselves in the sea were there either because they had fallen in or because their ship had sunk beneath them.

Language and the stock of concepts do not change only by the addition of new terms, however. The meanings of old terms change behind the façades of continuing locutions. This has notoriously been the case with the term "democracy," for example. People have not simply changed their minds in the last couple of centuries about democracy being on the whole a bad and dangerous thing. In the course of changing their minds, they have transformed the concept so that it now embraces the very constitutional provisions for due process, limited powers, and minority rights that it had formerly so objectionably ignored.

People who were regarded as humane by their contemporaries used to be very nearly indifferent to the physical sufferings of animals, children, and military offenders. Bulls were baited, children were caned, and soldiers and sailors flogged without anyone protesting much. By contrast, the modern concept of humanity embodies scruples about pain, whether suffered by human beings or by animals, that past ages would have despised as squeamish. They might not even have found them intelligible, since the associated change in concepts has been very extensive, affecting, for instance, our whole conception of the animal world—shown by the way in which the terms "beast" and "brute" have fallen into nearly complete disuse as ordinary terms for members of the animal kingdom. Would a Society for the Prevention of Cruelty to Beasts or Brutes have much chance of attracting funds or sympathy?

The difficulty with the received ideals of method, in connection with the pervasive fluidity of values, is not that the ideals do not allow for change of mind. They are in fact compatible with assuming that a deductive system or welfare function will require continuous revision, but they grossly underestimate the dimensions of the revisions involved. And they fail on a practical point: If such a system or function is difficult for the analyst to approximate, even with stable values, how much more difficult it is to keep up with continuous re-evaluation.

If we denote the dependence of evaluations on changing experience as "chronological instability or fluidity," we also need to identify, perhaps by such a term as "projective instability or fluidity," the dependence of evaluations on the concrete circumstances in which choices must actually be made. Quite often we find that we simply do not know what our values are on some points because we have never had to face a concrete choice in which we could ask ourselves the question and test the answer. Our conception of the circumstances in which a hypothetical choice will have to be made tends to vary from moment to moment; so do the values that we call to mind and project into the situation. With what competence can an individual who has never tasted either decide his preference for a hypothetical dinner of guinea pig or armadillo? In connection with the construction of a rational-deductive system or a welfare function, with what competence can an analyst who has experienced neither choose between two alternative hypothetical possibilities or social states such as are posed in some of the stock dilemmas of ethics? Or between alternatives that no one has ever confronted or experienced in history? Would it be better to have equality in material welfare without freedom in styles of life or freedom at the expense of misery for one-third of the population? It is an illusion to suppose that we ever encounter a choice posed in such clear terms. Would it be better to have a social state in which all appetites were satisfied or quiescent or one in which there are challenges and risks and deprivations?

When we hypothesize circumstances for unprecedented choices, we loosen the bonds of tradition and at the same time relinquish the clues of experience. Every time we return to considering such a choice, our attitudes are liable to fall into a different pattern—since so many patterns are possible and since we can only guess what we would do if we really had to make the choice.

4—Conflicts among Values and Combinations of Values

A further difficulty, especially familiar to economists, is that of formulating values in such a way as to take account of the costs of achieving them. Whenever values are in conflict—that is, whenever one has to give up some of one value in order to achieve some of another value—a full statement of a goal value requires that its ranking or position in a deductive system be related to the cost of achieving it. Thus, an analyst says little of worth—even to clarify his own mind—if he declares that he values full employment. He must also specify how much inflation he would be willing to suffer in order to raise the level of employment by some given degree and how much of various other values he would be willing to forgo.

The observable fact is that, given certain choices open to him, the analyst, as a practical man, prefers and will actually choose a high level of employment in some situations and not in others. To develop a set of deductive propositions sufficiently rich and operational to guide the analyst in this highly fluid context would be to accomplish what many analysts believe is well beyond human capacities. Although developing a welfare function that covers the various possibilities is formally a much easier task, since ranking all possible social states indicates all possible responses to various cost situations, the number of different possibilities that must be ranked is staggering.

Evaluation is also complicated by complementary relations among values. As Duncan Black has pointed out, there are no rock-bottom preferences; all expressions of preference presuppose that other values are satisfied to a degree.[2] Values, therefore, have, in the terminology of economics, variable "marginal utility." It has been suggested that the increase in the private purchase of life insurance after the passage of the Social Security Act in the late '30's can be accounted for by, among other factors, the higher value individuals came to place on modest expenditures to contribute to family security after the legislation had put a floor under it. Similarly, modest expenditures for family security had earlier been regarded as wholly inadequate—money down the drain. Only when social security provided a floor did private expenditures seem worthwhile.

Frequently, however, achieving some degree of a specific value diminishes the intensity with which more of it is pursued relative to other values that now become attractive, that is to say, some kinds of policy are marked by diminishing marginal utility. As increasingly high levels of employment are reached or expected, we value each additional percentage rise in employment somewhat less than we did similar percentage increases from lower levels. Or we value a squadron of military aircraft or of missiles at one level if our total makes us barely equal to Soviet military strength and at another level if we have supplied ourselves with a comfortable margin of superiority.

In short, both because values sometimes conflict and because they sometimes complement each other, those actually relevant to policy choices are values of increment or decrement, that is, marginal values—rather than abstractions such as defense, full employment, liberty, or better highways. Hence, in attempting to employ a rational-deductive system, the analyst must find a way to state these marginal values in a set of interlocked propositions. His propositions must not simply indicate when one abstract principle applies rather than another but must accomplish for each value what the economist aspires to do in the case of a commodity—construct a schedule that shows the values to a consumer of increments of the good for each of all possible quantities of the good.[3] It is probably safe to say that the rational-deductive ideal achieved its respected position in ethics without due attention being given to this complication.

In ranking all possible social states for a welfare function, one implicitly achieves marginal evaluation, for in ranking two almost identical social states, the analyst is distinguishing the small area in which they differ and is therefore identifying the increment in some value that accounts for the difference between the two states. Although the accomplishment of marginal evaluations is therefore in principle possible through the welfare function, the specification and subsequent ranking of social states must be endlessly detailed.

The same reasoning that supports the necessity for marginal or incremental evaluation of goal values leads to the conclusion that side values and foregone values or costs also require marginal or incremental evaluation. Hence the complications of evaluation introduced by the necessity for incremental evaluations are widespread, but the classical ideals of method do not indicate how to deal with these complications.

If one aspires (as in the rational-deductive ideal) to the construction of a set of principles sufficient to generate an answer for each specific evaluative problem, then one must recognize either the need for a fantastic number of principles or the possibility that beneath the apparent flux in the choices of individuals and groups —in which values seem to vary according to stages of learning, degrees of ignorance, cost of achievement, and extent of satiation—there lies, in every case, a stable value structure of which the variant forms of expressed preference are merely complex manifestations. In the latter instance, for example, one would assume that a stable attitude toward full employment underlay any particular set of evaluations, made in actual choice situations, that sometimes opted for more employment and sometimes did not. It is perhaps partly because of doubts that such stable systems could be constructed soon enough in the future to be interesting that some analysts have turned to the social welfare function with its much simpler formal requirement that "all possible social states" be ranked. But this escape is not without its costs, and we want to point out two special difficulties that confront the analyst who uses the welfare function.

One difficulty is that the analyst who ranks the possible must know at any one time what lies within the range of the possible. To evaluate, he therefore requires prodigious empirical information. He must know in an objective sense both what states of affairs can be achieved and also what values are represented in each. Such information is not required of those who follow the ideal of rational deduction.

But a social state that is not possible today may become possible tomorrow. In the actual pursuit of policy-making, we uncover new and sometimes less costly means of achieving goals. For example, an important effect of the Keynesian revolution in economics is often said to lie in the demonstration that economic activity can, to an important degree, be stabilized by methods much less drastic and threatening to widely accepted values than had earlier been believed. Thus, in addition to making the revisions in his ranking of social states necessary on grounds already established, the welfare-function analyst must incessantly revise in order to take into account what might be called the new "technological" possibilities of policy-making. If he wishes to escape such a task of revision, he is faced with the discouraging necessity of ranking all social states that are conceivable rather than merely all social states technologically possible.

5—Social Disagreement

Any one individual can, of course, evaluate policies even if no one else agrees with his evaluations. Logically, therefore, social agreement is not required for policy evaluation. But social agreement on values is highly prized by most analysts. Some expect to find the same benefits in agreement on values that they find in agreement on facts in scientific description. Or they see a political virtue in a degree of agreement on values.

Analysts find that the received ideals do not go far toward assuring social agreement on policy values. To be sure, the construction of a rational-deductive system might well commence by reaffirming those lofty ethical principles on which, at least in a given culture or civilization, almost everybody agrees, partly as a result of centuries of religious and philosophical effort to win agreement. But the movement from these abstractions to the applicable intermediate principles with which one decides, for example, whether the United States Supreme Court's decisions on desegregation are better or worse than an even more gradual policy of integration is a movement in which agreement begins to break down. There is little in the rational-deductive ideal itself to maintain it.

On the contrary, practitioners of the deductive ideal impose special difficulties on themselves in seeking agreement, for they ask, in effect, not only for agreement among analysts on policy, goals, and acceptable costs and side conditions but for a more ambitious agreement among them on the deductive system in which these agreements would be incorporated. If their ultimate principles are to generate specific applied values on which they can agree, the ultimate principles of each analyst must agree with those of every other analyst (or be so nicely related to the others as to produce in each application the same results).

As for the social welfare function, it offers nothing beyond its own precision as a basis for agreement. That is to say, if you and I as social scientists each should construct a social welfare function, we would not necessarily reach agreement on our rankings. No doubt study of various hypothetical social welfare functions, not even limited to those that approximately express current value judgments, can help clarify values or preferences, as a flourishing literature attests; and clarification may possibly encourage agreement. But the mere ability to write social welfare functions offers no present basis for agreement, and, paradoxically, political scientists have even argued persuasively that a clear perception of preferences is inimical to widespread agreement.[4]

Economists may be thought to enjoy an agreed value base in their use of formal utility theory, and it has been suggested by a growing literature on decision theory that utility theory might be made more generally an agreed value basis for policy-making. But economists do not find formal utility theory useful for policy evaluation except among alternative policies, none of which is morally reprehensible, which means that at best its scope is drastically limited. And even for this limited class of policy alternatives, the application of utility theory is usually limited to situations in which the pattern of income distribution is not at issue. Hence it fails to meet one of the big difficulties on which social agreement is quick to founder.[5]

It is sometimes suggested that, even if analysts cannot agree on the values themselves, they can and do agree on the principles, rules, or procedures for their reconciliation. Of course, such values as those pertaining to justice, equality, and reciprocity are themselves principles for reconciling conflicts of value; and to say that analysts agree on principles for reconciliation is to say that they can and do agree, after all, on enough important values to eliminate the problem of social agreement. But they do not agree sufficiently: Everyone knows that social scientists do not wholly agree on values directly, on overriding principles, or on conciliatory processes. There remains, therefore, a continuing significant problem of obtaining a higher level of social agreement than the classical methods have obtained.

One principle or process is so highly valued in the United

States that it might be thought to solve the agreement problem. Do we not agree that government shall take as its working objectives those that are preferred by the majority? Consequently, do we not enjoy a working agreement on objectives of governmental policy?

This is a question of fact, and for several reasons the answer is no.

In the first place, most policy choices that are open to government, almost all budgetary choices for example, will not even have been raised as issues in a recent election campaign. An analyst is therefore without a clearly defined objective or set of values; they have not been put to the test of majority opinion.

Second, it has been shown that it is not possible for a majority to express its preference on more than one issue at once, except under specially simplified conditions. If a combination of issues is presented to the voters at one time—which is the usual practice in campaigns—the results are generally ambiguous.[6] If a winning candidate differs from his defeated opponent on an issue in foreign policy (among many issues that divide them), it does not follow that all those who vote for him favor his stand on the foreign policy issue. After a vote, neither the winning candidate nor anyone else can say which specific policy objective or value is, by majority preference, to be taken as the government's objective. In short, if values are put to the test of majority opinion, the results are ambiguous.

Third, even in principle we do not agree on majority rule as a basis for a working agreement. For, in a large number of decision-making situations, citizens differ over how far the equality principle implicit in majority rule ought to be compromised to take account of differences in the intensity of preference among citizens, of differences in their circumstances, or of minority rights. We have moved so far from equality in the United States that we subject some policy decisions to a vote in which only farmers in particular categories participate. And, of course, the Constitution makes numerous systematic provisions for inequality among individuals, as in the basis for election of Senators and the bicameral legislature.

Finally, it is necessary to point out, in order to avoid misunderstanding, that when a policy analyst needs an agreed-upon set of values to advise himself or others how best to cast a vote or otherwise express preferences to lawmakers, it does not help him to say that he can infer what values are agreed upon from a democratic opinion that is still only in the making.

One must, of course, draw a distinction between majority rule as a practical device for resolving social conflict and majority rule as a guide to relevant values. Many thoughtful people would accept it on the first count but, not able to accept that whatever the majority wishes is right, would reject it on the second.

In the next chapter, we turn to further fundamental difficulties in evaluation and decision.

CHAPTER 3

THE SYNOPTIC CONCEPTION
OF PROBLEM SOLVING

1—Synoptic Policy Analysis

What general conception of policy analysis or problem solving[1] underlies a commitment to the rational-deductive ideal or the ideal of the social welfare function? To what kind of policy analysis are they adapted? Because the two methods are both restricted to the strictly evaluative as against the strictly empirical aspects of decision-making, we would expect their advocates to endorse a decision-making system in which fact and value elements are quite sharply separated. Because the two methods aspire to a high degree of comprehensiveness (deductive propositions should cover all possible situations and a welfare function should rank all possible social states), we would also expect an endorsement of policy analysis that is in all its aspects comprehensive. And, in fact, we find exactly that: Advocates of the two methods and, for that matter, analysts in general endorse just such a decision-making ideal.

For an illustration, we can turn to some specifications of the policy-making process outlined by the Dutch economist, Jan

Tinbergen. In his *Economic Policy: Principles and Design*,[2] he prescribes the following procedures for an ideal analytical process: (1) The policy-maker should pursue an agreed-upon set of values (pp. 11 ff.); (2) the aims of policy should be clearly formulated in advance of choosing among alternative policies (p. 6); (3) the policy-maker should attempt a comprehensive overview of policy problems and of alternative policies (p. 8); (4) co-ordination of policy should be made the explicit function of the policy maker (p. 220); and (5) economists as policy analysts should be comprehensive in considering economic variables and values (p. 8). Such a conception of ideal policy analysis is not unusual; its prescriptions are so "obvious" as to be the first things that come to anyone's mind.

This conception appeals not only to economists like Tinbergen. Writing about problem solving in public administration, Marshall Dimock endorses fundamentally the same ideal method:

First, there are always the problem and the issues. Second, there are the facts and analyses that need to be applied to the issues. Third, there is the setting forth of alternatives and the pros and cons applicable to each possible solution—all this in the light of larger institutional goals and objectives. Fourth, there is the decision proper, which depends upon choosing among alternatives. . . .[3]

If Tinbergen and Dimock differ in emphasis and even on some particular points, they nevertheless appear to be endorsing processes that are fundamentally alike. Both call for a systematic canvassing of possible alternative policies, for a similarly systematic analysis of the consequences of each possible alternative possibility, and for policy choices to serve goals or objectives somehow separately established.

The emphasis of both on comprehensiveness or on analyzing, in Dimock's words, "the pros and cons applicable to each possible solution" is often endorsed even by those who would question some of the other particular prescriptions encompassed in the ideal. For example, although he is renowned for disagreeing with those like Tinbergen who insist that the choice of goals be separated from the analysis of means, John Dewey endorses the ideal of making exhaustive surveys of all possible alternatives.[4] The advocacy of comprehensiveness may soar beyond any sense of practical moderation: In proposing reforms in the budgetary process in the United States government, Arthur Smithies, for example, declares that no claim on the budget should be acted upon until all competing claims can be considered.[5] Taken literally, this rule calls for superhuman comprehensiveness.

Comprehensiveness is often seen as logically necessary for rational choice; in fact, rational choice comes close to being defined as a choice that, *inter alia*, responds to a comprehensive consideration of all relevant variables. Herbert A. Simon has written, "Rational choice will be feasible to the extent that the limited set of factors upon which decision is based corresponds, in nature, to a closed system of variables—that is, to the extent that significant indirect effects are absent." [6]

It is generally conceded, of course, that such comprehensiveness is an ideal rather than an achievement. This qualification is sometimes partly recognized in models of problem solving, as, for example, when it is specified that not all alternative policies but only all important alternative policies are to be canvassed. Similarly, the impossibility of achieving a completely full account of the consequences of each alternative policy under analysis is sometimes conceded. Still, the ideal remains, and the policy analyst is still told: Be comprehensive!

As for separation of fact and value, although everyone recognizes that in problem solving the choice of objectives is in fact influenced to some degree by the choice of means, we have seen, especially in Tinbergen's statement, an insistence that as an ideal the specification of objectives precedes the final choice of means. To solve a problem, it is generally believed, its conditions must be finally fixed. Hence even if for a time fact suggests value and vice versa, at some point values must be fixed so that choice can then be made.

James G. March and Herbert A. Simon have described (though not endorsed) the same general conception of decision-making as it appears in the literature of statistical decision theory and economics, where, incidentally, it explicitly includes a social welfare function:

1. When we first encounter him in the decision-making situation, he [the decision maker] already has laid out before him the whole set of alternatives from which he will choose his action. . . .
2. To each alternative is attached a set of consequences. . . .
3. At the outset, the decision maker has a "utility function" or a "preference-ordering" that ranks all sets of consequences from the most preferred to the least preferred.
4. The decision maker selects the alternative leading to the preferred set of consequences. . . .[7]

In its best and now most current formulations, the concept of problem solving that we are describing is adapted to risk and uncertainty. In the case of certainty, according to the March-Simon version the rational problem solver chooses the maximum position on the welfare function; in the risky case, he chooses that alternative for which expected utility is greatest; and in the case of uncertainty he chooses according to some such rule as "minimax risk" or "minimax regret." [8]

Note further that under this conception of problem solving, ideal policy-making, rational decision-making, policy analysis, and rational problem solving are synonymous. The ideal way to make policy is to choose among alternatives after careful and complete study of all possible courses of action and all their possible consequences and after an evaluation of those consequences in the light of one's values. That is to say, ideally one treats the policy question as an intellectual problem; one does not look upon a policy question as calling for the exercise of something called "political" forces. Although it would be a mistake to identify policy-making, policy analysis and decision-making in every case with problem solving, it is nevertheless conventional to equate them in their ideal forms.

In this study, we shall call this method of problem solving "synoptic," for the sake of convenience, although it has generally borne no specific name, being accepted almost everywhere not merely as one of several types of rational decision-making but as *one* process of rational decision-making. This acceptance is not surprising, for almost everyone takes it for granted that one cannot be rational about a problem without understanding it, and, as we observed, understanding requires comprehensiveness of information and analysis. Similarly, one cannot be rational without first knowing what one wants and proceeding from there to a systematic examination of alternative means of attaining these wants. Moreover, this method of decision-making is consistent with scientific canons, including the prescription that purely scientific analysis must be kept free from contamination by ethical components of the problem-solving process. In every respect, what we call "synoptic analysis" appears to correspond to good sense, fundamental notions of rationality, and scientific procedure.

It would be gratifying to offer a convincing example of synoptic analysis. Except for very nicely circumscribed problems, however, the method is an ideal, not an accomplishment. Consequently, we cannot cite a well-developed historical example of its employment in policy analysis. Significantly, its advocates do not ordinarily use even an hypothetical example in expounding it. An abbreviated hypothetical example would be banal. For an extended example sufficiently detailed to begin to indicate the dimensions of a problem attacked synoptically, the task of illustration becomes impossibly tedious. To illustrate the point, for example, that alternatives and the consequences of each are exhaustively explored, it would be necessary to list multitudes of possible links in multitudes of possible chains, with the phrase "and so forth" endlessly repeated. As was true for the rational-deductive method and the method of welfare function, the synoptic method is not even a blueprint of what has to be achieved; therefore, an illustration of it cannot even detail an interesting strategy through which one seeks to approximate the comprehensiveness to which the method aspires. The illustration is all list—no tactics, no strategy, no sequences—and no structure except the formal and symmetrical structure of exhaustive lists of alternative policies, consequences, and values.

2—Strands of Anti-Synoptic Thought

J. S. Bruner, J. J. Goodnow, and G. A. Austin report an experiment in problem solving that throws light on the presumed virtues of the synoptic method as an ideal.[9] The experimenter tells the subject that, with respect to a specially printed deck of cards, he (the experimenter) has in mind a subset whose characteristics he would like the subject to discover. For example, the subset might be all the red cards, all the cards with borders, or all the black cards with borders. All the cards in the deck are displayed simultaneously to the subject, and the subject is permitted to select single cards in any order he wishes and to ask whether or not they are members of the subset.

In their report, Bruner, Goodnow, and Austin identify four possible strategies chosen by the subjects for solving the problem:

1. *Simultaneous scanning.* The subject attempts to develop all possible hypotheses identifying the subset, to keep in mind as he proceeds just which hypotheses have been invalidated and which remain, and to estimate which of all possible requests for information about a particular card would test a maximum number of remaining hypotheses. In the language of this chapter, the experimenter is synoptic in his attempt to be comprehensive and systematic.

2. *Successive scanning.* The subject tests a series of hypotheses one at a time by asking his question each time about a card that bears on the one hypothesis then under test. Inevitably, the subject will finally identify the subset, but he may be a long time in doing so. In the language of this chapter, he is synoptic in the exhaustiveness with which he examines "the pros and cons of each alternative possibility."

3. *Conservative focusing.* The subject finds a positive instance, a card to which the experimenter responds affirmatively; he then makes a sequence of choices each of which alters only one attribute of the first positive instance to see whether the change yields a second instance or not. It will be noticed that this strategy focuses exclusively on the kind of increment or margin of difference that (as pointed out in Chapter 2) the rational-deductive method and the method of the welfare function do not facilitate. This is a nonsynoptic strategy in its incremental, noncomprehensive features.

4. *Focus gambling.* This strategy is like number three except that the subject takes risks by altering more than one attribute at a time. Although risky, it is worth attempting if time is short. It too, in our language, is nonsynoptic.

The experimenters report that scanning imposes a great cognitive strain and that simultaneous scanning imposes so great a strain that it is not feasible. It requires the subject to grasp and calculate beyond his capacities. In focusing, they report, subjects achieve great cognitive economy. The results are that scanners' performances degenerate under conditions of increasing difficulty while focusers show little or no change. These conclusions hold for such changes in conditions as shortening the time allowed, increasing the number of alternatives, and reducing redundancy.

Thus, at least under the circumstances of this experiment, it is not true that the best way to solve a problem is to be comprehensive; and, at least in some circumstances—when time is short, for example—it may be best to trust to a degree to luck. The experiment also suggests not only that scanning is less successful than focusing but also that it is not a serviceable ideal—one would not advise a subject who wished to improve his performance to push scanning to the maximum. The experiment therefore challenges synopsis as an ideal.

The results are not at all surprising. Despite the prestige of the synoptic method as an ideal, all of us have long known that, in a number of respects, the ideal is vulnerable. It is well known, for example, that the mind flees from comprehensiveness, that an "object of perception, or judgment, is referred, not to the whole world, but to a specific background or framework." [10] Fully developed, such a proposition leads to the position that our minds do more than merely throw out what is unaffected by their activity and irrelevant to present difficulties—if that were all, there would be no challenge to the synoptic ideal. Rather, our minds determine what is relevant and irrelevant, by imposing a structure upon the problem situation. This structure tends to vary from mind to mind; and though it is true that on occasion people can be brought to adopt similar structures, it usually occurs at the expense of comprehensiveness and may mean that the most useful insights are abandoned together with the structures of assumption and interpretation that furnished them.

In a study of research on agricultural problems, Charles M. Hardin documents the fact—hardly unfamiliar—that different research groups have quite different insights [11] and that this phenomenon is not merely an occasional intellectual aberration but is both desirable and in many ways inevitable. At least as early as 1910, John Dewey was making the point that "We do not approach any problem with a wholly naive or virgin mind; we approach it with certain acquired habitual modes of understanding, with a certain store of previously evolved meanings, or at least of experiences from which meanings may be educed." [12]

It may be contended that the use of frames of reference, preliminary structuring, habitual modes—whatever they are called—does not seriously challenge the synoptic ideal. Everyone knows, it may be said, that we all have to organize our minds; organization means selection, and selection means noncomprehensiveness. The comprehensiveness called for in the synoptic ideal, it may be added, means comprehensiveness only within such an intellectual organization as every man must achieve. It is not a foolish call for omniscience.

To this argument we reply that it is either a foolish call or a very uncertain one. If the synoptic ideal does not call for omniscience, what degree of comprehensiveness does it call for? What kinds of element are to be included in analysis and what kinds are to be excluded? What does the ideal actually specify when we read that "all alternatives are to be considered, and all the consequences of each are to be traced" if the specification cannot really mean "all"? An ideal that either specifies the impossible or fails to specify at all is a dubious ideal.

There are other strands of antisynoptic thought. In an amusing example, Michael Polanyi calls attention to the difference between specification of a problem-solving strategy, on the one hand, and of a solved problem, on the other. To ride a bicycle, he says, it is necessary at any given angle of unbalance for the rider to give a turn to the front wheel that is by some measure inversely proportional to the square of the speed at which he is proceeding.[13] If this method specifies a solution for the cyclist, would anyone try to ride by making these calculations? At its best, the synoptic method is roughly analogous to riding by Polanyi's formula. It states conditions whose attainment would imply that a solution was at hand, but it gives no clue as to how people actually deal with problems. What is worse, those who advocate the ideal have not often drawn even Polanyi's distinction.

For example, in synoptic analysis with a social welfare function, one needs to draw a distinction between showing that an ideal decision is formally equivalent to maximizing such a function, on the one hand, and describing the actual or idealized pursuit of a maximum on the other. Consider the distinction between conceptualizing rational consumer behavior for some analytical purposes and describing rational consumer behavior. Although economists describe rational consumer behavior by reference to utility surfaces, indifference curves, demand schedules, and the like, a rational consumer need know nothing about them even ideally. He need not first determine his indifference curve for oranges and apples and subsequently decide his purchase policies accordingly. Nor need he first try to comprehend all possible product mixes (the relevant social states for him), next decide which one he prefers, and only then make the purchases necessary to attain the preferred mix. The rational consumer proceeds directly to marginal comparison of alternative specific purchases. The way in which economists can, for their own professional purposes, conceptualize some aspects of consumer choice obscures the great difference between what the consumer can be conceived as having done but does not actually do—ascertain a function, then choose so as to maximize it—and what he actually does— simply compare policies at the margin and choose directly the preferred policy.

Karl Popper sounds still another antisynoptic note. Many of his objections to large-scale social reform or, as he calls it, utopian engineering, constitute criticisms of the synoptic method, which utopian reformers implicitly assume to be both necessary and possible. He stresses the limitations both of man's intellectual capacities and of his available knowledge and argues that both preclude comprehensiveness in analysis. Similarly, he argues that the close interplay between fact and value precludes the separation of factual and evaluative parts of analysis to the degree required in utopian reform. Above all, he insists that a decision-making system must be adapted to the experimental nature of social reforms, in which ends are as much adjusted to means, through reappraisal of objectives in the light of success or failure with policies, as means are to ends.[14]

Others have dissented from the synoptic ideal because they have perceived that the character of actual and ideal decision-making is dependent upon the level of the decision-maker's aspiration and is consequently altered in ways quite foreign to the synoptic method. The best known example of this type of alteration is Herbert A. Simon's model of the "satisficing" process, where one aims at a tolerable level of satisfaction rather than at maximization.[15] On still another tack, Richard C. Snyder and Glenn D. Paige, on the basis of an intensive study of the American decision to fight in Korea, suggest that analysis should ideally sometimes revolve around single policy alternatives to the exclusion of others. This was true of some of the major decisions on Korea.

Snyder and Paige write,

Perhaps the hypothesis would be: when the decision-making process must be compressed into a short time period and the situation is a crisis thrust upon the decision makers from outside, single alternatives rather than multiple alternatives will be considered. If this holds true, it suggests a different dialectic from that which is usually assumed. . . . One possible consequence of the single alternative process may be . . . to provide a way of *simplifying a situation to the point where action is possible*, thus avoiding the complexities of estimate involved in discussing multiple alternatives.[16]

It would be a mistake to dismiss Snyder and Paige's suggestion as a make-shift method suitable only for emergencies, when a single possible alternative may be a better focus than multiple alternatives because time is short. In public policy-making, time is never a free good; it is always short to some degree. Ideals, as well as practices, need to be adapted to that fact.

For a last illustrative dissent from the synoptic ideal, Martin

Meyerson and Edward C. Banfield make a persuasive case against thoroughgoing examination of the problem situation, of alternative courses of action, and of consequences in their case study of policy-making with respect to the location of public housing in Chicago. Of the Chicago Housing Authority, they write,

> As the case study shows, the Authority made little use of social science or of any technical knowledge regarding social phenomena. . . . No one, for example, had precise or systematic knowledge of the ends that people entertained regarding public housing. . . . It might be that the clearance of slums in one place created new slums or worsened old ones somewhere else. No one knew. . . .

> To have assembled a useful amount of information on even these few matters would have required a large staff of highly trained researchers . . . more of a staff certainly than it would be reasonable to expect the Authority to employ.[17]

In short, information is extremely costly and is not always worth its cost. Hence, comprehensive analysis is not always worth its cost.

Nor can this fundamental, if obvious, criticism of the synoptic system be dismissed on the ground that, costs aside, one should still aspire to comprehensiveness as an ideal. One should never ever be "as comprehensive as possible," whatever that means. For in fact one cannot now or in any calculable future put costs aside; the costliness of analysis is a fundamental fact that all analytical strategies should face up to. What Meyerson and Banfield's point suggests is that we need an analytical strategy or decision-making method that would give some guidance as to what steps to take in the light of the costliness of the analysis, whether in terms of the analyst's own time and energy or in terms of a research budget.

3—Failures of Adaptation

These dissents from one or another point of the synoptic ideal are no less persuasive than the outline of the ideal itself. What is to be inferred from the conflict between the two? Simply that one should try to realize the ideal as fully as possible? The dissents suggest very strongly that analysts do in fact find alternative strategies that can sometimes be exploited with great skill. Thus, in the experiment with the cards, the subjects adapted to unreasonable demands on their cognitive faculties by "focusing" rather than "scanning." Simon's "satisficing" model is another adaptation to limited cognitive faculties and costliness of search, just as Popper's now familiar "piecemeal engineering" is an adaptation to the discrepancy between the complexity of the problem and the capacity of the human mind.

The key concept here is adaptation, adaptation of the problem-solving method to certain troublesome characteristics of problems and problem-solving situations. A decision-making method is adapted to a specified difficulty in decision-making only if it contains some prescriptions that give specific guidance in overcoming such difficulty. And the conclusion that we urge at this stage of the argument is that the synoptic ideal, like the rational-deductive and welfare function methods, is distinguished by its failure to incorporate adaptive features. To expose the poverty of this ideal more fully with respect to adaptive features, we can summarize the dissenting notes in the form of a list of failures of adaptation, at the same time extending the list to identify still other failures.

In all these failures of adaptation, the synoptic ideal displays the same confusion between conceivability and practicability, or between operability in principle and operability in practice, that we found in the rational-deductive method and the method of the social welfare function. The following propositions can be read as applicable both to the synoptic method taken as a whole and to the two evaluative methods considered by themselves. We can subsume under one proposition or another each of the specific difficulties in evaluation identified in Chapter 2.

1. *The synoptic ideal is not adapted to man's limited problem-solving capacities.*

The mind, as everyone likes to say, is a wonderful mechanism, and we do not yet understand very well the astonishing ways in which apparently impossible problems are converted, by simplifying tactics, into manageable intellectual tasks. We sometimes get useful answers from our mental processes when questions are posed that cannot possibly be analyzed in any articulated systematic way—how to hit a target with a stone, for example. Yet it is easy to find puzzles and games, some of them simple to arrange, that go beyond the capacity of any man's mind to solve synoptically. Nor can they always be solved synoptically with the help of electronic computers. A. L. Samuel's checkers-playing machine would require 10^{21} centuries, supposing that it worked as fast as the fastest imaginable computer, to explore every possible path leading to the end of a game of checkers.[18] Hence calculation would not be practical unless it departed from synoptic principles.

The kinds of problems encountered in analyzing public policies stand high on the list of problems requiring simplification. Here, even the form of the problem is difficult to discern. One has, as it were, to find the game—to decide upon a form for the problem. Given the form, one might still have too many possible solutions from which to choose to proceed synoptically. This is the general situation in which policy analysts find themselves. The issues before them are susceptible of infinite variation as attention shifts among different values and different facts. How can they do anything effective about problems of evaluation unless they have some way of achieving what Bruner, Goodnow, and Austin aptly call "cognitive economy"?

But the synoptic approach ignores the need for such economy. We are not asking that problem-solving prescriptions include "Think with your blood!" or that they propose to substitute conditioned reflexes for conscious analysis. Rather, we are suggesting that the synoptic ideal is deficient because it fails to provide quite respectable simplifying tactics such as those illustrated by the tactic of "focusing" in the experiment referred to above; because it does not prescribe a method for selecting which aspects of the problem to analyze when cognitive strain requires that some lines be abandoned; and because, to cite a final example, it fails to specify just how a solution is to be qualified or limited in practice to allow for the inevitable omissions of analysis.

We have, of course, pointed out that the ideal can, to a degree, be adapted to certain kinds of risk and uncertainty, as in statistical decision theory. At best, however, these adaptations respond to certain difficulties in knowing consequences when the alternative policies have been identified. They do not respond to problems of identifying alternative policies in the first place or of identifying the values that these policies are designed to serve.[19] To be sure, these are also elementary simplifying devices that any advocate of the synoptic ideal would no doubt expect an analyst to exploit: for example, written language, theory construction, quantification, classification, subdivision, and factoring out. In the analysis of the difficulties of the synoptic method, we have simply been assuming that an analyst employs all such very general devices. Beyond these usual devices, however, the synoptic ideal not only fails to incorporate simplifying strategies but compounds the analyst's difficulties by insisting on comprehensiveness of analysis. To insist on comprehensiveness is to rule out at the start many techniques for simplification, since omission is a chief principle of simplification.

2. *The synoptic ideal is not adapted to inadequacy of information.*

3. *The synoptic ideal is not adapted to the costliness of analysis.*

Just as man's finite intellectual capacities call for methods of simplification and other devices to reduce cognitive strain, so the unavailability of information and the costliness of the individual or group processes by which information is gathered and analyzed call for adaptations that economize on information and analysis. We need not repeat the summary line of argument on adaptation to man's limited intellectual capacity; we need do little more than recall the illustration of impossibly costly analysis from Meyerson and Banfield's study of the Chicago Housing Authority. In any problem-solving application of analytical effort, the value of the solved problem imposes some limit on the energies worth expending to achieve the solution; and a problem-solving method patterned, as seems to be the case for the synoptic ideal, after analytical methods in pure research, where the research activity is valued for its own sake, is irrational by any ordinary standard of rationality.

Information, moreover, is costly in a special sense that is worth noting because it illustrates the need for some strategic adaptation. Adequate information often provides an embarrassment of riches; if it can be had, it will sometimes burden the analyst with problems of ordering and calculation that go beyond his capacities. On the one hand, he cannot follow the tenets of the synoptic ideal if he lacks adequate information; on the other hand, he cannot follow them if he has more information at hand than he can manage.

March and Simon's critical exposition of the synoptic ideal, to which we referred above, calls particular attention to the fact that alternative policies are somehow assumed to be known to the analyst. How the alternatives are discovered is unspecified. Since the search for alternatives is an especially demanding and costly part of the problem-solving process, the fact that advocates of the synoptic ideal have not usually identified the search for alternatives as a central part of problem solving points even more strongly to failure in adaptation than does the lack of an adaptive feature for facilitating the search.

4. *The synoptic ideal is not adapted to failures in constructing a satisfactory evaluative method (whether a rational deductive system, a welfare function, or some other).*

The principal problem here was posed in Chapter 2, where the particular difficulties of constructing a satisfactory rational deductive system or welfare function were discussed. As we pointed out there, no one has yet constructed either. Indeed, attempts much more modest than the construction of a welfare function—to construct relatively simply criteria for problem solving in operations research, for example—are typically only partially successful.[20] Neither the prescriptions of the two evaluative methods nor the prescriptions of the synoptic ideal specify how to proceed when one cannot actually push through the construction of deductive system or welfare function.

It might be doubted that any adaptations are possible in value difficulties: Either one has formulated values to provide a satisfactory criterion or one cannot solve the problem; there is no third alternative. But most of us know that we do solve problems, that we solve them in ways that we subsequently sometimes endorse, and that we do so without rational-deductive system, welfare function, or any other formal prior organization of values. Somehow all of us have found at least a third alternative. As for adaptations to social conflict over values, at least one adaptive alternative is worth mentioning as assurance that they exist: It is both logically possible and empirically commonplace for men who cannot agree on values to agree directly on policy choices.

5. *The synoptic ideal is not adapted to the closeness of observed relationships between fact and value in policy-making.*

Except to observe that fact and value occupy separate compartments in the synoptic ideal, we have so far said little on this point. But we can explain this particular failure of adaptation in the light of what we have said about the synoptic ideal in general and about the two evaluative ideals in particular. If we remember that every actual policy choice is accompanied by a new flow of information about values and, similarly, that even the contemplation of alternative imminent policies stimulates new insights into values, we shall not derive much help from a prescription that states: At some point, turn off the evaluation, stabilize the values, and make the choice in the light of them. Moreover, in actual practice continued contemplation of alternative means is often empirically inseparable from continued contemplation of values.

It is not logically impossible to prescribe a separation between establishing one's values and choosing in their light, but we maintain that to attempt to follow such a course does not help the analyst who does not want to disregard any of the new insights into values that his contemplation of concrete means gives him. One might conceive a round of successive approximations in which the analyst permits means to act upon end and end upon means until he reaches a position of stability in value, if he ever does. Although such a procedure would be helpful, it is neither prescribed nor forbidden by the synoptic ideal; nor is any other strategy indicated by which the rich interplay of fact and value might be harnessed.

6. *The synoptic ideal is not adapted to the openness of the systems of variables with which it contends.*

We have already taken note that for synoptic problem-solving it is difficult or impossible to define rationality except in relation to a closed system of variables. But the would-be synoptic problem-solver aspires to comprehend all interacting variables except, perhaps, those whose interaction is infrequent or for some other reason can be regarded as trivial. Yet in actual policy-making situations it is not always possible to find a closed system of variables sufficiently comprehensive to cover the problem, and the analyst is therefore left with an open analytical system mirroring the far-reaching interactions that his analytical system is designed to encompass.

Now, while it is common to say that the analysis should be completed—presumably by someone else who has the time, energy, competence, and interest—and that, in the meantime, the conclusions should be considered as tentative, the fact is that scholarly thinking is very loose both on how completion could be accomplished and on how the conclusions so far achieved should be handled pending closure. For the synoptic ideal does not include prescriptions that deal with these problems.

7. *The synoptic ideal is not adapted to the analyst's need for strategic sequences of analytical moves.*

As we have said before in different ways, the synoptic ideal demands a great deal but provides very little. For an analyst faced with a problem of magnitude and complexity, the ideal is little more than a description of what, if he aspires to the ideal, he should have completed by the time he calls his problem solved. It is not a body of prescriptions that guide his first steps, direct him through a sequence of subsequent moves, and specify the details of a dynamic process in such a way as to convert an impossible task into a feasible one. One might view each of a number of the itemized failures already discussed as a failure to find a strategic sequence capable of dealing with the itemized problem. If so, we are now simply taking account more generally of failures in adaptation that assume the specific form of failure in developing strategic sequences.

In pure research and in some of the purely empirical parts of applied analysis, an analyst can organize his task by following widely endorsed sequences as, for example, in mathematical problem solving, in statistics, and in the formulation and testing of hypotheses. In organizing a policy problem as a whole and in pushing past the purely empirical components of his task into the latter stages of applied analysis, however, a policy analyst runs beyond those agreed-upon and partially codified sequences.

8. *The synoptic ideal is not adapted to the diverse forms in which policy problems actually arise.*

The synoptic view of a public policy problem is heavily influenced by the common and useful concept of a problem that is expressed in the two following definitions, taken from two different authors:

A person may be said to have a problem if he is motivated toward a goal and his first goal-directed response is unrewarding.[21]

A problem is a situation which for some reasons appreciably holds up an organism in its efforts to reach a goal.[22]

These definitions can easily be altered to fit some public problems like national security. Despite a relatively homogeneous body of opinion, achievement of a widely shared goal is thwarted. (If this seems a slight oversimplification, it is not something of which we wish to make an issue.) For many other problems, however, the familiar situation is that a number of diverse individuals and groups are each thwarted in different ways in the pursuit of diverse and sometimes conflicting goals. "The problem" is in fact a cluster of interlocked problems with interdependent solutions.

Of course, the would-be synoptic analyst can occupy himself exclusively with one problem of one of these diverse groups, while trying to turn his back on problems of interdependent solutions. In this case, he faces the problems discussed under the last proposition on the openness of systems of variables. Or he may solve a problem for one of the groups, simply doing his best for the one group at the expense of the others.

The more typical situation is one in which the analyst attends to what might be called a synthetic problem, one that represents a reconstruction of the problems of individuals and groups who are meeting frustration in pursuing their goals. For a cluster of interlocked problems can always be formally envisaged as one problem, in which "the problem" is to find a reconciliation of the diverse groups on terms that provide a measure of satisfaction for each.

Public policy problems like inflation, unemployment, social security, reform of the judiciary, relief of urban congestion, and segregation are single "synthetic" problems each of which encompasses a host of disparate but interlocked individual and group problems. We might add that they quickly lose their synthetic character in practice; once formulated, they become deeply felt problems to those individuals and groups whose own important goals include reconciliation and a wide sharing of satisfactions in society. To these people (the group includes many policy analysts) these problems are no less real than the subproblems out of which they were constructed.[23]

The consequence of focusing on a synthetic problem is that the problem is no longer a simple situation in which goal achievement is thwarted but an extremely complex adjustment-of-interests situation. This fact is familiar, but its implications are not always perceived. Problem solving becomes a more continuous process than is ordinarily thought. Whether or not a possible reconciliation today is satisfactory will depend not solely on the characteristics of today's problem but also on what yesterday's pattern of reconciliation was and what tomorrow's might be.

On the one hand, then, the possibilities of shifting the pattern of reconciliation from day to day do not so much pose an additional difficulty to policy analysts as they provide freedom and a greater degree of flexibility. On this score, the synoptic ideal is too rigid in its prescription that a "solution" be found for a problem, where all that is actually required and all that can at best be defended as a right "solution" is that a series of reconciliatory moves be made.

On the other hand, however, a continuous attack on a synthetic problem also creates new difficulties in analysis. A problem of reconciliation of interests is not a stable, well-formed problem that retains its outlines so firmly that "all consequences of all alternatives" can be investigated. The public policy problem, in contrast to less complex problems of the conventional kind, is highly fluid. The synoptic ideal, as we have already seen, is even less well adapted to this fluid problem than to a static one.

A further failure of adaptation of the synoptic ideal to the way in which public policy problems arise stems from the fact that the need for analysis is often triggered not by identification of an unachieved goal but by identification of a new policy proposal. When this happens the problem-solving process is turned upside down. Policy problems are often forced upon policy analysts because an individual or group pushes a policy proposal with sufficient influence to stimulate public discussion—or because a useful new means comes to hand for achieving a variety of ends. Examples of new means are the union shop, minimum wages, legislative reapportionment, deficit financing, and artificial satellites. The focus of attention is the means; its sponsors hope to persuade other individuals or groups that it suits *their* goals, but they do not suppose that all potential supporters of the means will want it for the same reason.

That is, in the pursuit of the objectives for which the proposal is to be evaluated, there can be no examination of alternative policies to reach agreed objectives. Such questions as, Is the union shop the best of alternative ways to attain its objective? or, Is landing a man on the moon the best way to achieve its objective? hardly make sense. There are no alternatives to reach whatever combination of objectives these means pursue, and, on the other hand, we cannot identify any agreed-upon "objective" in either of the questions. Still, these policies need study; it is not foolish to ask whether they are worthwhile.

Similarly, the need for policy analysis often springs from dissatisfaction with existing institutional arrangements—government agencies, for instance—where no particular problem in the ordinary sense of the word has been identified, let alone agreed upon, but where nevertheless it seems clear that "something needs to be done." Of national water resources administration James Fesler writes, "Many official inquiries attest that the federal government is poorly organized for the development and execution of water resources programs. There is less agreement on what should be done. This is, in large part, because there is no consensus on a definition of the problem. . . ." [24]

Here, as when a policy is made the focus of analysis, analysis requires the examination of alternative possible objectives in the light of which administrative organizations and their efforts can be justified or in the light of which amended organization and policy can be justified. Again, the problem, conceived as an exercise in selecting among alternative means to achieve a given set of goals, is turned upside down.

4—Evaluation and Decision-Making

We confess to a special reason for stressing the interconnection between evaluative methods and the synoptic method more generally. The strategy of evaluation that we are going to present in Chapter 5 is not part of a decision-making system in which, as for the two ideals we have been discussing, evaluative and empirical aspects of problem solving are sharply separated; on the contrary, evaluation and empirical analysis are closely intertwined. Hence, in presenting a strategy of evaluation we shall in fact have to outline a problem-solving or decision-making strategy more generally. In short, we have been setting the stage for a strategy of evaluation that is inseparable from a general strategy for decision-making. We conceive this strategy as a set of adaptations in policy analysis both to the specified difficulties of evaluation identified in the preceding chapter and to the points identified in the present chapter on which the synoptic method fails in adaptation. It is because it is a set of adaptations, incidentally, that we refer to it not as a method but as a strategy.

But we must first consider further the relationship between analytical method and political environment, for we have seen in the last few pages that conceptions of problems and strategies must be adapted to the political circumstances in which "problems" arise.

PART TWO

OBSERVED PRACTICE IN POLICY EVALUATION AND DECISION-MAKING

CHAPTER 4

MATCHING PRACTICES TO
POLITICAL CONTEXTS

In view of the obstacles frustrating an approximation to the synoptic ideal, it is not surprising to find problem solvers exploiting in quite systematic ways, adaptive strategies for decision-making. They do not simply give up. A commonplace strategy is one to which we give the name "disjointed incrementalism." It is not the only set of adaptations to the difficulties of policy analysis—others range from coin tossing to the employment of game theory—but it is undoubtedly a most important one, no less important for not having been explicitly codified. Our aim is not to present it in the spirit of invention but to show that it is indeed an observable system—despite the fact that social scientists tend to employ it apologetically, as though their deviations from the synoptic ideal were regrettable.

Our first move in presenting the strategy, however, is indirect. Disjointed incrementalism is best understood in terms of the kinds of political decisions and situations to which it is adapted. The patterns of decision-making that circumstances allow vary from situation to situation, and the principal characteristics of the pattern that we identify as the strategy of disjointed incrementalism display themselves more emphatically in some kinds of situations and decisions rather than others. At this point, therefore, we shall look into a variety of situations and decisions.

1—Decisions Effecting Small Changes

In some situations, political decisions effect large changes and in other situations effect only small ones. For our purposes, this distinction is so crucial that we must take the time necessary to make it more precise.

When is a change small? When is a difference in social states small? Is a change in the Federal Reserve's rediscount rate a small change? A change in eligibility for unemployment compensation? Dropping a bomb on Hiroshima? Limiting the President of the United States to two terms in office? Building a national highway network? Integrating public schools? If "small" seems easy to define, consider the difficulty that arises if we declare that restricting the President to two terms in office is only a small reform —and you declare that the restriction, through its effects on the balance of power between President and Congress during his second term, will seriously weaken the Presidency, drastically impair the nation's capacity to act vigorously in foreign policy, and finally threaten our survival in the cold war. Or consider the possibility that we regard a change in habits of church attendance as small because we find it unimportant, while you consider it large because you deem it important.

These examples suggest that, whether a change is called "large" or "small" depends on the value attached to it, and this value can vary from person to person. But the notion of "small" is not so subjective and personal as this conclusion implies, for in any society there develops a strong tendency toward convergence in estimates of what changes are important or unimportant. The convergence is of a particular kind that gives the judgment of "importance" an objective quality. Convergence develops for two reasons: because, while people favor (or disfavor) contrary things, they make issues of the same topics and because they tend to agree on which factors are important for theoretical explanations of change.

"Theoretical" may be too elegant a word; "ideological," on the other hand, is too abusive. What we mean to say is that individuals in a society have ways of describing and explaining important social change, ways that give prominence to some factors rather than others, including factors that affect people's values. These ways of describing and explaining tend to be roughly the same for most members of the society. Thus, in the United States, almost everyone would assume such factors as private property, the two-party system, separation of church and state, civil liberties, and American attitudes toward personal success to be relevant to a description and explanation of important social change. Almost everyone would also agree that such factors as rate of progression in income taxation, school lunch programs, a particular election, or parental attitudes toward comic books belong to a discussion of somewhat less important social change. And almost everyone would dismiss such factors as today's weather, a particular municipal election, or the current popular evaluation of a recent movie as appropriate only to the discussion of the most trivial social change. At this extreme, one might even refuse to think of such a discussion as descriptive of social change at all.

We come very close here to suggesting that our distinction between "small" and "large" change is the difference, as it is sometimes put, between structural changes and changes within a given structure. We prefer our formulation because we are not confident that the difference between structural changes and intrastructural changes can be established objectively. Depending on one's view of society, a change, for example, in language habits could be structural (for what social pattern is more fundamental than language?) or not structural (for ways of speech can and do change without evident consequences either for other elements of social structure or for the community's values). The view of society we take for purposes of defining "large" and "small" change, then, is the converging view that rests on widespread agreement concerning what is or is not important change.

We have advanced in our task of definition only to the point where we now propose to say that a "small" change is a change in a relatively unimportant variable or relatively unimportant change in an important variable. To introduce another term we shall want to use heavily, we add that a small change in an important variable will also be denoted as an "increment of change." We consider the introduction through public policy of what is considered to be a new and important element (in the combination of elements to which people refer in explaining important social change) to be a large or nonincremental change. On the other hand, a somewhat greater or reduced use of an existing social technique or a somewhat higher or lower level of attainment of some existing values is a small or incremental change.

It could be argued that any change is nonincremental if one counts its indefinitely cumulating consequences from here to eternity. We therefore wish to specify that a small or incremental change is one that, within some short time period, such as five years, is small or incremental, regardless of the indefinite future.

We draw no sharp line between the incremental and nonincremental; the difference is one of degree. Hence we imagine a continuum between, at one extreme, quite trivial changes (either because no important variables are altered or because the change of important variables is of trivial magnitude) and, at the other extreme, large changes in important variables. In such a continuum, we would place the kind of change we wish to identify as small toward the left. At the extreme left, however, are changes of such little importance that they do not even raise policy problems. Strictly speaking, they are incremental; but we take no interest in them, for they include such public problems as—to mention a popular example of triviality—what kind of paper clips the Department of Agriculture should purchase.

Within the range of incremental changes, two types are worth distinguishing. The first is social change that largely repeats (with respect to the elements altered and with respect to the character and scope of the changes) frequent previous change. Changes in

interest rates, tax rates, severity of court sentences, school cur-
ricula, budget allocations to various public services, or traffic
regulations achieve changes of this kind. On a continuum, the
more repetitive the change, other things being equal, the more it
is incremental. It is, of course, not logically necessary for a repetitive change that stays within a given range to be considered
small or incremental. Sometimes repetitive changes of this kind
can, because of changed circumstances, be regarded as nonincremental. The typical situation is, however, that repetitive changes
become part of a game played by rule; they are not viewed as
important in "theories" of social change, even if they are important from other points of view. In example, manipulation of the
interest rate, while of no small consequence in maintaining full
employment, represents only small social change.

The second kind of incremental change is the nonrepetitive
change that is viewed either as a permanent small alteration in
policy or as one small step in an indefinite nonrepetitive sequence.
In the United States, present desegregation policies are achieving
changes that might be termed incremental, although some people
would argue that they go beyond the incremental; the changes
contemplated in recent revisions of the antitrust laws and laws
on federal funds for research, agricultural prices, and foreign aid
are also within the incremental spectrum.

One can distinguish very roughly between changes in patterns of behavior or policies that are limited by their containment
within another "larger" pattern of behavior or policies—and
changes in the "larger" pattern that are held in turn to be variations within another still "larger" fixed pattern, and so forth.
Viewed in this way, incremental changes include any changes
permitted within the smallest set of patterns, as well as some of
the smaller changes within the larger patterns, including very
small changes in the very largest. Thus any change in the rediscount rate authorized by the Federal Reserve System, most
changes in rules governing congressional procedure, some changes
in the major governing principles of the U.S. Constitution, and
very minor changes of degree in fundamental political attitudes
would be considered marginal or incremental.

2—Political Decision-Making

Imagine now another continuum, on which political decisions can be arrayed according to the degree to which the decision-makers can be supposed to understand all the features of the problem with which they are faced. Near one extreme, information is generally lacking; values (goals, objectives, constraints, side conditions) are neither well understood nor well reconciled, and intellectual capacity generally falls far short of grasping and thinking through the problem. Near the other extreme, all aspects of the problem are quite well grasped in the decision-maker's mind.

We can combine this continuum with the first by altering the latter to refer explicitly to *decisions* that achieve a range from small to large change. We now have four recognizable types of decisions: (a) decisions that effect large change and are guided by adequate information and understanding; (b) decisions that effect large change but are not similarly guided—hence, at an extreme, blind or unpredictable decisions; (c) decisions that effect only small change and are guided by adequate information and understanding; and (d) decisions that effect small change but are not similarly guided, being therefore subject to constant reconsideration and redirection. In Diagram 1 these types appear in quadrants 1, 4, 2, and 3, respectively.

To what kinds of political situation can we match each of these kinds of decision?

With respect to the first quadrant, the likelihood that decisions can accomplish large social changes and, at the same time, be guided by a high level of intellectual comprehension of the problem is slim. Such decisions require prodigious feats of synoptic analysis, beyond human capacities. To be sure, we are competent enough to produce catastrophes; with nuclear energy in our hands, we may be able, if we choose, to extinguish human life on earth—a very large change indeed. The kinds of large changes that lie within the range of what a government might wish to ac-

DIAGRAM 1

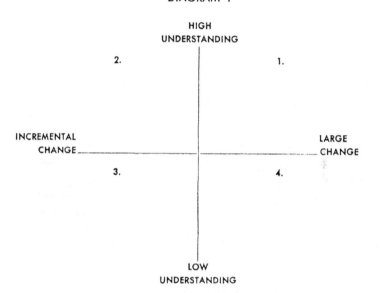

HIGH
UNDERSTANDING

2.   1.

INCREMENTAL   LARGE
CHANGE   CHANGE

3.   4.

LOW
UNDERSTANDING

complish, however, are immensely more difficult, for reasons outlined in the preceding chapter. For although one needs to be able to predict only one disastrous consequence of a policy decision in order to be sure of a disaster, to attain some positive large-scale change, one needs to predict (unless one counts on luck) that none of a number of possible disasters will ensue.

Decisions designed to achieve desired large changes are, of course, made: for example, the decision of the southern states to secede from the Union and the decision of the Lincoln administration to use force to stop them; the Soviet decision to move rapidly to the collectivization of agriculture; or the decision of some high-ranking French officers in Algeria in 1961 to challenge the authority of the civil government. That decisions to achieve large change are not guided by a high level of understanding, however, is illustrated by these very decisions, all of which brought quite unanticipated consequences.

Although we can think of many decisions to accomplish large

changes that produced consequences subsequently applauded by the decision-makers—including some of the examples already given—is there a single example of a decision for which it can be claimed both that it accomplished a large change and that its implications were comprehensively and clearly understood beforehand?

In short, the only political context in which a decision of this kind could be made is the imaginary society of the philosopher king or some other utopian society in which, as in B. F. Skinner's *Walden Two*,[1] one group in the society—in Skinner's book, the psychologists—has achieved extraordinary comprehension of social change. One might, of course, argue that when circumstances are intolerable enough, available understanding is sufficient for large—specifically revolutionary—social change. An analyst might believe, without denying his incompetence to trace through the consequences of revolution, that any new situation likely to develop is preferable to the *status quo*. Aside from this possibility, however, the first quadrant is the realm of superhuman decision-makers.

Decisions in the fourth quadrant, decisions marked by large change and quite imperfect understanding, are not rare, even if they are not the typical instrument of policy-making. Nor are such decisions made only in error or by foolish decision-makers. On the contrary, such decisions are sometimes inescapable, forced on decision-makers by circumstances. In addition, such decisions are sometimes deliberately taken by decision-makers because the potential rewards seem attractive enough to outweigh the perils posed by imperfect understanding. If, in an important sense, Pearl Harbor forced the United States into war with Japan, nothing similar forced the United States to bomb Hiroshima and Nagasaki.

The political situations or circumstances that stimulate decisions effecting large but poorly understood change include crises, some revolutions, and war, as well as what decision-makers might call "grand opportunities." (Lest we fail to appreciate the blindness of such decisions, let us note that crises, wars, and revolutions are often the results rather than the antecedent circumstances of such decisions.) The political locus for decisions of this kind lies in the deliberations of policy-makers and their advisers at the highest level. There is some circularity in such a statement, for anyone who carries off a revolution becomes a top-level policy-maker, even if he was not recognized as such before. All we mean to say is that, typically, the decision effecting large change is not made at the lower levels of government, nor, specifically, is it made in the middle or lower ranks of the administrative service.

The fourth quadrant, therefore, is clearly not the area or context of politics as usual, not even in the dictatorships, where the large decision seems more feasible than it normally does in the democracies. In the Soviet system, for example, decisions do not typically fall into the fourth quadrant: Foreign policy, for example, is typically carried forward by endless small moves; economic planning too is a process of unending calculation and step-by-step adjustment.

What is the political context for decisions in the second quadrant, decisions that effect small or incremental changes on the basis of a high level of intellectual comprehension of problem and decision? In the first place, it appears that decisions effecting only small or incremental changes are the daily business of governmental machinery: decisions to build a new veterans' hospital, increase foreign aid to Latin America, amend our farm-price legislation, schedule a summit conference, continue with a small increase or decrease of the annual appropriation to the navy, liberalize benefits under Old Age and Survivors' Insurance, provide health insurance for the aged, lower the banking system's reserve requirements, call a conference on the problems of small business, order office equipment or furniture for government offices, assign tasks to administrative subordinates, provide paid sick-leave for government employees, deny or grant workmen's compensation to an applicant, undertake an anti-trust action against a corporation, condemn a building, reroute traffic, make a loan, or arrest a speeding motorist. Even if we drop from this list all those decisions that are not to be dignified in the name of policy, the remaining items and countless other examples that could be cited leave no doubt that policy is usually made through decisions that in any given instance achieve only small or incremental changes.

But for how many of these decisions can we say that the decision-maker attains a high level of understanding of his problem, including the implications of all the various alternative possible decisions? Not for all, certainly. When policy makers, fearful of inflation, opt for higher taxes, they know that before the new legislation can be implemented, business conditions may call for antidotes to recession rather than for curbs on inflation. They can only hope to have an opportunity to act again if they are in error; they can hardly hope to read the future with confidence. When policy-makers try to woo Latin America with more generous foreign aid, they act largely on the supposition that more funds will not do any damage to our relations with the American republics and might help. How often can they be said to have diagnosed correctly the particular ills they wished to remedy and to have predicted what the direct and indirect consequences of the new flow of funds would be? Even when policy-makers attempt something so simple as grants-in-aid for state highway construction, they cannot foresee the whole range of important consequences for urban congestion and the amenities of life. We need only call to mind the arguments of the preceding chapters to establish that, even for decisions effecting only small changes, information and understanding will be limited.

Where a decision effecting an incremental change does indeed seem to fall within a recognized competence—rather than to depend largely on imponderables or preferences—the decision is often delegated to a specialized group: engineers, economists, physicians, accountants—or one or another subgroup of that very large and internally differentiated group of experts on small policy decisions, the public administrators. We can say, therefore, that for decisions of the second quadrant, the decision-maker is typically not at the highest levels of the government bureaucracy and may be a professional specialist of some sort.

Bearing in mind the difficulties of comprehending a problem as envisaged in the synoptic ideal, however, we should recognize that many decisions of the administrative service of government, even at middle and low levels, and many decisions of professional experts are not decisions of the second quadrant. If a decision is a second quadrant decision, it is probably an administrative or professional decision, but many administrative and professional decisions are too complex to fall into the second quadrant.

3—Incremental Politics

We are thus brought to the third quadrant: decisions effecting small or incremental change and not guided by a high level of understanding. These decisions, we now see, are the decisions typical of ordinary political life—even if they rarely solve problems but merely stave them off or nibble at them, often making headway but sometimes retrogressing. Decisions like these are made day by day in ordinary political circumstances by congressmen, executives, administrators, and party leaders.

Let us describe this kind of political decision-making in more detail. It is decision-making through small or incremental moves on particular problems rather than through a comprehensive reform program. It is also endless; it takes the form of an indefinite sequence of policy moves. Moreover, it is exploratory in that the goals of policy-making continue to change as new experience with policy throws new light on what is possible and desirable. In this sense, it is also better described as moving *away* from known social ills rather than as moving *toward* a known and relatively stable goal. In any case, it is policy-making that chooses those goals that draw policies forward in the light of what recent policy steps have shown to be probably realizable; the utopian goal, chosen for its attractiveness without thought of its feasibility, is not a heavy influence on this kind of policy-making. In the frequency with which past moves are found wanting and new moves debated, it reveals both man's limited capacities to understand and solve complex problems and an unsettled, shifting compromise of conflicting values. Woodrow Wilson describes the process at its best:

We shall deal with our economic system as it is and as it might be modified, not as it might be if we had a clean sheet of paper to write upon; and step by step we shall make it what it should be, in the spirit of those who question their own wisdom and seek council and knowledge, not shallow self-satisfaction or the excitement of excursions whither they cannot tell.[2]

Incremental policy-making is illustrated less flatteringly in legislation for old-age security in the United States. Our "program" for the aged is not a program at all; it is not a comprehensively considered and co-ordinated policy. Rather, it consists of Old Age and Survivors' Insurance, special provisions for the aged under the income tax law, old-age assistance provided through the cooperation of state and federal government, and county and municipal provision of medical care and other particular services for the needy aged. It is therefore a product of a number of small, specific moves. It has been developed—and goes on developing—as a sequence of decisions, illustrated in the endless stream of congressional decisions that liberalizes benefits and extends incrementally the coverage of Old Age and Survivors' Insurance.

To pursue the illustration, policy-makers have never been confident—and certainly have never agreed—on what goals for old-age income and security they wish to pursue. Nor have they understood exactly what consequences would flow from their decisions. During the great depression of the 1930's, they were stirred into important steps to appease a politically restless group of aged voters, and they were stirred again to remedy the real reduction in old-age benefits that attended post-World War II inflation—and to head off an increasingly strong movement for industry-financed pensions that trade unions were pushing at the bargaining table. During all these years, decision-makers have presumably also been motivated by their perceptions of the ways in which programs existing at any one time still left the aged inadequately cared for. The proportion of those uncared for has no doubt diminished, but the programs are incomplete while some remain; furthermore, new matters of concern appear once all the aged have been assured the minimum decencies. Never sure how far they wished to go in liberalization, policy-makers nevertheless have known what they wanted to move away from. Increases in coverage of OASI have clearly been influenced by growing skill in administering the program—a clear example of goals following the emergence of means.

We shall call this typical pattern incremental politics for two reasons. In the first place, we have referred to its preoccupation with small or incremental changes as one of its defining characteristics. Secondly, some of the other characteristics of this pattern of politics are rooted in its preoccupation with small or incremental change. In short, the incremental character of this political pattern is central and fundamental, even if it does not wholly characterize it.

For a democracy like the United States, the commitment to incremental change is not surprising. Nonincremental alternatives usually do not lie within the range of choice possible in the society or body politic. Societies, it goes without saying, are complex structures that can avoid dissolution or intolerable dislocation only by meeting certain preconditions, among them that certain kinds of change are admissible only if they occur slowly. Political democracy is often greatly endangered by nonincremental change, which it can accommodate only in certain limited circumstances.

In incremental politics, political parties and leaders compete for votes by agreeing on fundamentals and offering only incrementally different policies in each policy area in which they wish to compete. Since this phenomenon has been frequently demonstrated to be a prerequisite for the survival of democracy itself, it can hardly be questioned as a characteristic of political life in the Western democracies. Moreover, each of the competing political parties shifts its own policies only incrementally at any one time. Such incremental alteration of party policies is in fact the normal, though not invariable, rule in all two-party democracies and in some multiparty democracies.[3] In addition, policy-making proceeds through a sequence of approximations. A policy is directed at a problem; it is tried, altered, tried in its altered form, altered again, and so forth. In short, incremental policies follow one upon the other in the solution to a given problem.

These are easily recognizable fundamental processes in American democracy and indeed in most, if not all, of the stable, deeply rooted democracies of the world. To be sure, ideological rhetoric pervades political debate and runs through general statements of purpose in legislative enactments; but the preponderance of incremental politics is evident from the manner in which the legislators themselves, as well as administrators and judges, implement those purposes.

It becomes clearer now why political policy, in its focus on increments of change, also shows the other characteristics—it is remedial, serial, and exploratory, for example—that we identified as part of incremental politics. To pursue incremental changes is to direct policy toward specific ills—the nature of which is continually being re-examined—rather than toward comprehensive reforms; it is also to pursue long-term changes through sequences of moves. Avoiding social cleavage along ideological lines, which is exacerbated when issues of ultimate principle are raised, incremental politics explores a continuing series of remedial moves on which some agreement can be developed even among members of opposing ideological camps.

Even though we speak of small or incremental changes as the kind of change that is made in incremental politics, we should like to caution against identifying incremental change only with change that is immediately acceptable to political decision-makers. Discussing national water resources policy, James Fesler goes through a list of possible administrative reorganizations and reaches the conclusion that

The indications that Congress cannot be appeased by any administrative arrangement so far devised simplifies our immediate task of drawing conclusions about national water resources administration. Until further political analyses disclose a way in which Congress might accommodate the patent need for more reasonable arrangements for consideration of water resource programs, we can revert to relatively apolitical modes of analysis.[4]

He proceeds to discuss, in despair of finding any program on which Congress might look favorably, the possibility of organizing water-resource administration into a single major national department with program formulation at the secretarial level of the contemplated department. These suggestions remain, despite their immediate political unacceptability, within the bounds of incremental politics as we define the term.

Just how far the practice of incremental politics permeates the activity of our government can be illustrated even by decisions that, on superficial inspection, appear to be nonincremental. The decision to convert from a peacetime to a wartime economy would, at first glance, appear to be one of the largest and most consequential decisions a nation might make, hardly an incremental decision. Yet, in the United States, the actual process of transformation was incremental.[5] A sequence of decisions began in fact before the country was actually at war, when this country took up the task of supplying its future allies from "the arsenal of democracy." The Neutrality Act was revised in November, 1939, to permit "cash and carry" purchases of arms by the Allies, and the federal government set up an interdepartmental committee to co-ordinate foreign and domestic purchases. The government began applying informal pressure to expand the machine-tool industry, even before Congress authorized new appropriations for "defense"; after these appropriations were made, "educational contracts" were issued "through which industry was led into war production step by step, somewhat against its desires, if not against its will."[6]

The President reacted to the Nazi triumphs in the spring of 1940 by declaring a state of "unlimited national emergency." What this meant, immediately, was a number of incremental moves— a demand for "night and day production" of machine tools; creation of new administrative agencies to deal with petroleum and food; and the founding of an Office of Civilian Defense. Other developments came soon after. In addition to passing increased appropriations, Congress made various laws to facilitate the financing of war contracts. The Selective Service Administration commenced operations. (At roughly the same time, the United States exchanged fifty destroyers for island bases within the British Empire.) As the summer of 1940 ended, voluntary priorities on military orders began to give way to regulation; the Council of National Defense established a Priorities Board.

In January, 1941, the President put forward the "lend-lease" program, which was approved by Congress in March. An Office of Production Management was set up. As agitation began for the conversion of the automobile industry to aircraft production, the government began acting to expand steel and aluminum capacity. To speed up the conversion of existing plants to war production, a Supply Priorities and Allocations Board was superimposed in August, 1941, on the Office of Production Management, which in its several months of operation had proved unable to deal effectively with "the military opposition to lend-lease and . . . industrial opposition to war conversion." [7] An Office of Price Administration began functioning, although it did not obtain specific statutory powers until some months later. The first Liberty ship was launched, nonessential building was brought to an end, and steel plate was put under "complete allocation."

All these steps were taken before the war officially began; it was in the midst of an unfinished series of such developments that the Japanese struck at Pearl Harbor. The War and Navy Departments had prepared an industrial mobilization plan against the eventuality of being officially at war, and the plan was revised as late as September, 1939. This gesture at over-all planning was not, however, effective in the sense of producing a plan that was actually applied—even though, in making the gesture, the planners had foreseen most of the functions that the government would have to take on in a wartime economy. The planners had not envisioned—even during the revisions of mid-1939—what Gulick calls "our crab-like progress into 'defense' and war." Equally important, they had not realized how complex and extensive—and how variable—the institutions necessary to organize mobilization would turn out to be. They underestimated the importance, for example, of political leadership by the President, omitted to consider the need for a food administration, and treated price controls as an optional possibility. Apparently they did not contemplate any "economic dealings with allies"—thus ignoring what became, as we have seen, the leading stimulus to industrial mobilization before the war officially began.

The incremental pattern of mobilization continued as an accelerated process after the United States became fully involved.

Indeed, one could hardly hope for more spectacular evidence of incremental adjustments than the continual reorganizations of the war production agencies themselves. The Office of Production Management, as we have seen, was superseded, at least in part, even before the war began by the Supply Priorities and Allocations Board. The co-ordinating functions of those two agencies were taken over, once the war began, by still another *ad hoc* agency—the War Production Board; then by the Office of Economic Stabilization; and finally by the Office of War Mobilization. The last became, as new needs emerged, the Office of War Mobilization and Reconversion. Waves of reorganization also characterize the history of other wartime agencies. Gulick claims to detect in these waves a "sequence of evolution" or "rhythm of growth and adaptation,"

starting with (a) planning and advisory agencies, (b) passing to action agencies with extensive power of issuing coordinating directives to other action agencies, (c) improvising bottleneck-breaking agencies for individual programs and then (d) correcting the conflicts thus engendered by setting up co-ordinating agencies of limited jurisdiction, and finally (e) creating a super co-ordinating agency in the White House, with complete authority over the domestic economy.[8]

We may append to this account Gulick's comment, "Our administrative structure for war . . . was not established like a new building and completed before occupancy, but was built while occupied and remodeled from time to time as we waged the war."[9] Whether or not large-scale operations like mobilization are launched according to a general plan, there seem to be indefeasible incremental features about them.

The incremental character of political policy-making is often disguised, more often in the Soviet Union than in the United States, by much talk of plans and planning. Often a plan is no more than a loosely stated set of goals and possible steps. It is relevant to the kind of actual decision-making we have been describing, but its goals and steps ordinarily have to be reformulated with each policy move. Even in the Soviet Union, economic planning is highly sequential and incremental like the kind of policy-making we have been describing for the United States.

4—Types of Decision-Making

We can now ask, What methods for analysis are suitable to each of the kinds of decisions and situations represented in the four quadrants? We are going to present the strategy of disjointed incrementalism as an analytical strategy adapted, as the name we give it suggests, to the third quadrant—adapted, that is to say, to incremental politics.

DIAGRAM 2

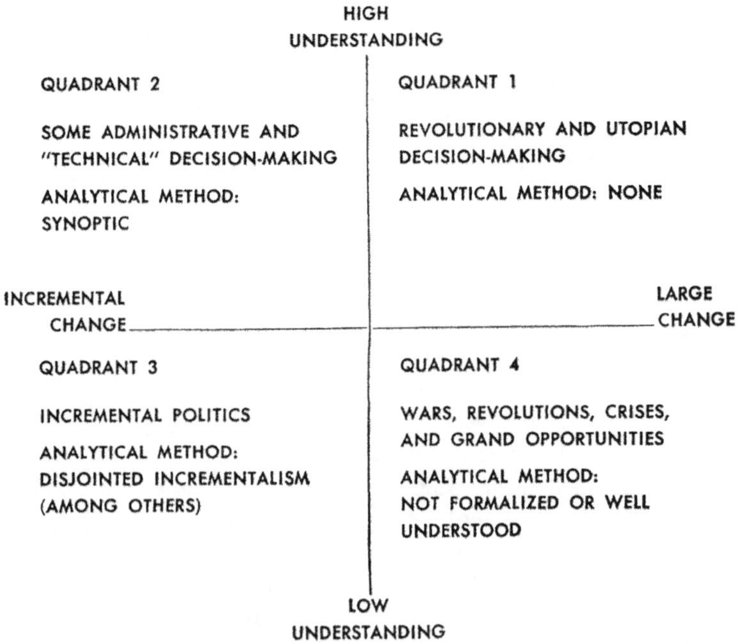

HIGH
UNDERSTANDING

QUADRANT 2	QUADRANT 1
SOME ADMINISTRATIVE AND "TECHNICAL" DECISION-MAKING	REVOLUTIONARY AND UTOPIAN DECISION-MAKING
ANALYTICAL METHOD: SYNOPTIC	ANALYTICAL METHOD: NONE

INCREMENTAL
CHANGE_____LARGE
CHANGE

QUADRANT 3	QUADRANT 4
INCREMENTAL POLITICS	WARS, REVOLUTIONS, CRISES, AND GRAND OPPORTUNITIES
ANALYTICAL METHOD: DISJOINTED INCREMENTALISM (AMONG OTHERS)	ANALYTICAL METHOD: NOT FORMALIZED OR WELL UNDERSTOOD

LOW
UNDERSTANDING

Synoptic methods, we suggest, are limited to the second quadrant, that is, to those happy if limited circumstances in which decisions effect sufficiently small change to make synoptic under-standing possible. Synoptic methods are called for in the first quadrant, to be sure; for all the reasons given in this and the preceding chapter, however, the information and comprehension requirements of synoptic problem-solving simply cannot be met for large-scale social change. It is of course the careless assumption that man's competence is unlimited that makes utopian reconstruc-tion so attractive.

As for the fourth quadrant, crises, wars, revolutions, and grand opportunities call for kinds of analytical strategy quite different from the synoptic, but we cannot claim that the strategy of dis-jointed incrementalism is suited to these situations. At the present juncture in the study of decision-making, one would be hard put to formalize the methods appropriate to that quadrant. We repre-sent these conclusions roughly in Diagram 2.

Now we are ready to outline the strategy of disjointed incre-mentalism as it can be observed in actual practice.

CHAPTER 5

THE STRATEGY OF
DISJOINTED INCREMENTALISM

We are now finally ready to outline a strategy that many policy analysts do in fact use to adapt to the difficulties of evaluation and decision-making.

Even though we attach great importance to the strategy, we are quick to acknowledge—again—that it is only one of many possible sets of adaptations. When a man sets out to solve a problem, he embarks on a course of mental activity more circuitous, more complex, more subtle, and perhaps more idiosyncratic than he perceives. If he is aware of some of the grosser aspects of his own problem solving, as when he consciously focuses his attention on what he has identified as a critical unknown, he will often have only the feeblest insight into how his mind finds, creates, dredges up—which of these he does not know—a new idea. Dodging in and out of the unconscious, moving back and forth from concrete to abstract, trying chance here and system there, soaring, jumping, backtracking, crawling, sometimes freezing on point like a bird dog, he exploits mental processes that are only slowly yielding to observation and systematic description.

We do not attempt to make any direct contribution to the growing literature on the phenomenal patterns of mental processes. In presenting an outline of what we call disjointed incrementalism, we do not presume to know in any detail or with any degree of intimacy how men think; neither do our generalizations imply that we have found that one man's mental processes are necessarily quite like any other man's. When we speak of disjointed incrementalism as a strategy for analysis, we mean only to describe one set of practices that, however subtly and idiosyncratically each mind works, represents a point of convergence for policy analysts in their adaptations to the difficulties of problem solving and evaluation. The set of adaptations is relatively simple, crude, almost wholly conscious, and public; it can be discussed with the same concepts and language that were employed in discussing the synoptic ideal. We do not need to use the language, for example, of sensori-motor coordinations, perceptive organizations, or concept formation (as psychologists study it).

As to what the adaptations are, they become familiar as soon as they are named. Our purpose in collecting them together under the label of disjointed incrementalism is only, as we have said before, to show that, taken together as a mutually reinforcing set of adaptations, they constitute a systematic and defensible strategy. Since the adaptations are commonplace, some of them have been recognized in the literature. Perhaps because they are often taken for granted and their mutual reinforcement is overlooked, they are not generally identified as a system. In his concept of "piecemeal social engineering," however, Karl Popper gives recognition to a number of these adaptations. Popper rightly holds that the problem of evaluation is simplified by a concentration on social evils rather than on utopias; that limits on man's competence are acknowledged in reforms that alter only relatively small parts of the social structure at any one time; that continuity in readjustment diminishes the need to be right in any single decision; that aims change with experience with policies; and that experiments in social reform teach some things that cannot be learned in any other way.[1] For our purposes, he has, however, underplayed the significance of his insights, missing their general applicability and reducing them in his own analysis to no more than supporting arguments in an attack on planning.

In describing the strategy, we shall draw repeatedly on two examples of policy analysis: one contained in Charles S. Hyneman's *Bureaucracy in a Democracy*, the other in W. W. Rostow and Max F. Millikan's *A Proposal: Key to an Effective Foreign Policy*. If the adaptive methods are to be seen combined as a systematic strategy, we must show how they interconnect in single pieces of policy analysis; hence we are precluded from relying for illustration solely on scattered examples from different pieces of analysis.[2] Hyneman's is an analysis of bureaucracy with a sustained though not exclusive policy interest. He analyzes the policy problem of the proper place of bureaucracy in democratic government. Rostow and Millikan focus exclusively on policy. They have written their book to push a specific proposal: that the United States take the leadership in organizing and financing a long-term program to lend to underdeveloped countries in the free world on such a scale as "would make available . . . sufficient additional capital and technical assistance to satisfy all likely demands for such assistance which meet fairly high standards of eligibility based on the prospective productivity of investment" (p. 126).

In this chapter we shall simply lay out the strategy, leaving for the following chapter fuller exposition of how it accomplishes the adaptations lacking in the synoptic ideal.

1—The Strategy Outlined

Margin-Dependent Choice

Policy analysts always begin somewhere, not *ab nihilo* as when God created the world. They have an idea of present conditions, present policies, and present objectives. They seek to improve their idea of present conditions, policies, and objectives by obtaining more information about them. It is conspicuously the case—although not logically necessary—that they often do so by comparing alternatives all of which are similar to the status quo. It is equally clear that they derive information about alternatives from historical experience, from contemporary experience in other societies or locations, and from imagination stimulated by experience. A dominant characteristic, then, of their investigations is that they focus on the increments by which the social states that might result from alternative policies differ from the status quo. To put the point in other terms, their investigations are concerned with margins at which it is contemplated that social states might be changed from that existing. They are focused on incremental alteration of existing social states, as it is defined in the preceding chapter.

They are accordingly occupied with the kind of change that is the usual product of incremental politics, and they are sometimes quite explicit in recognizing the connection between incremental politics and the pattern of their own analysis. In commenting, for example, on the kinds of policies for the control of government bureaucracy that he intends to discuss, Hyneman writes,

> It seems to me unwise if not futile to urge the American people to make radical departures from their present political system and venture into relationships and ways of doing things that are completely foreign to their experience. This is not to urge conservatism in governmental reform on the ground that fundamental changes cannot be made to appear attractive and be sold to the people. It is rather to say that a nation that is devoted to democratic government should, to the extent possible, forego revolutionary change in favor of gradual adaptation; that a quick installation of fundamental changes, even when we are caught flat-footed by the deficiencies of existing arrangements, is likely to defeat the very purposes which cause it to be advocated. The people, who must ultimately indicate their satisfaction or discontent with the way things are going, can only do so with confidence if they feel at home among the institutions available to them for exerting influence. If fundamental understanding about the form and methods of government are upset, the people will flounder in their efforts to participate in political life (pp. 563–564).

So far as his empirical analysis is concerned, a policy analyst need not and often does not attempt to comprehend strictly and literally present states of affairs or the consequences of present policies. Nor does he try to comprehend strictly and literally new possible social states or all the consequences of new policy possibilities. He attempts no more—later we shall show that he attempts even less—than to understand the respects in which various possible states differ from each other and from the status quo.

We can say that he concentrates his evaluations on what we call margins or increments, that is, on the increments by which value outputs or value consequences differ from one policy to another. He need not ask himself if liberty is precious and, if so, whether it is more precious than security; he need only consider whether an increment of the one value is desirable and whether, when he must choose between the two, an increment of one is worth an increment of the other.

He will sometimes recognize, even explicitly, that his evaluations are what we call marginal. In Hyneman's statement on democracy, for instance, he converts the question of the value of respect for the individual into a question of more or less: "The essence of democracy, as that word is used in this book, is respect for the individual . . . In a democracy, any man who manages to be born is entitled to consideration. The next question is, *how much consideration?*" (p. 11, our italics).

In another illustrative passage, Hyneman explicitly recognizes that it is what we call marginal values that count in policy determination. Referring to the value, "control over the bureaucracy by elected officials," he writes, "This basic presumption is no doubt accepted by all thoughtful observers and students of government. But there is substantial difference of opinion as to how pervasive and how compelling that relationship should be" (p. 48).

Several features of incremental or margin-dependent choice need to be distinguished. Altering the order in which they were first introduced, we note first that only those policies are considered whose known or expected consequent social states differ from each other incrementally. But one can imagine that a set of policies meeting this condition might be expected to bring about some social state differing drastically and nonincrementally from the status quo. Hence we add a second feature: that only those policies are considered whose known or expected consequences differ incrementally from the status quo. The third feature of incremental choice, however closely it seems to follow from the first two, is logically independent of them: that examination of policies proceeds through comparative analysis of no more than the marginal or incremental differences in the consequent social states rather than through an attempt at more comprehensive analysis of the social states. To this list we add a final feature, again logically independent but implicit in our exposition of incremental choice: choice among policies is made by ranking in order of preference the increments by which social states differ.

Incremental evaluation is clearly quite different from the construction of a rational-deductive system. Its demands on the analyst are best estimated, however, if we compare it with the method of the welfare function, to which it appears more closely related, since there is a kind of formal equivalence between ranking all social states and choosing among increments of value. (No doubt this equivalence is sometimes simply assumed by advocates of the welfare function.) If all conceivable social states are enumerated for ranking, then each social state differs only incrementally from at least some other social states. If it were possible to rank them explicitly, therefore, one would be responding to the increments in value consequence by which each social state differed from the others most like it. One immediate and major difference between the two concepts of evaluation is that, where the welfare function requires a ranking of all social states, the strategy restricts evaluation to social states only incrementally different from the status quo. The strategy is less demanding than the method of the welfare function.

The strategy also differs from the social welfare function in that, strictly speaking, ranking social states is not necessarily the same as ranking incrementally differing alternatives. If, for example, one proposes to rank all possible social states—rather than all conceivable states—then whether or not the states differ only incrementally from at least some other social states on the list depends on what variety of social states one assumes to be possible.

Assuming, however, that each social state ranked in a function is incrementally different from at least some others, there is a further subtle but important difference between the two systems.

The strategy of identifying increments by which consequences of policies differ and of responding to these differences in one's choices actually achieves in practice an implicit ranking of social states. One does not need to conceptualize "social state" before doing so—nor does one need to face up to an explicit choice among such difficult-to-grasp complexes as social states. The ranking of social states is merely a by-product of incremental comparisons. By contrast, discussion of social welfare functions is usually characterized either by the prescription that the policy analyst rank social states directly, rather than epiphenomenally as in the strategy, or it is silent on the point. In either case, the method of the welfare function is not adapted in this respect to describing or prescribing in actual policy analysis.

On this point, the consumer analogy is again helpful. We can imagine a consumer trying to respond to a request that he rank all possible social states he could achieve by spending his income in one way or another. We can imagine his despair. Yet he achieves such a ranking implicitly whenever he chooses among alternative increments of value for which he spends increments of his income. In this respect, every consumer practices the strategy in spending his income.

Furthermore, as a guide to performing the task of evaluation, the prescription to rank social states does not commit an analyst (or consumer) to incremental analysis, and it may lead him to an impossibly ambitious program of comparisons. Instructed to compare social states, an analyst may make an ambitious attempt somehow to comprehend alternative social states as abstractions to be compared with one another. He may completely miss the fact that only comparison of increments will do the job for him. Although economists, who originated the idea of the welfare function, are unlikely to make such a mistake, others less familiar with marginalism might easily do so.

It may further clarify the incremental character of the strategy to point out the forms in which value conflicts arise in any one analyst's mind, although we have already suggested the answer. Conflicts take the forms of questions about the analyst's or evaluator's trading ratios at the margin between pairs of values.

The resolution of a conflict over two values is not expressed by a principle, as in the rational-deductive method, nor by a priorities list—nor is it implicitly embodied in a ranking of social states. It can best be expressed by stating how much of one value is worth sacrificing, at the margin reached in a given situation, to achieve an increment of another.[3] As an illustration, we may ask again whether anyone can say that he prefers, for example, unemployment to inflation or inflation to unemployment when they are in conflict? Some individuals think they know which they prefer, but it can quickly be shown that they cannot arrange even two such values in order of priority. Almost everyone prefers unemployment to inflation if unemployment is small enough and inflation great enough. Yet almost everyone prefers inflation to unemployment if unemployment is great enough and inflation small enough. One's preferences between unemployment and inflation can therefore be expressed as a set of trades or as a set of terms on which one is willingly exchanged for the other.

Restricted Variety of Policy Alternatives Considered

If the analyst limits his attention to policies that differ only incrementally from the status quo, then it follows that he attends to a smaller variety than all the possible policies that might be imagined. There exists, of course, an infinite number of incremental policies; but, given discontinuities in the adjustments by which policies can be varied, given certain characteristics in the ways individuals describe and explain policies, and given failures in imagination and other restrictions on the infinite multiplication of alternative policies, restriction to policies that offer only incremental changes is indeed a great restriction of the possible variety.

For those who suspect that this limitation of attention to policies that differ only incrementally from present policies reduces the rationality of problem solving by neglecting desirable nonincremental alternatives, we shall provide a full statement of how disjointed incrementalism meets this objection at a later stage in the argument. For now, a brief comment will suffice. One answer is that nonincremental alternatives, even if desirable in some sense, are often politically irrelevant, for reasons set forth in the preceding chapter. Preoccupation with incremental alternatives is suitable when a society is practicing incremental politics. Another answer is that, while one can speculate on nonincremental alternatives, an analyst is often without adequate information, theory, or any other organized way of dealing systematically with nonincremental alternatives. Observation of recent policy steps throws little light on them, and they call for competence beyond the capacity of contemporary social science. They cannot be very rationally explored, therefore, even if one wished to try.

It is hardly necessary to illustrate the relatively tight logical connection between an incremental focus in policy analysis and a consequent reduction in the variety of policy alternatives to be considered. Hyneman's preoccupation with relatively few alternatives is implied in our first quotation from his book; in Rostow and Millikan's analysis, their proposal for foreign aid simply excludes other proposals. Presumably, they considered a variety of such proposals before settling on that particular form for their own, even though the deliberations are not reported in the book itself. We can be fairly sure, however, that, consistent with their expressed intention to present a plan similar to policies already in effect or under discussion, they restricted themselves to relatively few alternatives. Unspecified numbers of alternatives are written off in passages like the following, in which they argue that policy-making cannot range over the whole spectrum of what might at first be thought possible:

In the face of the obvious possibility that the political and psychological effects of economic assistance programs can be contrary to our interests, would it not be better to leave the people of the underdeveloped areas of the world in a state of placid stagnation rather than arouse expectations that neither we nor they can possibly satisfy and thus expose their societies to the risk of social and political upheaval? The question implies a choice that is not in fact open to us. The unprecedented spread of communication throughout the world in the last twenty years has already created new images of the future in the minds of the bulk of the world's population. The process of expectations are already aroused, and the economic, political, and social revolution of the underdeveloped areas is already inexorably on the march. Even if the Communists were not everywhere promoting and encouraging this revolution in order to serve their own ends, its world-wide movement would be accelerated in the coming decades. The alternative of supporting semifeudal stability is a mirage (pp. 24–25).

Restricted Number of Consequences Considered for Any Given Policy

The third attribute of actual analysis, although it bears a certain relationship to the attribute just discussed, is not logically implied by any of the foregoing. Sometimes the analyst explicitly restricts his examination of policy consequences, as when an economist declares that certain aspects of his problem go beyond his competence and belong to the jurisdiction of the psychologist, sociologist, or political scientist. Sometimes restriction on analysis is not explicit but is, nevertheless, deliberate, as when an analyst studying the consequences of a certain federal highway building program feels free to disregard certain indirect consequences for social mobility or family solidarity.

One misses the significance of this feature of the strategy if one dismisses it as no more than a recognition that unimportant consequences are to be neglected, as in the synoptic ideal. In neither of the above illustrations are the neglected consequences necessarily unimportant. Highway building could, for example, have striking indirect effects on the cohesion of family groups, through its direct impact on population mobility. To be sure, incremental analysts do neglect the unimportant consequences of policies, but among those they concede to be important, they often rule out of bounds the uninteresting (to them), the remote, the imponderable, the intangible, and the poorly understood, no matter how important. Of course, they also sometimes omit inadvertently some important consequences.

The strategy does not necessarily encourage neglect of long-run consequences in favor of exploring short-run effects. The strategy is used for both and should not be identified simply as a strategy for attending to the short run in the hope that the long run will take care of itself. On this point, we shall, however, have more to say in a later section on political attitudes.

This third attribute of the strategy—restricted examination of consequences—is, perhaps, the most puzzling of all its features. To be sure, omitting consideration of one set or another of important consequences greatly simplifies the analyst's task. To omit is often to make manageable, and to aspire to completeness is often to do a bad job of everything attempted. Still, it may be asked, how can society expect to avoid suffering serious adverse consequences if policies are chosen without careful consideration of all consequences? We shall answer this question later. If this third attribute of the strategy seems alarming, we have not at all forgotten our intention of showing that these attributes interrelate in such a way as to constitute a systematic, understandable, and defensible strategy for problem solving generally and for evaluation in particular.

How complete is the Rostow-Millikan analysis of consequences? It does indeed cover an impressive array of the implications of their proposal. Nevertheless, we can easily point to important possible consequences of implementing their proposal that they have not considered. Although they have considered some possible Soviet reactions to the United States' inauguration of the policy they propose, they have not analyzed the possibility that, if the Soviets are contemplating attack on the United States at some future date, they might be driven to attack earlier by fear of a strengthened United States position. If this possibility seems remote, it is nevertheless a serious possible consequence of their program. Furthermore, the authors have not carefully analyzed the possibility that their proposal might push underdeveloped nations into heavier reliance on central planning than might otherwise be the case—even though it suggests that applications for loans show that the recipient country has worked out a "consistent national development program" (p. 65). Nor have they considered the possibility that their proposal will put a premium on deceit as it has been alleged that the Marshall Plan motivated recipients to manufacture balance-of-payments deficits in order to qualify for aid.

In one explicit passage, Millikan and Rostow take note of some aspects of their problem not embraced in their own study; hence their omissions are not to be dismissed as oversights:

Some would emphasize the importance of organizational arrangements for collective security—a better structure for the United Nations; a system of bilateral, multilateral, or world-wide international agreements; institutions to reduce the importance of national sovereignty like European Union, World Federalism, and the like. Some would emphasize ideological considerations—the necessity to counter and expose systems of thought like communism which have a built-in commitment to violence as an instrument of change; the importance of restating systematically and promulgating widely the values of Western democratic liberalism in a form which would be irresistibly persuasive to peoples everywhere. Some would emphasize the importance of creating social, economic, and political conditions in which violence and protest would lose their appeal because more attractive methods were available for satisfying personal and collective aspirations. Obviously all these approaches and others besides are needed (pp. 3–4).

Hyneman provides another example of incomplete examination of consequences, by boldly declaring his inability to pursue the implications of his problem in every direction and to every possible distance:

Human relationships do not have a starting place and a stopping place. . . . Everything that is going on at any moment bears some relation, however remote, to a vast range of other things that are going on at the same time. . . . Any discussion of the place of bureaucracy in the structure of a democratic society is therefore of necessity only a fragmentary treatment of the problem in its whole implications. My decisions as to what to include and what to exclude in this study are accordingly arbitrary . . . (pp. ix–x).

His preoccupation with democracy, the values of which he takes trouble to define in his first chapter, lead him to exclude certain other values important to a full assessment of policy consequences—although in this quotation he does not distinguish between omission of important consequences and other omissions. Note, however, the last sentence of the quotation: his decisions as to what to exclude are "arbitrary." He does not deceive himself that he has achieved a nice and nonarbitrary distinction between the important and unimportant, omitting only the latter. In his use of the term "arbitrary," he in effect emphasizes one striking feature of disjointed incrementalism: that what is omitted is often quite as important as what is considered. Hyneman's omissions, it should be noted, are not capricious.

Adjustment of Objectives to Policies

While the conventional view of problem solving is that means are adjusted to ends (policies are sought that will attain certain objectives), it is a significant aspect of policy analysis as actually practiced that, in certain specific ways, the reverse adjustment also takes place. Since the reverse adjustment is superimposed on the conventionally conceived adjustment of means to end, the net result is a reciprocal relationship between means and ends or between policies and values that is different from that envisaged in the synoptic ideal.

Although there is a fundamental sense in which ends govern means, there is an equally fundamental sense in which the proximate ends of public policy are governed by means. We can aspire to fly without mechanical aids, to eliminate boredom, to prevent pain and the occasions for it, to bring democracy to the Soviet Union next year, or to safeguard the atmosphere against radiation while simultaneously testing nuclear weapons. None of these is our policy objective, however, because we have neither means to its achievement nor any likely prospect of finding them. Clearly what we establish as policy objectives we derive in large part from an inspection of our means. It was once an American policy objective to be able to fight any war without serious damage to life and property within the continental United States; it is no longer an objective. The objective shifted with the shift in possible means.

Policy objectives shift not only because an old objective becomes impossible or a new one possible but because the cost of achieving an objective changes. In fact, "impossible" often means no more than "prohibitively costly." When, for example, we say that it is impossible to eliminate automobile accidents, we mean that most people would view the elimination of automobiles, which is the best possible method of eliminating automobile accidents, as too great a sacrifice or cost. Usually, of course, the costliness of achieving an objective does not disqualify the objective but merely makes its relative importance dependent on the means at hand with which to pursue it.

In the last excerpt but one from Rostow and Millikan, in which they rule out a do-nothing policy for underdeveloped areas, they make clear their belief not only that some kinds of policies are impossible under present circumstances but that an objective like "supporting semi-feudal stability" is a mirage. There is no longer any feasible means of supporting such stability, even if we wished to do so.

In the light of this fundamental dependence of ends on means, the way in which adaptation takes place can be explained as follows:

1. The analyst chooses as relevant objectives only those worth considering in view of the means actually at hand or likely to become available.

2. He automatically incorporates consideration of the costliness of achieving the objective into his marginal comparison, for an examination of incremental differences in value consequences of various means tells him at what price in terms of one value he is obtaining an increment of another.

3. While he contemplates means, he continues at the same time to contemplate objectives, unlike the synoptic analyst who ideally must at some point finally stabilize his objectives and then select the proper means.[4]

The incremental strategy on the third point is worth illustrating with particular care. Let us see, for example, how Hyneman specifies objectives simultaneously with means. Having introduced his presumption that control over the bureaucracy by elected officials is an essential objective and then immediately declaring that, to be meaningful, the objective has to be stated in terms of "how much control," he goes on to indicate how to attack the "how much" question. The principal questions, he declares, involve presidential-congressional relations:

Here is the parting of the ways for students of theory of administration. The issue is both one of theory as to where we shall place authority for making public policy and one of theory as to where we shall place authority for directing and controlling administration. The Constitution, in locating certain grants of authority in Congress and in the President, respectively, offers a limited amount of guidance toward the resolution of the issue. But the words of the Constitution are far from conclusive and the courts have not yet written any definitive meaning into the document so far as this matter is concerned. The question of how President and Congress shall divide between themselves and share together the direction and control of the bureaucracy is therefore an issue in political theory, to be resolved for each man in terms of what kind of direction and control he would like to see made effective upon the bureaucracy and in terms of his supposition that either President or Congress or the two together will most certainly provide that direction and control (p. 71).

With this statement, Hyneman has completed his introductory materials; the remainder of the book treats this issue at length. Whether we seek further evidence of ends or values in specification of the meaning of "respect for the individual," which is Hyneman's most abstract formulation of the democratic value; in specification of desirable degrees of popular control over bureaucracy, which is his less abstract formulation of particular objectives; or in specification of how Congress and the President should co-operate in controlling administration, which is the set of specifications that occupies him in all his subsequent analyses—we find it only in the detailed consideration of means that makes up the bulk of his analysis and in his concluding remarks, where a summary commitment on ends is indistinguishable from a commitment on means.

In the following paragraph, taken from the last page of the book—where it is clearly a product of, not a preface to, analysis —Hyneman's conclusions are simultaneously a judgment on means and a further specification of his ends or objectives:

The conclusion to be drawn from what has just been said is that Congress provides, and must continue to provide, the brake on the President and the administrative branch which keeps the policies of the national government within limits that are acceptable to the American people. Any departures that we make in the relations between Congress and President must not be allowed to impair the understanding that Congress is never under a legal or constitutional obligation to make effective the wishes of the President. Our political system must be so regulated that the man who is chosen by the people for the nation's highest office can lay his program before the representative assembly in a way that permits no doubt as to what he wants and can make a dramatic appeal to the people for support in his demand that Congress adopt his program. But the individual Congressman, even those who are in the President's own party, must at all times feel free to weigh the evidences of public demand which the President can produce against the evidence which comes to them that the people of their respective constituencies will or will not go along with the President. A system of government that is entitled to be called democratic will let the final decision lie in the judgment of the elective representative assembly (p. 568).

For many subjects of policy, there is apparently no possibility of arriving at a precise conception of one's objectives independent of specific policy choices. For example, how can one conceive of his objectives relevant to restrictions on the right to strike? One can, of course, believe that he favors the right to strike, although not without limits. He can also believe that he favors uninterrupted production, although again not without limits. But how does he conceive the limits? In the final analysis, he can conceive his objectives only by specifying particular policies restricting the right to strike that he is more willing to accept than certain interferences with production and, conversely, by specifying the interruptions of production he is more willing to accept than certain policies restricting strikes.

Moreover, since the pairing of limits on strikes against interferences with production is an endless process because all kinds of pairs might be imagined, he cannot express all his preferences for all possible alternatives. He is reduced to stating his preferences in the form of choices among those relatively few policies that are under active consideration. In short, he finally conceives of his preferences by choosing among a limited number of incrementally different policy proposals.

Many objectives like peace, higher farm incomes, reform of

the judiciary, better schools, a higher rate of economic growth, containment of the Soviet Union, or plugging up loopholes in income tax legislation have very little meaning unless one can see just what some degree and kind of accomplishment of the objective looks like. To concretize these values in this way tends to make the value indistinguishable from a particular policy.

To the three listed aspects of the ends-means relationship in the strategy, we add finally a fourth. In synopsis one conceives a panel of alternative policies being examined for their suitability to a set of objectives. The strategy, however, examines a panel of objectives for their suitability to a given fixed alternative or small group of alternatives. Hyneman's presumption that the problem of control over bureaucracy has to be attacked through control by elected officials, is an example. It organizes the entire analysis around the values of one important group of means to effective control over the bureaucracy—rather than around a systematic attempt to formulate ends precisely and then examine possible means to the formulated ends.

Even more explicitly than Hyneman, Rostow and Millikan approach alternative objectives in the light of their given policy. To be sure, their proposal did not spring from nowhere; it was presumably devised with problems or objectives in mind. But it is clear that, having committed themselves to examination of their own policy, their concentration on its features opens up for them new insights into possible objectives. The final justification of their policy is based, it appears, on a group of objectives possessing these very interesting characteristics: (a) Some of the objectives became relevant only after the means was decided upon, and (b) the group excluded certain objectives relevant to foreign aid policy only because they were irrelevant to the one means decided upon.

The latter is already demonstrated in their second chapter, in which several objectives are discarded because the proposal under discussion is not a suitable instrument for attaining them. The objectives are discarded, not the policy. For example, they ask: Should aid bring us friends? The answer is no, not because friends are of no value but because "The grantee's sense of dependence often produces feelings of resentment toward the grantor which may worsen rather than improve relations between the two" (p. 10).

To the question, Should aid guarantee reliance on private enterprise? they also answer no, not because private enterprise is not desirable but because "crude attempts to force a free private enterprise philosophy on recipient countries as an explicit or implicit condition for aid are almost certain to be self-defeating . . ." (p. 15).[5]

Reconstructive Treatment of Data

The mutual adjustment of means and ends is important enough to be designated as a separate feature of the strategy. It may also be viewed, however, as a particular application or illustration of another feature of the strategy—its active, reconstructive response to data. Evaluation under the strategy requires firm and definite starting points, but it is not rigidly bound to treat problems in their original forms. On the contrary, it transforms problems in the course of exploring data. Old possibilities are discarded, and new urgencies appear. Fact-systems are restructured as new ones are discovered. Policy proposals are redesigned as new views of the facts are adopted. As fact-systems are restructured and proposals redesigned, shifts occur in the values deemed relevant to settling the questions in hand. But the process is reciprocal. It might equally well be described as starting with shifts in values, which then affect both the design of policies and the attention given various orders of fact.

Such shifts in values are both encouraged and facilitated by a widespread tendency, already noted in Chapter 2, to express values as themes of concern without formulating definite rules of prescription or prohibition. Evaluators typically do not insist that "Any policy with the feature F is prescribed." Instead, they tentatively mention F as "an important consideration"—along with G and H, whose relative importance remains to be determined.

The common use of themes rather than rules is a most important means of realizing the reconstructive feature of the strategy on the value side. Furthermore, the transformations of view that occur on the fact side are shaped in part by changes in evaluative themes and reflect in part analogous shifts in factual conceptions, which are often no less flexible. For example, the facts about certain agencies of the federal government will almost surely be restructured (and amplified in different ways) when interest in them shifts from their connection with efficient performance of their avowed functions to their connection with the upkeep of party organizations. This shift reflects a change of evaluative theme.

In its preference for dealing with themes, the strategy seizes the reconstructive opportunities that are latent in the multiplicity and fluidity of values. Multiplicity and fluidity are by no means absolute drawbacks to rational evaluation (though they must seem so in a synoptic approach). Fluid themes invite, as settled sets of rules do not, exploratory responses—attempts to meet concrete demands of specific circumstances as imaginatively as is compatible with meeting them appropriately. Evaluators working with themes, as evaluators using the strategy do, can easily extend, develop, combine, and recombine conceptions of value on a given issue and can explore a variety of combinations of subordination and superordination among values and the facts connected with them. In dispensing with rules, evaluators preserve a maneuverability they would not otherwise enjoy.

Serial Analysis and Evaluation

It is difficult to speak of the margin-dependent feature of the strategy, difficult also to speak of its restructuring of data, without implying that policy-making under the strategy proceeds through long chains of policy steps. This serial procedure is an important feature of the strategy in its own right.

Analysis and evaluation together follow a series of steps. The strategy is thus adapted to continual changes in incremental politics. The Social Security Act, for example, is amended every few years to increase incrementally the level of benefits, scope of benefits, and categories of coverage. Similarly, labor legislation has undergone a long series of changes, each one incrementally different from those preceding and succeeding it. The same is true of legislation on public education, publicly supported research, grants-in-aid to state governments, and almost any other policy area one might mention. The return of analysts, time after time, to approximately the same values at approximately the same margins of choice and to confrontation of the same analytical and evaluative problem in a highly familiar context, though perhaps implicit in the incremental and exploratory character of analysis, is sufficiently important to merit the emphasis it receives here.

It is a characteristic of political processes in most governments that any single office, organization, or agency pursues a never-ending series of attacks on more or less permanent, though perhaps slowly changing, problems that lie within its field of interest or authority. In the serial attack on the insecurities of old age in the United States, it is Congress that repeatedly legislates on the problem, with advice from administrative organizations whose responsibilities for administering welfare legislation require that they too repeatedly analyze and suggest policies in the area. Private organizations are also often organized around problem areas so that they can be expected to undertake serial analyses and evaluations in their problem areas. They do not organize to solve a problem and then disband. Instead, they take it for granted that their problems will rarely be "solved" but only alleviated.

In the light of this commonplace, it is clear not only that policy analysts in these public and private organizations return time and time again to much the same problems but that social scientists and other unaffiliated analysts also find themselves returning repeatedly to the same problems they analyzed last year or last decade. The social scientist or other analyst, however diligently and imaginatively he works, does not imagine that he is "solving" such problems as strikes, juvenile delinquency, control of nuclear explosions, war, poverty, traffic congestion, insecurity. He looks instead for appropriate moves in a series he expects to continue.

The series of analyses and evaluations that typically characterize problem solving in the field of public policy is not always a tidy series, not always explicitly identified as a series, not always recognized as a series. Sometimes frames of reference shift in the course of a series, in some cases so much so that new steps take on the superficial appearance of an entirely new line of problem solving. But this appearance should not obscure the continuity that often exists below the level of superficial observation. For example, a shift in congressional attention from income-tax legislation to sales-tax legislation might reflect a continuing concern and a serial attack on certain problems of income distribution. Shifts in attention from controversy over large aircraft carriers versus bombers to a missile program to public policy on basic research to federal aid to education should not obscure an underlying continuity of interest in national security—even though the consideration of federal aid to education requires attention to many issues other than national security.

Hyneman, not pretending to solve a problem but attacking it, not pretending to finish a job but getting on with it, comments on one of his own proposals (for a new and powerful council of party leaders headed by the President):

It seems to me that the time is now ripe for one innovation in the relationships at the top of our government that promises to give the President a firmer hold on the loyalty of his party in Congress and at the same time give Congress a better opportunity to tell the President in advance what it will and will not tolerate. Some persons may see in the proposed arrangement a first step toward a parliamentary system. It certainly will not erect an obstacle to later moves in that direction. The proposal is made, however, without concern for its relation to the parliamentary style of government; I put it forward because it promises to improve working relationships at the top of our government that seem to me badly in need of improvement (p. 571).

Over many years a problem may, of course, come to be regarded as solved; if so, the accomplishment is a product of a long series of policy actions. And there is always another series. Rostow and Millikan clearly assume the serial nature of policy-making in the following two statements. Describing the past, they write,

The United States is now within sight of solutions to the range of issues which have dominated its political life since 1865. Our central problem has been to reconcile the fact of industrialization with the abiding principles of democracy. The farm problem, the status of big business in a democratic society, and status and responsibilities of organized labor, the avoidance of extreme cyclical unemployment, social equity for the Negro, the provision of equal educational opportunity, the equitable distribution of income—none of all these great issues is fully resolved; but a national consensus on them exists within which we are clearly moving forward as a nation . . . (pp. 149–150).

Describing the future, they write,

The nation will have to sustain association with other nations over many years, bringing to bear its taxes and its talent, its sympathy, curiosity, and understanding. It will have to learn much of other peoples and come to know problems which the United States has long since outgrown or which it never faced (p. 151).

Remedial Orientation of Analysis and Evaluation

Since policy analysis is incremental, exploratory, serial, and marked by adjustment of ends to means, it is to be expected that stable long-term aspirations will not appear as dominant critical values in the eyes of the analyst. The characteristics of the strategy support and encourage the analyst to identify situations or ills from which to move *away* rather than goals *toward* which to move. Even short-term goals are defined largely in terms of reducing some observed ill rather than in terms of a known objective of another sort. For example, values attached to the distribution of income are not likely to be the attainment of any desired pattern of distribution. They are most likely to be the amelioration of a specific social evil, represented by the proportion of the country's children living in poverty or by the proportion of the population disqualified for appropriate education solely by inadequate incomes.

These characteristics of the strategy again parallel a feature of incremental politics. Policy aims at suppressing vice even though virtue cannot be defined, let alone concretized as a goal; at attending to mental illness even though we are not sure what attitudes and behavior are most healthy; at curbing the expansion of the Soviet Union even though we do not know what positive foreign policy objectives to set against the Kremlin's; at reducing the governmental inefficiencies even though we do not know what maximum level of competence we can reasonably expect; at eliminating inequities in the tax structure even though we do not agree on equity; at destroying slums even though we are uncertain about the kinds of homes and neighborhoods in which their occupants should live.

We do not deny the currency of ideological objectives like freedom and security. We suggest, however, that these abstractions only establish the orientation that most analysts in a particular country or culture share. To influence policy choices at points on which analysts differ—or to play any other direct role—they must first be transformed into the more specific values involved in actual policy choices. In the process of that transformation they turn into remedial values.

Some positive themes are indeed displayed in the thinking of those who practice the strategy. An analyst may, for example, introduce the theme of equality into his consideration of policies affecting the distribution of income. If and when he does so, however, the difference between the synoptic and the incremental process remains rather sharp. Where the would-be synoptic analyst introduces equality or some specific degree of equality as a rather firm value, the incremental analyst is aware that marginal preferences among values are constantly shifting for various reasons—shifting with, for example, degrees of achievement of each value. He therefore hesitates to generalize about any specified degree of equality as a value and is more concerned instead with specific respects in which intolerable situations can be identified as negative values.

Hyneman's preoccupation with ills to be avoided is revealed in such passages as the following:

The importance of maintaining a system of government which subjects the bureaucracy to elected officials in whom the people have confidence can be fully appreciated only if we have some understanding of the things which the bureaucracy can do to the injury of the people. What are these things—specific acts, standing practices, underlying policies, states of mind—that singly or collectively may defeat the public will and undermine our democratic system of government? Some of them are things which we think of as spontaneous action of men and women in the lower ranks of the bureaucracy—personal qualities and working habits which result in what we commonly call inefficiency, for instance. Some of them are things into which the great mass of lesser officials and employees may be led by men who occupy the higher offices of the administrative branch. Still others are things which will only come about if the President or other men who occupy high places of political leadership set about using the bureaucracy to further their (private) ends. If the possibilities of abuse which are pointed out in the following pages appear worthy of serious concern, it will be necessary to consider whether they can be avoided by safeguards within the administrative branch, or whether the measures for their prevention must be found in the political system of the country (pp. 25–26).

Rostow and Millikan also take a remedial approach. Their final specification of objectives is dominated by dangers or ills to be avoided. They are less concerned with pursuing a better world than with avoiding a worse. This attitude is indicated by their preoccupation with the Soviet threat to the free world, which, although it does not preclude their occasionally discussing objectives in nonremedial terms, never hides the connection between objectives and the Soviet threat. One central statement of objectives, for example, runs as follows:

There are two priority tasks for U.S. foreign policy. The first of these is to meet effectively the threat to our security posed by the danger of overt military aggression. . . .

The second . . . is to promote the evolution of a world in which threats to our security and, more broadly, to our way of life are less likely to arise (pp. 2, 3).

Social Fragmentation of Analysis and Evaluation

Finally, it is integral to our concept of the strategy that analysis and evaluation are socially fragmented, that is, that they take place at a very large number of points in society. Analysis of any single given problem area and of possible policies for solving the problem is often conducted in a large number of centers. A problem as many faceted as national security, for example, is under study in at least hundreds and perhaps in several thousand different centers—government agencies, universities, private organizations, committees, and other institutions. Furthermore, regardless of certain notions about efficiency, each of many different approaches is taken simultaneously by dozens or hundreds of centers in imperfect communication with one another. Even for a more specific subject area like income taxation, a large number of centers of analysis can be found, including various taxpayer associations, government agencies, universities, research institutes, and individuals.

For this attribute of disjointed incrementalism, it is not necessary to draw a contrast with the synoptic ideal; synoptic problem solving would proceed, of course, in a large number of centers. We can, however, distinguish between the character of fragmentation in the two cases. In the synoptic ideal, aside from precautionary duplication, different analysts would handle either different problems or factorable subordinate parts of a given problem. But one can factor out only those relatively independent subtopics or aspects of a problem that can be understood and solved with little or no attention to the problem solving directed at other aspects of the problem. In the strategy, however, subdivision is not restricted. Specifically, where interdependencies often prohibit factoring out in the synoptic ideal, they do not prohibit fragmentation when the strategy is in use.

We have already taken note of Hyneman's "arbitrary" exclusions from his analysis. Clearly he did not ask a coordinator's permission to attack only those aspects of bureaucracy that his book encompasses; nor did he attack only a clearly factorable independent subdivision of a larger problem; nor did he take it upon himself to see to it that others attended to what he neglected. This behavior is typical in policy analysis and in social science as a whole. Gaps, overlaps, every man for himself—at least superficially, social science appears to be a chaos of laissez faire.

It is primarily this feature that has led us to use the apparently pejorative and deliberately awkward term "disjointed" in denoting the strategy. Analysis and evaluation are disjointed in the sense that various aspects of public policy and even various aspects of any one problem or problem area are analyzed at various points, with no apparent co-ordination and without the articulation of parts that ideally characterizes subdivision of topic in synoptic problem solving. Of course, analysis and evaluation are in a secondary sense also disjointed because they focus as heavily as they do on remedial policies that "happen" to be at hand rather than addressing themselves to a more comprehensive set of goals and alternative policies.

In explaining why social scientists and other policy analysts employ the strategy, we accept its appearance of disorder, its apparent inattention to needs for completeness and co-ordination. Is not fragmentation, in particular, an obstacle to co-operation? How can a coherent attack on a problem be mounted without a common plan? We are not trying to suppress these objections. In fact, we deliberately stress them in the terms we use to denote the strategy. What we want to make plain is that the objections are not conclusive. Disjointedness has its advantages—the virtues of its defects—chief among them the advantage of preserving a rich variety of impressions and insights that are liable to be "co-ordinated" out of sight by hasty and inappropriate demands for a common plan of attack. There are circumstances to which no one plan is especially suited.[6]

2—The Variable Political Coloring of the Strategy

It is easy to misconceive the strategy as having an indelibly conservative color. Is not a distaste for large plans and sweeping changes the very essence of a conservative attitude in politics? Is it not characteristic of conservatives to insist on clinging to established policies? Are they not in the habit of arguing that it is unnecessary to do more than remedy the defects that turn up in established policies, using the most economical and least disruptive means of remedy when remedy finally cannot be avoided? Do they not mean to renounce novel opportunities for social benefit?

The cautions and renunciations embraced in the strategy may seem to be cautions and renunciations that would please only conservatives. A similar consideration, which also may encourage people to associate the strategy with conservative political attitudes, appears in the analogy (which may well have struck many readers already) between the features of the strategy and the procedures of legal decision-making, especially the procedures followed in English-speaking countries in applying the common law. The fear of "system," which some authors [7] find characteristic of the English legal outlook, and the opposition of English jurists to comprehensive codifications, which the same authors [8] find so notable, seem to be directed against much the same objects as our criticisms of the received ideals of evaluative method. No one could sound more like an adherent—a convinced adherent—of the strategy of disjointed incrementalism than the English jurist as characterized by Gustav Radbruch. Radbruch writes,

The English jurist . . . is inclined to believe that the individual case comes with the law that applies to it already built into it, and he believes that the formula *"ex facto ius oritur"* ("the law comes out of the fact"), if it is to be a fruitful ground for methodological thinking, should be taken to signify that the concrete necessity of deciding a genuine case has considerably more interest for the creative energies of judges than the phantoms of imaginary future cases could, floating about in the mind of a codifier who is trying to formulate a general principle of law. Because of this, the English jurist distrusts highly generalized theories in legal philosophy—he does not want to preempt the place of the individualized law that appears in single cases; he does not want to become insensitive through preconceived ideas to the lessons of an infinitely changeable and unforeseeable course of future experience (p. 53).[9]

For the light that it throws on English legal methods, Radbruch cites from Macaulay an account of English methods of legislation that seems both to capture the essence of the strategy and to stamp it with an indelibly conservative spirit:

To think nothing of symmetry and much of convenience; never to remove an anomaly merely because it is an anomaly; never to innovate except when some grievance is felt; never to innovate except so far as to get rid of the grievance; never to lay down any proposition of wider extent than the particular case for which it is necessary to provide; these are the rules which have, from the age of John to the age of Victoria, generally guided the deliberations of our two hundred and fifty Parliaments.[10]

The quotation brings us back from law to politics—where we must insist that, compelling as these reasons for associating the strategy with conservative political attitudes may seem, there is another side of the story. It is possible to have quite a different impression of the strategy—indeed, the reverse impression. Is not the strategy prepared for a world of unremitting change—the same sort of world for which John Dewey said education must be designed, thereby scandalizing conservative people? Once launched with the strategy on a course of changing policy, where is the stopping-place? Is there any limit to the changes to which it might lend itself? The very word "incrementalism" may awaken the same sort of fears that call forth declamations against "creeping socialism." Surely (from this point of view) it cannot be regarded as a coincidence that the New Deal should be fertile in examples of the strategy's being applied.

From this point of view, the synoptic approach to evaluation, or at least that specific version of it that is represented by the rational-deductive ideal, may well seem more conservative than the strategy. Unlike the strategy, it seems suited to taking a stand on fixed principles. That is at least one reason why conservatives might be inclined to claim the synoptic approach for themselves. There are also reasons why progressively minded people might be inclined to assign the synoptic approach to them. Does not the synoptic approach encourage the assumption that every detail of an innovation ought to be shown to be theoretically adequate before a move is made?

Even the legal analogy can be given the opposite color. It is easy to imagine circumstances in which a codified law would be used to obstruct legal innovation—and conversely to imagine circumstances in which common law procedures would be used to facilitate change. They might even be the same circumstances, except for the varying character of the judges: Suppose that the judges working with the codified law are less socially enlightened and less courageous than those working with common law. Codes may require revolutions to change them; the common law may be changing all the time without appearing to. English jurists may claim that the highest merit of English law is that it is fixed and certain—and kept that way by following precedents. It is just this claim that adherents of codified systems find most surprising,[11] and they are not alone in doubting it. Radbruch reminds us of a familiar remark of Sir Henry Maine's regarding "judge made law": "The fact is that the law has been wholly changed, the fiction is that it remains what it always was." [12]

The considerations that we have given on both sides—for associating the strategy with conservative attitudes or with progressive ones—do not warrant a conclusion that the strategy is in fact neutral respecting those attitudes. We have discussed the points on both sides only far enough to bring out their powers of suggestion. They would have to be examined much more carefully to determine what the suggestions actually amount to. The question of attitudes associated with the strategy is in large part an empirical question, and needs to be treated as such. Whatever the a priori possibilities, how much more likely in fact are people using the strategy to be conservative in political attitudes than people who approach evaluation in other ways?

The strategy specifies nothing about the social states in which activity about a given issue is desired to terminate; it could equally well be used to travel toward complete laissez faire or toward pervasive governmental regulation of the economy; it may well be used without adopting any idea at all of a terminus. Secondly, the strategy specifies nothing about the speed with which change is to be carried on—at any rate, nothing if, to take this point separately, we suppose that either we are comparing the speed of running through whole sequences with the same number of steps, or the speed with which the second steps of different sequences are to succeed the first, and the third the second, etc., which does not require that number or character of the remoter steps be known in advance. Conservatives may want to travel more slowly, though this is not necessarily true, if travelling slowly costs more, or if there is a temporary prospect of seizing an opportunity of stabilizing an institution that is threatened with change unless certain precautions are taken quickly. Whether they wish to travel slowly or not, however, it is possible that they will use the strategy to evaluate each step; but progressives may use it equally well, and equally well whether they wish to move fast or slow.

It is true that in requiring small steps, the strategy demands extra time for consultation and negotiation. It is sensible to suppose that so far as the strategy is exploratory and experimental, some time will be required between each two steps to inspect the results of the latest move. Let us not conclude from this that the strategy is conservative. Whether allowing for time in this way means moving so slowly that only conservatives will keep their patience depends on the accustomed rate of change in the particular society considered. In a society suddenly launched on the path of change, after centuries of somnolence, it might not prevent things from moving with alarming rapidity. Even in a society like that of the United States which is used to change, to allow no more time than is required to evaluate the last step before moving on to the next may well mean moving much faster than the accustomed rate of change.

In the argument just presented, we have again treated the strategy and synoptic analysis as alternatives. We again wish to forestall any implication that synoptic analysis (which we regard as generally impractical anyway) is the only alternative to the strategy. We disclaim any intention of presenting other practical approaches besides the strategy—though we suppose others to exist.[13] We also wish to emphasize that, given the present state of research into methods of evaluation and decision-making, we believe we can afford to leave open questions about the role in evaluation of vaguely stated aspirations, whether conservative or progressive; of utopias—whether reactionary or radical; and of highly abstract and would-be comprehensive conceptions of value. It is enough to observe that whatever use they make of such aspirations and values, policy analysts also practice the adaptations that we have described in this chapter. How these adaptations help to overcome the difficulties of problem solving that were discussed in Chapters 2 and 3, we shall now examine.

CHAPTER 6

WHY ANALYSTS USE THE STRATEGY

Taken one by one, each attribute of the strategy identified in the preceding chapter is familiar—distressingly familiar to those accustomed to thinking of at least some of them as regrettable features of policy analysis. We step onto more controversial ground in suggesting that the attributes taken together comprise more than a heterogeneous bundle of dubious analytical tactics. The controversy is in part already behind us, for merely specifying some attributes of the strategy is enough to indicate why analysts employ such devices and the grounds on which analysts might defend them. It is unmistakable, for example, that the strategy permits analysts to adapt to the kinds of troublesome interdependencies between fact and value first discussed in Chapter 2 to which the received ideals of evaluative method were not adaptable. It is also unquestionable that the strategy accomplishes an enormous simplification of the analytical task, compared to the rational-deductive ideal, the method of the welfare function, or the general synoptic approach. An analyst who practices the strategy does not even attempt the heroic tasks prescribed by these ideals.

This last point indicates one of the aspects that remain to be covered. The simplification accomplished by the strategy may appear to some readers to have been accomplished at too high a cost and may even appear to be so arbitrary as to undermine immediately any possible defense of the strategy. The implicit defense of the strategy contained in the previous chapters does not suffice. If we defend it no further, the strategy may appear perverse to some, irresponsible to others. Indeed, without further defense, the strategy may not be fully understood even by those inclined to favor it. Consequently, as we turn to further amplification of the strategy, we shall be more explicitly concerned with justifying it.

In this chapter, we shall confine ourselves to a discussion that abstracts, as we have been abstracting throughout, from the *content* of the values with which the strategy may be concerned. We want to show that the strategy does not merely relinquish idle ambitions regarding comprehensive information and comprehensive solutions to policy problems. We want to show, on the positive side, that it exploits unique advantages respecting the effective use of information, and we want to show that, while it leads people to ignore some information (as part of the price of being able to use other information effectively), its use does not amount to flagrant irresponsibility. It could amount to irresponsibility, if persons using the strategy pretended to reach comprehensive solutions for the policy problems they were investigating. Analysts and evaluators do not adopt the strategy because they expect to reach comprehensive solutions, however, but because it helps them to deal with various difficulties that the synoptic approach cannot solve. There are no perfect guarantees—the choice is between a combination of practical devices that offers some chance of headway and pedantic prescriptions that will not even succeed in getting the anchor lifted.

In the preceding chapter, the strategy was described as having eight distinct features. With respect to evaluation and analysis, it was shown to be incremental, restricted (both with respect to variety of alternatives and to variety of consequences for each alternative), means-oriented (in a number of complex senses), reconstructive, serial, remedial, and fragmented. We want now to show just what these attributes signify in regard to coping with the difficulties of evaluation specified in Chapter 2 and avoiding the failures of adaptation charged against the synoptic approach in Chapter 3. The specific difficulties of evaluation are those arising from multiplicity and fluidity of values and from social disagreement about values. Description of these difficulties was amplified and incorporated into the description of the failures of adaptation that characterize the synoptic approach to problem solving in general. The strategy is a response to those failures of adaptation. We shall therefore examine each attribute of the strategy in the light of the enumerated failures of adaptation.

The synoptic ideal, it will be remembered from Chapter 3, does not adapt in any specific way to

1. man's limited intellectual capacities
2. his limited knowledge
3. the costliness of analysis
4. the analyst's inevitable failure to construct a complete rational-deductive system or welfare function
5. interdependencies between fact and value
6. the openness of the systems to be analyzed
7. the analyst's need for strategic sequences to guide analysis and evaluation
8. the diversity of forms in which policy problems actually arise.

1—Intellectual Capacities, Information, and Costs of Analysis

To begin with a summary of what is already apparent, the strategy drastically reduces both the demands made on the analyst's intellectual capacities and on his needs for information. The strategy is thus adapted to man's limited intellectual capacities, to limited information, and to the costliness of analysis. Nothing we have said in describing the strategy assigns to the analyst any such task as constructing a rational-deductive system or welfare function. Not only does he not have to undertake such tasks as these but his burden is lighter in other ways, both obvious and subtle.

A—Adaptation through Incremental and Limited Analysis

Simplification through omission. The most obvious group of specific adaptations to limited capacities, limited information, and the high costs of analysis are the simplifying omissions to which both the specifically incremental character and the restricted scope of the strategy lead. The practitioner of disjointed incrementalism simply omits from his analysis (a) nonincremental policies, (b) many important consequences of a given policy, (c) objectives that are not attainable by present or potential means, and (d) all those aspects of alternative policies and consequences that do not represent the increments of difference among them. Here then are four adaptations by omission, each reducing the demand for intellectual capacity and information.

Such simplifications by omission cannot be rejected as intolerable simply because they neglect analysis of factors that are presumed to have great importance. The strategy, as explained earlier, is limited in application to incremental politics where the neglect of the nonincremental is the neglect of the irrelevant. The omission of impossible objectives is again a restriction of analysis to the politically relevant—values and objectives not formulated in the light of policies at hand or potentially available can have at most only indirect significance for policy-making. These values are suitable for speculative discussion but not for integration into the analysis of public policy.[1]

The omission by the strategist of important consequences of any one policy does indeed appear to be alarming. If, however, one could be reasonably confident that what one analyst neglects at any one step in a serial policy-making process would be attended to in a later step or by another analyst, this neglect would no longer seem such a major imperfection in the strategy. We shall discuss such a possibility at some length below.

Granting that simplification can be achieved by omission, what is the difference, it may be asked, between the inevitable omissions of the analyst who pursues the synoptic ideal knowing that he cannot in fact attain it and the omissions of the incremental strategist? There are two significant differences. First, the synoptic prescription is "Be as complete as possible!" If it is to mean anything at all, therefore, the analyst must substitute extensiveness for intensiveness—or at least give priority to formal completeness over other goals of analysis. The prescriptions of the strategy are different: they recognize that one may achieve a higher level of competence by not spreading oneself too thin. Second, even where omissions are admitted to be necessary, the synoptic ideal fails to specify what to omit, while the strategy both prescribes that the analyst omit the nonincremental and suggests other guidelines that will emerge in this chapter.

Other simplifications. Besides the four adaptations by omission, there are other methods of simplification. In the strategy, what *is* analyzed is adapted in various ways to man's capacities, to available information, and to the costliness of analysis. If the analyst limits his attention to incremental policies, to the increments by which policies and consequences differ, and to objectives achievable by available or nearly available means, the materials he must analyze are relatively concrete. He has therefore made a specific adaptation to such difficulties as the elusiveness of abstract values, the difficulty of knowing one's values except in concrete choice situations, and the instability of values. We noted how Hyneman moved his analysis from concern for an impossibly abstract "respect for the individual" through less abstract concern for popular control over the bureaucracy to an operating or working concern, finally, with the concrete values of and possibilities for achieving joint congressional-presidential control over the bureaucracy. He formulated his value problems as questions of how much and what kind of control and only then found them manageable.

Moreover, if the analyst limits his attention to incremental policies and to attainable or nearly attainable objectives, he necessarily limits his analysis to what is familiar to him. It is a commonplace that an analyst solves problems by finding elements in the new problem like those of older problems already solved. He makes a specific adaptation to such difficulties as evaluating the unknown and the readiness with which values shift with each new experience. He also makes use of the soundest, least speculative information available, since his focus is on the present and on the familiar.

If the analyst limits his attention to increments, it follows that he will also forswear the extraordinary difficulties of finding a utopia or the maximum of a function and will ask himself only for evidence of a step forward. An appreciation of the difficulties in finding the ideal solution and of the strategic merit in simply continuing to make some kind of headway against problems runs through most policy analyses. It is frequently revealed, for example, in the excerpts quoted in the preceding chapter from Rostow and Millikan and from Hyneman.

In limiting himself to consideration of the increments by which policies and consequences differ, the practitioner of the strategy takes other elements of social structure and policy as given for the moment, regardless of their stability or instability. If they are in fact fluid, he may subsequently have to take them into account, but he will then treat them incrementally too. For the time being, however, they are the parameters of his problem. As evaluator using the strategy does not try to deal with all the dimensions of fluidity simultaneously. He reduces the fluidity that he must take into account at any one time to one very small segment of social structure and policy.

In doing so, he is taking advantage of the fact that institutions and values change at various rates. Many incremental changes are occurring within relatively short intervals of time. The shorter the time interval with which an analyst concerns himself, the more justified he is in treating a great number of elements, even changing elements, as stable. Many changes occur at a rate that will make no appreciable difference in the period being considered. An analyst may reasonably ignore decennial population shifts and trends toward using the telephone in preference to the mails when he is trying to find a way to satisfy complaints about slow mail service among cities in the Northeast.

It must by now be unmistakably clear that, if an evaluator limits his attention to incremental differences among policies and consequences, he is automatically in possession of a tactic for determining the costs of attaining policy objectives. Comparing the incrementally different value outcomes of incrementally different policies tells him precisely how much of one value has to be sacrificed to win an increment of another. He has thus adapted to a most troublesome feature of evaluation that has loomed large in our discussion of obstacles to the success of the synoptic ideal.

The role of theory. Further light can be shed on the ways in which the incremental and limited features of the strategy adapt to limited intellectual capacity, limited knowledge, and the expense of analysis—by considering the affinity between the use of theories to solve problems and the aspiration toward synoptic methods in evaluation. The synoptic approach not only takes scientific theories as models for evaluation; to succeed, it also depends on their being available in the subject matters of policy problems. The synoptic approach makes such comprehensive demands for information and analysis that theories are desperately needed merely to discipline the gathering of information and to organize the multiple implications of whatever evidence is gathered. Yet theories of this sort, highly structured bodies of generalizations that systematically employ concepts offering some approximation of axiomatic treatment, have simply not been developed for most of the topics that fall within the field of public policy evaluation. Rudimentary theories are sometimes available, and they are sometimes susceptible of further systematic development. At present, however, one almost never encounters enough of a system to impose a suitably comprehensive formal structure on the relevant problems. Nor is there much chance that the situation will quickly change. There is more explicit formal theory in economics than in the other social sciences, yet it is clear from the variety of political aspects surrounding every problem of economic policy, that economic theory can organize only a part of the information and analysis that the synoptic approach requires. The lack of theory paralyzes the synoptic approach even at the fact-gathering stage, to say nothing of its requirements regarding full and consistent treatment of values.

By contrast, the strategy remains free to operate. Although theories can be enormously helpful when they exist, the strategy can adapt itself to the absence of theories—it is a way of getting along without theory when necessary. Theories offer generalizations on various topics, and the analyst searches among these until he finds the generalizations that apply to his policy problem. He tries to subsume his problem under a more general one that theory has clarified. If he succeeds, he will have substantial findings to offer on at least one aspect of the policy problem at hand. Behind the theory which he applies in his analysis lie many observations and a structure of derived implications embodying the generalizations found relevant. He takes this structure ready-made; it cannot ordinarily be worked up on the spot. What is he to do if the observations have not been made, or the structure of derivations formulated and tested? This would be a crisis for the synoptic approach. Under disjointed incrementalism, such crises can often be avoided. The prior observations and the derived generalizations are often not required, for the analyst proceeds directly to ascertaining by the comparison of increments the relatively few relationships that need to be examined for his particular problem.

The strategy thus sharply reduces the analyst's need for either a wide-ranging body of empirical generalizations or the propositions of a large formal theoretical system. He can dispense with comprehensive theories about the workings of large institutional complexes because he limits his analysis to changes in which the variables involved are fewer and less consequential—and by which those large complexes are only tangentially affected. The strategy also reduces his need for high-level generalizations on the fewer variables that he does treat. He does not require full information about relationships extending over large domains because he can be satisfied with understanding a relationship within the more restricted domain of changes in a few variables.

What we have just said should not be mistaken for an attack upon systematic formal theories in social science. The strategy is not a rival of scientific theories. It shows what to do when scientific theories are not available, yet effective use of information is required. It shows what to do when the systematic—synoptic—model of evaluation analogous to scientific theories cannot successfully be applied. These moves tend in no way to discredit scientific theory.

One kind of theory, the very large-scale or grand integrating theory, can perhaps be helpful in a particular way to a practitioner of the strategy, while its failures of completeness or of specific applicability are not so crippling as they would be in pursuit of the synoptic ideal. A Walrasian or Keynesian theoretical framework for economic analysis, for example, can serve a useful orienting function for the analyst even though he attacks problems for which they do not provide a solution. The harbor pilot of a ship does not have to know about the shape of the earth, its motion, its magnetic field, the density of its atmosphere, or the heat-absorbing qualities of land and water. Nevertheless, such knowledge may help him to be intellectually oriented, as to a degree every literate person is, in physical theory. (The case of the navigator is different, of course. But the navigator is an example of the synoptic problem solver who operates with a theory adequate for his purposes. He has no counterpart among those who attack complex policy problems.)

B—Adaptation through Means-Orientation and Fragmentation

The strategy also adapts to limits on intelligence and information through its achievement of a close reciprocity between means and ends. Enough has already been said about the strategy to make much elaboration of this point unnecessary. Briefly, however, the preoccupation with means—the simultaneous determination of means and ends and the relative dependence of value choices on costs of achieving values—reinforces other ways in which the strategy makes the most of limited information.

In the close interrelationship between fact and value that characterizes the strategy, there is some assurance that objectives and values will not fail to keep abreast of policy possibilities as they often will in the synoptic approach. Obsolete values do not persist and unnecessarily complicate the policy problem. In the strategy, values—not all values, but those most immediately relevant to differentiating between policies—are seriously reconsidered with each new policy choice because values and policies are chosen simultaneously.

In the same way, the fragmented character of disjointed incrementalism increases its adaptability to man's limited capacities and information and to the costliness of analysis. To aspire to the synoptic ideal, an analyst must choose a policy problem whose solution is independent of the solutions to other problems, or he must somehow take account of the subsequent need for coordinating his solution with others that are related. Although he may, in despair of achieving this ideal, take this responsibility lightly, the responsibility is nevertheless his and calls for extremely delicate adjustments. Since it is characteristic of the strategy that subdivision or factoring occurs in an unrestricted variety of ways, without regard to lines along which interdependency can be minimized, no such obligation is undertaken by the practitioner of the strategy.

C—Adaptation through Serial, Remedial, and Reconstructive Features

There are major adaptations to limited capacity, limited information, and costliness of analysis that supplement the enormous simplification achieved by incremental and limited analysis. They are achieved through the remedial and serial character of the strategy, two features that have not yet figured in the present discussion. In the first place, we can see that the serial nature of strategic problem solving, like the focus on the incremental, holds analytic attention to the familiar. The penalties incurred in non-serial evaluation are nicely illustrated in this comment on a bill in Parliament:

The only reason that the Bill, which seeks to substitute a large number of petti-fogging restrictions for the present general ban on cash betting off the course, had so shaky a time during this week's debate was that the Government has been shirking its duty to amend an obviously out-of-date law for too long. Instead of moving with the times, the Government had turned a blind eye to them; the law had become so archaic that nobody had any clear idea of what to put in its place.[2]

We can also see that the serial and remedial character of analysis supports its incremental character in contributing to the modesty of analytical aspirations. As we have observed in other connections, the analyst practicing the strategy does not try to achieve an optimum or maximum of a particular value; he does not try to "solve" his problem, does not ask what a solution would require. At the most, he attempts comprehension of a suitable remedial next step in a series. To satisfy himself that a new policy remedies a perceived ill and is superior both to present policy and to some relatively small number of alternative policies does not require him to undertake the immensely more difficult task of establishing that the new policy solves the problem or drastically reduces its intensity. He always expects to take another step.

We can take note, too, of the peculiar importance of both the remedial and serial, as well as the reconstructive, character of the strategy in the face of fluidity. Since circumstances, values, and possible policies change constantly, the analyst knows that to attempt to solve a problem is to run the risk of achieving tomorrow a solution to yesterday's problem. He copes more successfully with fluidity therefore by attending to those changing social ills that a series of steps may remedy than by postulating more positive goals and aspiring to more fully conceived solutions. He does not imagine that his analytical work is anything more than a continuing problem-solving process, itself fluid in nature. An excellent illustration of the sorts of difficulty to which explicitly remedial, serial, and exploratory analysis can be seen as a corrective response is provided in this complaint by the staff head of the Chicago Housing Authority:

By the time the researchers had defined the problem, debated about proper methodology, taken their observations . . . made a highly refined and scientific analysis and prepared their report, the emergencies which had given rise to the research had already reached a climax several months earlier. . . .[3]

We can also note that, because of the serial nature of analysis, the strategy itself, when applied to incremental politics, generates the kind of information it requires. What is required is information specifically adapted to the clarification of policy steps incremental to steps already taken. This requirement follows from the fact that policy-making is serial and incremental and that, consequently, today's and tomorrow's problems are very much like yesterday's. Information is generated about the consequences of the policies that have been inaugurated, appraised as their consequences were revealed, and altered serially. More specifically, a series of changes offers analysts the opportunity to observe with some precision which incremental changes in policies produce which incremental changes in results. Thus it offers them the opportunity to obtain exactly that information required for next steps in a series.

To return to the difficulties of the Chicago Housing Authority, Meyerson and Banfield suggest that, given the complexity and fluidity of the problems faced, "the way to discover and evaluate the advantages and disadvantages of slum rehabilitation as an alternative to slum clearance, for example, was actually to rehabilitate a few blocks and appraise the results with care." [4] The advantages of practical experimentation are also the advantages of remedial, serial and reconstructive analysis. That is to say, when the analyst operates in circumstances under which he can return again and again to further remedial steps in a series of policy decisions, taking a reconstructive attitude toward the values in question, he achieves the advantages to which Meyerson and Banfield refer. [5]

We still have not hit, however, upon one of the main accomplishments of serial and remedial analysis in adapting to complexity, limited information, and costliness of analysis. We have alluded to but have not quite identified the critical interconnection between the limited and incremental character of analysis, on the one hand, and its remedial and serial character, on the other. For when these four characteristics of the strategy are combined in a political environment where policy making is incremental, remedial, and serial, a greatly simplified intellectual reorganization of the problem-solving process is also achieved.

Imagine first a society in which values or preferences and available means do not change. In such a hypothetical society, we can see one essential element in the problem-solving process: The difference between the intellectual organization of the problem-solving process under the synoptic ideal and under the strategy roughly parallels the difference between solving a mathematical problem by exact computation and by successive approximation. The advantages of the strategy would be similar to those of successive approximation, which is superior when exact computation is too difficult—and which is necessary when exact computation is impossible.

Seen this way, the concept of problem solving by the strategy is this: The analyst makes an incremental move in the desired direction without taking upon himself the difficulties of finding a solution. He disregards many other possible moves because they are too costly (in time, energy, or money) to examine. For the move he makes, he does not trouble to find out (again, because it is too costly to do so) what all its consequences are. If his move fails or is attended by unanticipated adverse consequences, he assumes that someone's (perhaps even his own) next move will take care of the resulting problem. If his policy-making is remedial and serial, his assumptions are usually correct.

To be sure, his assumptions are not always correct, and sometimes a great deal of permanent damage can be done before a corrective next step can be taken. We do not, of course, believe that the strategy is infallible. But analysts often do find it a desirable and unavoidable method of adaptation in view of the failures of the synoptic method. Their view of problem solving as successive approximation is a practical and sophisticated adaptation to the impossibility of attaining the synoptic ideal. It represents a practical alternative concept of problem solving when a synoptic computation fails to be more than superficial and leaves them with a poorer solution than can be had with successive approximation.

For the society we live in, where preferences and means change constantly, the concept of policy-making through successive approximation needs some amendment. It needs to be emphasized that the analyst using the strategy in an actual society, where goals and means change, cannot approximate a "solution" in the conventional sense that is integral to the synoptic ideal. (It is in their conception of social ills as well defined "problems" with "solutions" that, as we have already pointed out, aspirants to the synoptic ideal go wrong.) In a nonstatic society, objectives and other values continue to shift and so do actual possibilities for change. The process we have outlined for the strategy does not, therefore, successively approximate any "solution" but continues to change with changing values and policy possibilities. What we have said about the static society is even more relevant to a nonstatic society. The obstacles to the successful practice of anything approaching exact computation loom increasingly large, and the advantages of moving in a series of remedial steps seem increasingly appropriate.

D—The Problem of Neglected Consequences

We can no longer defer an exposition of how, in the strategy, consequences neglected in any one analysis are accounted for. We have emphasized the ways in which simplification of analysis is achieved by omission. We want now to show how what is omitted at one point in an analytical system can be accounted for elsewhere. At the same time, we can show more generally how harmful failures in analysis are "corrected" despite the relative narrowness of analysis by any one analyst at any one time.

We distinguish between a) adverse consequences and failures in policy unanticipated because of limited analysis, and b) adverse consequences and failures at least roughly anticipated but nevertheless not permitted to influence the analyst's choice among policies. If the analyst's approach to his policy area is both remedial and serial, he can catch either kind of neglected consequence or failure in policy as it begins to show itself and he can at that time devise policies to cope with it. And if policy-making organizations like government agencies approach their problems serially and remedially, as they do in incremental politics, they can attack these consequences as they arise.

The analyst or policy-maker can also actually anticipate ways of meeting problems posed by the second kind of neglected consequence or failure. Why, then, if he can be expected to anticipate the emerging problems and deal with them does he neglect these consequences in the first place? The answer is that he cannot, on top of his other burdens, incorporate an analysis of the neglected consequence and ways of coping with it in his original policy analysis, but he can make it the focus of a subsequent policy analysis. He can cope with two quite separate successive policy problems where he cannot cope with an integrated problem.

A city traffic engineer, for example, might propose the allocation of certain streets to one-way traffic. He may be quite unable to predict how many serious bottlenecks in traffic will arise and where. Nevertheless, he may confidently make his recommendations, assuming that, as bottlenecks arise, appropriate steps to solve the new problem will be taken at the time—new traffic lights, assignment of traffic patrolmen, or further revision of the one-way plan itself. He may also correctly anticipate certain other consequences, such as business losses in certain locations from rerouting customer traffic. Some of these consequences he will nevertheless ignore in drawing up his traffic plan. Instead, he will, in separate consideration of each of various anticipated problems, decide to alter parking regulations, ease pedestrian traffic in certain areas, or turn some other policy to reduce the business losses ruled irrelevant to his first policy problem.

At centers in which general responsibility for a wide variety of problems is located—the Presidency or the Congress, for example—some decisions will be made in the light of some values to the neglect of others. Subsequent decisions will exclude the first group and permit the previously neglected values to dominate. The values of national security, for example, dominate some decisions to the neglect of the values of price stability and low taxes, while other decisions at other times promote price stability or fairer taxation without regard for the values of national security. So long as the process continues, none of the three values is neglected.

In short, when analysis and policy-making are remedial and serial, anticipated adverse consequences of any given policy can often be more effectively treated as new and separate problems than as aspects of the original problem. Unanticipated adverse consequences can often be better guarded against by waiting for their emergence than by futile attempts to anticipate every contingency as required in synoptic problem solving. "It is better to answer as many questions as possible in advance" [6] is not an acceptable axiom for decision-making.

The process can even be speeded up by assigning to each of various policy-making and policy-analyzing agencies, groups, or individuals the responsibility for studying a specified type of policy failure or adverse consequence. The process can be further refined if these centers of responsibility develop skill in actually anticipating certain kinds of failure and adverse consequence. It is possible to develop such skill, since no one is required to anticipate all possible failures and adverse consequences. Nor is he required, as he would be by the synoptic ideal, to view anticipated consequences as objections to the policy he is considering. Instead, he simply designs a next step to deal with the anticipated failure or adverse consequence of the last step.

Despite all that we have said, some readers may still feel that the strategy does not take adequate account of consequences neglected by any one analysis. Such a feeling may reflect a misconception of the policy-making process and especially of the kind of problem that is characteristic in the field of public policy. If one falsely imagines that for the sort of problem with which the strategy deals all the relevant items of information are specifiable and fixed, then it may appear that the analyst perversely omits items x, y, and z, knowing that they will not merely modify his conclusion but show that it is dead wrong. One might falsely compare the analyst to a judge and jury who decide a question of guilty, while refusing to consider certain evidence that can be plausibly claimed to show the guilt or innocence of the prisoner.

In the practice of the strategy, the problem-solving situation is in fact quite different. Typically there is no "yes" or "no" answer but only more or less successful answers. What is relevant to the problem cannot for several reasons be predetermined, and one of these reasons is that *there is no one problem*. In addition, in deciding to attack his problem in a certain limited perspective, the analyst is making a claim about relevance that he expects will be assessed against other claims. Finally, he does not ignore information relevant to accomplishing his task, but instead he defines his task so as to leave out some consequences. We shall have more to say in a later chapter about some of these fundamental features of the strategy and their implications for the problem of tracking consequences, for, as we have said, this is a long-standing problem in ethical theory.

E—Further Adaptation through Fragmentation

When we mentioned the possibility of speeding or refining the process through which neglected consequences are attended to, by assigning to various agencies and groups the responsibility of guarding against—and anticipating if possible—certain kinds of failure and adverse consequence, we omitted for simplicity's sake the possibility of self-assignment. Fragmentation of analysis and policy-making is in large part, however, a result of self-assignment, and such fragmentation is especially adapted to non-static elements in society.

If analysis and policy-making are dispersed widely through self-assignment to many different individuals and centers, then the same kind of process that links a series of incomplete analyses by any one individual into more complete coverage of problems operates among the different individuals and groups. This kind of social fragmentation adds an important new element: the prospect that, if the values of one analyst or one policy-making group neglect indefinitely some kinds of policy consequence, other analysts and groups whose values are adversely affected will make these neglected consequences focal points of their own problem solving.

As explained in the previous chapter, the attack on the problem of income distribution in the United States, for example, is fragmented among various taxing authorities; social security agencies at the local, state, and national levels; trade unions; and business groups. All these agencies perform public services that affect the distribution of income, as well as the market, the market itself being a highly fragmented decision-making process. We attack educational inadequacies, to take an example of an apparently more specific problem, through a variety of public and private organizations, and we rely as well on the initiative of many different persons, each of whom analyzes some unique or overlapping aspect of the problem.

These various centers of analysis and decision-making differ in the values by which they judge policy. Organizations, as everyone knows, are often dedicated to interests or values that the members wish to protect. What one center ignores, another does not. Values neglected at one point in the policy-making process are central to the analysis carried on at another point. Consider an example: The President and some of his advisers agree on a greatly expanded program of highway expenditures. Their objectives include national defense, reduction of highway congestion for civilians, and economic development. Consequences of the program for the parity of the fifty states as recipients of federal funds are ignored, as are possible consequences for auto fatalities, design of automobiles, profits of existing toll roads, destruction of homes and recreational areas, sales of automobiles, sales of home furnishings, character of home life, participation in organized religion, and so forth.

When the program is presented to Congress, if not before, some of the neglected values will be defended, by representatives of the states or of toll-road authorities perhaps. These representatives may come to terms immediately with the original proponents of the program, not necessarily by each representative's taking into account the others' values but by direct agreement on modification of the program. Representatives of other interests will wait until congressional consideration of the program is underway, while still other interests will be brought to bear on the administrative officials eventually responsible for implementing the program. Finally, years later, when it becomes apparent to churchmen that too many people are out driving on Sunday, rather than attending religious services, they will stir themselves to find ways of combating this tendency. When they do, they will not necessarily attribute the tendency to the earlier highway program, and it is not at all necessary that they do so in order to deal with their problem.

To justify such a process, it is not necessary to show that all values are given equal consideration; even in the synoptic ideal, certain values, through intention or oversight, may be given short shrift. Nor is it necessary to show that their inequalities are systematic or understandable in terms of a particular formula; the synoptic ideal cannot live up to such a promise either. Nor is it necessary to show that all important values are somehow brought to bear on each decision, even if each decision-maker is not considering all of them. Sometimes neglect of a particular value will arouse no one to action until a decade later when it becomes clear that it is being endangered.

We have already drawn the distinction between dealing with a neglected consequence only when it appears and anticipating it. Where interested groups and agencies are many, both possibilities are open, just as they were shown to be open for any one policy analyst or policy-maker. Groups and government decision makers become watchdogs for values they fear will be neglected by others, and each decision maker develops great sensitivity to certain lines of consequence and becomes more competent to explore them than others for whom they are incidental to other objectives and values.

It ought to be emphasized that the individuals, groups, and agencies that undertake analysis and policy-making can be either public or private, either partisan or non-partisan. It ought also to be emphasized that the process we are describing is more inclusive than the familiar interest-group adjustment process, as it is often described. Moreover, we are calling attention here to the capacities of a process of fragmented decision-making for achieving not a decentralization of power, which is usually claimed for dispersion of policy-making authority, but a specific contribution to the completeness with which consequences of alternative possible policies are brought under consideration.

To the extent that these many individuals, groups, and agencies find themselves in overt conflict with one another, the overt conflicts themselves may seem to create policy problems than can only be resolved by final recourse to some higher authority that can govern their interactions in the light of a synoptic analysis of them. In fact, however, at least three other possibilities are open:

1. In some cases, the adjustment process proceeds without appeal to a higher authority. Overt conflicts are often settled by striking a bargain; by more discussion without a bargain; by an individual, agency, or group (public or private) overriding its adversaries on a particular issue; or by still other forms of interplay among conflicting groups, which produces a final adjustment.[7]

2. While representatives of conflicting interests sometimes appeal to a higher authority in government, they are often simply shifting the problem to another level at which adjustment by a number of fragmented policy-makers continues. Even at the highest levels of government in the United States, policy is a product of mutual adjustment among congressional leaders, congressional committees, powerful party officials, the President, and influential members of the executive branch. No one can claim pushing a decision up to the highest reaches of government is necessarily to put it in the hands of a synoptic policy-maker.

3. A single higher authority may conceivably take over the policy problem posed by the conflict and yet approach the problem through the practice of disjointed incrementalism rather than through synoptic aspirations. That is to say, it will move incrementally, remedially, and serially on a changing list of problems arising out of conflicts at lower levels.

Although one might hastily suppose that sooner or later such an authority would have to adopt a synoptic role to co-ordinate its solutions to these various conflict problems, it can in fact achieve co-ordination by attending to each of its subproblems in a sequence of remedial actions. If its actions on subproblem x create a problem in area y, it can attend to this problem when it turns to area y. If what is then done in area y creates problems in area z, it can subsequently attend separately to those problems.

Where no difficulties of co-ordination arise, the authority's attention will not be demanded; where co-ordination problems do arise, they can always be treated as special problems. In short, wherever lack of co-ordination produces identifiable, specific problems, the difficulties can be attacked through a sequence of remedial attacks on these identifiable, specific problems. The problem of co-ordination itself need not be attacked explicitly.

This third method of co-ordination can sometimes also take the variant form in which the adverse consequences of overt conflict are anticipated. Suppose, for example, that it is anticipated that intended farm price-support policies will be inconsistent with policies designed to remove marginal farms from cultivation and inconsistent also with the intention to reduce rather than aggravate income inequality among farmers. The conventional notion of co-ordination would encourage appropriate adjustments among these three lines of policy to eliminate their inconsistencies before enactment of the intended supports. In incremental, serial, and remedial co-ordination, however, the inconsistent policies would be inaugurated without modification. The anticipated conflicts would meanwhile be dealt with as several identifiable, specific, but quite separate policy problems leading to still other remedial policies. In pursuing co-ordination by means of the strategy, there is no distinction between problems to be solved, on the one hand, and solutions to be co-ordinated, on the other, as there is in the conventional concept of co-ordination through explicit central decision-making.

2—Inadequately Formulated Values

We have shown how various features of the strategy are adaptable to man's limited intellectual capacity and information, as well as to the costliness of analysis. How do they adapt to inadequacies in the structuring or ordering of values?

We do not think that we need dwell on the obvious ways in which attention to comparison of values at the margin directs the analyst's attention to that minimum of evaluation that he must accomplish—or on other equally obvious ways in which the strategy points the way to the solution of evaluative problems immediately at hand. In every respect in which the strategy simplifies, it points the way to working with whatever limited mastery of values the analyst can achieve.

A few points are worth special mention, however. We recall first that the strategy succeeds in minimizing the problem of aggregation because it makes the most, rather than the least, of existing constraints on the alternatives to be considered. A strictly synoptic analyst would discuss values without limitation, that is, he would abstract from all "practical" considerations. He would debate a question like ideal distribution of income after expressly ruling out limitations upon alternatives imposed by political relevance or the stickiness of social change. The strategy takes the opposite tack: The more limitations that can be applied to a choice, the fewer the factors that must be considered in making the choice.

The strategy also offers important specific aids to the analyst's attempts to accomplish the relatively limited amount of evaluation he cannot escape. For example, only a small part of the evaluating he must do on a problem need be done in any one decision situation. That is, in any one decision-making situation, the only values that must be weighed are those on which the alternative policies differ. Furthermore, because choice of value and choice of policy are made simultaneously, evaluation is achieved automatically in decision-making—the analyst does not first work out an evaluation and then apply to decision-making. In addition, he deals with specific features of observable situations, which we suggest can be evaluated regardless of whether there is any way to deal conclusively with the more abstract conceptions of value. Finally, because he deals with a succession of incrementally different policies, he acquires familiarity with the kinds of choice he faces, so that relative weights pose meaningful rather than remote and hypothetical questions to him.

An especially significant obstacle to synoptic problem solving, we found, however, is the inability of the analyst to find his way to criteria that would, in addition to meeting his own needs for a system, command agreement among his colleagues or even among a larger circle of interested people. How then does the strategy adapt to the desirability of at least some agreement?

We suggest, first, that much agreement emerges simply because the practitioners of the strategy share a common culture that disposes them to an important degree of consensus on values. To a lesser degree, this consensus also operates under the synoptic ideal. In the employment of the strategy, however, unlike that of the synoptic ideal, culturally conditioned agreement is not challenged by conflicts engendered by careful separation of value and factual components of analysis, by making value elements as explicit as possible, and by formulating values into hierarchies, systems of priority, or other constructions. We suggest that these elaborate and in a sense artificial operations on values lead analysts away from their common ground into formal differences and sometimes into idiosyncratic positions. In the synoptic ideal, differences in formulating values are crucial, particularly in formulating more abstract values.

On the other hand, the characteristics of the strategy that make the most of the common culture also tend to disguise the agreement achieved, to the degree that in appraising the strategy one might seriously underestimate it. The strategy leaves valuations in large part tacit and promotes agreements that are manifest in behavior without being explicitly arranged. Furthermore, agreement is usually quite consistent with explicit and elaborately articulated ideological disagreement that is, however, largely irrelevant to the actual choices being made. It seems to be a characteristic of policy discussions that value terms make the most of disagreement, while the quiet ways in which values are actually used indicate an important degree of agreement.

Beyond capitalizing on a common cultural background, the strategy contributes to social agreement in other specific ways, each reflecting specific attributes of this strategy.

In its preoccupation with increments of change, the strategy makes the most of existing constraints on policy to reduce the areas on which social disagreement is possible. Since typically only increments of change are politically relevant, using the strategy avoids provocations on an enormous range of politically irrelevant issues. Similarly, in its preoccupation with increments, the strategy often makes it logically possible for analysts to agree on evaluations of alternative policies, regardless of their disagreements on ultimate values. Ultimate values are irrelevant, except when they are weighed and employed in actual policy evaluations where quite different sets of ultimate values are logically consistent with the same policy. Two analysts can agree to liberalize old-age pensions even if they do not agree on their reasons for doing so. Liberalization of old-age insurance legislation in the United States in the past decade or so is a product of conservative consent, influenced by fear of union insistence on employer-financed pensions as an alternative to security by legislation—and of liberal consent, influenced by ideas of the welfare state. At the other extreme is the situation in which two analysts believe that they must agree on abstract values before they can permit themselves to ask whether or not they agree on the application of these values to policy choice.

Because the strategy is remedial and serial, it takes advantage of the frequency with which we find ourselves agreeing on what we are against (as in the Rostow-Millikan appeal to fear of the Soviet Union, for example), even though we cannot agree on what we are for. We agree that a commonly experienced situation is intolerable; we agree in large part on a "next step" designed to remove us from this intolerable situation; we disagree only on questions about more distant goals of policy that are increasingly detached from the kinds of policy choice that can be made for the present. Analysts can agree that disagreements on abstract values are often simply disagreements on utopias, from which policy choices are far removed.

Furthermore, because the strategy is serial, it gives to analysts in the same or related policy fields a common heritage of observation and often of participation in earlier moves in the series of policy steps for which they are studying a next step.

Because the strategy is marked by the mutual adjustment of ends and means, we suggest, in accordance with a favorite point of John Dewey's, that it again promotes agreement among evaluators. Adjustment in any direction is principally caused by observation of empirical discrepancies between given means and suggested ends. The means are too big or too small for the ends, the ends too ambitious or too limited for the means. Now, there are well-established techniques, accepted throughout the scientific community and beyond, for making observations of this kind. Analysts operating from very different premises respecting values can be expected to agree on these observations, and they are in effect then agreeing on the relevance or irrelevance of certain values. This fact may not imply agreement on the exact policy to choose, but it is certainly a step toward such agreement.

Because the strategy is reconstructive, we add that it discourages intransigence in the defense of values. To clarify this point, we can imagine a group of people engaged in policy discussion, and we can ask how the character of the discussion might differ according to the procedure they follow. What happens if they begin by invoking rules or principles, as they might in pursuit of the rational-deductive ideal, to deal with a fixed problem? And what happens if they begin, as in fact people usually do, by introducing value themes that permit a highly flexible restructuring of the data on the policy problem as discussion proceeds?

If people begin by advocating rules, they declare more in the way of belief in formulating a rule than they would in introducing a theme in some other way. Furthermore the more they declare, the harder it is for them to change without embarrassment. They are likely to feel that, in allowing their rules to be qualified (so as not to apply to the present case perhaps) or abandoned (as further discussion may suggest), they are confessing faults of ignorance or oversight, and lack of perspicacity. Rules are usually formulated in ordinary (nonphilosophical) discussions in terms of fundamental convictions. When a man says, "I believe that everything that is done in foreign policy should be calculated to make a maximum contribution to the economic well-being of the people of the world as a whole," he is ordinarily understood, from the formality and care of his phrasing, to be expressing a deep-seated and carefully pondered belief. Such implications make it all the harder for him to change.

This point about the way in which advocating rules limits flexibility and cuts off directions of free development is, of course, largely a psychological one—that is to say, it would theoretically be possible for an evaluator to shuffle through a whole series of different rules. He tends to stick with one, not necessarily because it would be unintelligent for him to change, but simply because changing is distasteful. The point is not entirely a psychological one, however. Once one has advocated a given rule, change can threaten to cause suspicions of inconsistency and, at worst, a breakdown in communication. To advocate a rule is to advocate the form of a general solution for a dispute over policy. It is to declare, at least, that any undesirable alternatives should be eliminated before taking any further steps. To change to another rule is to change to another basis for elimination. If an analyst changes too quickly and too often, it becomes impossible to tell what basis of elimination he means to propose; he has so many solutions to offer that one cannot tell what his answer is or even what the problem is supposed to be. The chief attraction of formulating a rule, however, is that it defines a problem and indicates a formal procedure for solving it.[8]

Once a rule has been formulated, any revision undertaken by its advocates is likely to be confined to making it more precise, not only because it would be embarrassing and unsuitable to *change* to other rules, but also because *combining* the initial rule with other rules quickly generates unmanageable complications. The rules will not lead to solution unless, in combining them, the mutual relations of the rules are made clear. This apparatus of qualifications and distinctions—the apparatus, it might be remarked, of the rational-deductive ideal—cannot ordinarily be provided in finished form, and attempting to provide it actually distracts attention from practical efforts to resolve the dispute in hand. People cannot combine themes once they appear in rule-like form—if the form is to be kept—without incurring large overhead costs in apparatus. If rules are kept out of the picture, nothing is easier. People acknowledge that this or that topic or theme must be considered, as well as the ones that they themselves have raised —and they can move toward giving them paramount attention without having to revoke anything that they have said. They may even drop a subject entirely, without embarrassment and with minimum confusion, since they have not committed themselves to saying that the issue should be decided by it alone.

In addition to generating agreement, the strategy makes still another and somewhat unexpected contribution to evaluation in the face of social conflict over values. Because each analyst excludes some important values from any given analysis and because the completion of analysis depends upon social processes rather than intellectual integration of parts, the need for social agreement is significantly altered by using the strategy. Agreement is still desirable among analysts working on the same policy problem with the same limited set of values. Among analysts working on different problems or on the same problem with different limited sets of values, however, agreement is unnecessary. It is unnecessary because none of these analysts need discuss his differences with any other analyst or come to terms with him.

Agreement on values among analysts is necessary only to the degree that agreement on policy is sought by an intellectual resolution of disagreement. To the extent that policy disagreement is resolved not in any individual's or group's mind but in a serial or fragmented political process—in which a line of policy emerges as the result of a series of steps or an adjustment among groups—analysts need not agree.

But is it not required, it may be asked, that serial and fragmented policy-makers themselves, if not the analysts on whom they lean, reach agreement on values? And does not their need for agreement impose some pressure on their advisers to reach agreement? Let us see.

In the first place, as we have seen, policy-makers need not agree on values; the most that is required is that they agree on policies. On this first count, then, their needs for agreement do not necessarily demand agreement on values among analysts. Secondly, policy makers need not attempt and often do not attempt to reach agreement through intellectual resolution of their differences; instead, they trade favors, threaten each other, make arbitrary settlements for compromise, and so forth. Since they anticipate such settlement of their differences, they do not require resolution through agreement among analysts.

Finally, policy-makers do not always need to agree even on policies. It is common that each policy-maker in a serial or fragmented policy-making structure goes his respective way, neither negotiating with other groups nor conceding to groups any authority in the area in which he operates. Tax authorities, unemployment-compensation administrators, and urban redevelopers can determine directions within their respective jurisdictions. To a significant degree, so can legislative committees in any one legislature. And, as noted above, a legislature as a whole can, at one stage in the policy-making process, pursue values that it then at a subsequent step chooses to ignore at a subsequent stage. In this respect, policy-makers are like fragmented or serial analysts who need not come to terms with each other.

Is all this merely to repeat the obvious—that if analysts cannot agree on decisions, some kind of agreement will emerge in the political process? No, the point goes beyond that. We are saying that where analysis and policy-making are serial, remedial, and fragmented, political processes can achieve consideration of a wider variety of values than can possibly be grasped and attended to by any one analyst or policy-maker. It is this accomplishment at the political level that makes agreement among analysts less necessary.

Consider again the example of public policy on income distribution. Income distribution is a consequence of serial and remedial public policies on taxation, social security, public education, national parks, highways, housing, agricultural prices, collective bargaining, veterans' problems, and many other subjects. All these policy areas are approached by analysts and policy-makers each of whom works with his own limited set of values. Income distribution thus reflects both a multiplicity of analyses and a multiplicity of policy-making groups. That economists in these different areas do not agree on values creates no problem of communication among them because they are not called upon to communicate with each other. Nor does their failure to agree discredit them in the eyes of those who use their analytical services, for each policy-making group realizes that it is approaching a problem from a limited set of values and is not distressed to find that the experts to whom it turns are doing the same.

Imagine in contrast a monolithic government in which, in the absence of fragmentation, income distribution is not the result of a multiplicity of conflicting and reinforcing decisions but is an object of explicit central policy. In this case, central policy-makers would attempt an intellectual resolution of all important values. It would therefore be important that each analyst be comprehensive in his consideration of values. If the analysts could not agree among themselves on values, their disagreement would undermine the confidence with which policy-makers could employ them.

3—Other Adaptations

The more we have said about the strategy's implications for any one difficulty in problem solving, the clearer its implications have become for all others, and we increasingly risk laboring the obvious if we continue. All that is required, we therefore suggest, is a mopping-up operation on those difficulties of problem solving to which we have not so far given explicit attention.

The remaining aspects of problem solving, to which the synoptic ideal does not adapt but to which the strategy can be seen as an adaptation, are listed at the opening of this chapter:

5. interdependencies between fact and value
6. openness of systems to be analyzed
7. need for strategic sequences to guide analysis and evaluation
8. the diversity of forms in which policy problems actually arise.

The strategy's adaptation to the first item on this residual list is, of course, immediate, direct, and apparent. Since we have defined the incremental strategy as including the orientation of ends to means—an attribute that encompasses in turn the simultaneous selection of means and ends and the adaptation of values to the costs of achieving them—it is clear from the definition itself of the strategy that it adapts to troublesome interdependencies of fact and value.

As for the synoptic analyst's need for a closed analytical system when in fact he is often faced with far-ranging interdependencies among real world variables, we can draw on the discussion just concluded. In showing that the strategy accomplishes a more complete problem-solving process than individual analysts themselves accomplish, we have actually shown that the remedial and serial character of the strategy, as well as its fragmented character, permits the practitioner of the strategy to "have achieved" closure of his own analytic system despite the openness of the real world system he analyzes. We say "have achieved" rather than "achieve" because, given the reconstructive feature of the strategy, his problem continues to shift as long as he works on it. Hence it is not until he has made a policy choice and can look back on the problem as it was just at the moment of decision that he can see that he has achieved a kind of closure on that momentary problem.

This accomplishment of the strategy illustrates a point emphasized in Chapter 4, that an analytical system has to be understood in its social context and that the social context for the strategy permits adaptations in analytical method that would not be permissible in another context. In seeing the strategy as adapting to open systems through its remedial, serial, and fragmented attributes, we in effect challenge a kind of fallacy of composition by which it is believed that analysis rises to no greater level of completeness than is achieved at the hand of one analyst or one co-operating group of analysts. To an important degree incompleteness in the work of any one analyst at any one time can be remedied both by appropriate political interactions among analysts and policy-makers and interactions among any given analyst's work at different points in time.

Now, of course, a division of labor takes place in the synoptic ideal too, and analysts may interact with one another. An analyst may factor out parts of his problem to himself, taking each part in turn, or to other co-operating analysts. The distinction is that in the synoptic ideal the integration of parts remains an intellectual task for the analyst, and whatever closure is accomplished is attributable to, and therefore limited by, his capacities to understand the relationship of the parts. In the strategy, however, integration of parts is not entirely—sometimes not at all—an intellectual accomplishment but a result of a set of specialized social or political processes. Strategic analysis therefore reaches closure beyond the level to which any analyst's mind takes it, and the possibility of closure is not so closely limited by intellectual capacities as in the synoptic method.

As for the penultimate difficulty on the list, the analyst's need for strategic sequences for guidance, the problem, it will be remembered from Chapter 3, is that, in contemplation of the impossibility of actually constructing an analysis closely approximating the synoptic ideal, the analyst needs to know what first and intermediate steps to take. How should he go about doing what lies within his capacities? Just what is most worth doing in analysis if he cannot wholly achieve the synoptic ideal?

Again, our earlier discussion has covered the point. Both in showing the various ways in which the strategy moves on from the here and now and in showing specifically how analysts attack evaluation in the absence of fully developed rational-deductive systems or welfare functions, we have said enough to show that the strategy is not, like the synoptic ideal, simply an unhelpful description of something unattainable. It is a set of adaptations that can be put into use immediately at any stage in the analytical process. It may be remembered that, for this very reason, we have called the collection of adaptations a strategy.

There remains, then, only the problem of adapting the analytical method to the forms in which policy problems actually arise, the problem being suggested by the identification in the synoptic ideal of public policy problems with problems as ordinarily defined. That the strategy adapts to this difficulty is demonstrated by the parallel at one point after another between incremental politics and the strategy. Incremental politics is itself incremental, remedial, serial, reconstructive, and fragmented, as outlined in Chapter 4. Being fragmented, for example, the strategy adapts to the way in which problems appear in clusters, which is one of the difficulties identified in Chapter 3; and, being reconstructive, remedial, and serial, it adapts to the continuity of problem defining and solving, which was another difficulty earlier discussed.

An especially troublesome feature of the synoptic ideal was its failure to adapt to the frequency with which problems arise not in situations where goal achievement is frustrated and alternative new routes are sought, even if this is the ordinary view of the problem situation, but instead in situations in which some new policy possibility is put forward. Here, it will be remembered, the problem situation, as conventionally described, is almost reversed. What is required is not new policies to reach a goal but new goals toward which to employ a policy. Such a development can occur either because a new "technological" possibility in policy-making opens up—that is, new means at hand stimulate speculation on new goals to accomplish, as when cloud seeding opened up possibilities for controlling weather. Or it occurs when some group in the society, finding a policy that suits *its* problems, compels other groups to give attention to that same policy in the hope that they will find grounds on which to accept the new policy. The union shop is an example of such a proposal, and so are oil depletion allowances, zoning, and tariffs.

While the question that must be asked in synoptic problem solving—What is the problem?—cannot be answered, the strategy adapts to the situation in ways that at this point hardly need explaining. As we saw in the Rostow-Millikan study, a single proposal is a quite feasible analytical focus in the strategy. Beyond that one illustration, we have also seen in the means orientation of the strategy its receptivity to analytical tasks posed by means at hand rather than by goals frustrated. Frequently, though not always, the strategy copes with situations in which all that is asked is whether a possible policy at hand moves away from an identified ill regardless of how it compares in efficacy with others that might be imagined. In such a situation, one policy alternative defines an appropriate "problem" even if goals remain to be discovered.

Other strategies may achieve adaptations in still other ways, including those strategies that we may not even realize that we practice. In delineating the strategy of disjointed incrementalism and its adaptation to difficulties of problem solving and policy-making, we hardly begin to suggest the richness of the human mind coping with its challenges. We attach importance to this particular strategy, however, because it seems clear that it is widely prac-ticed and can usefully be codified.

Moreover, the exposition of the strategy can be employed to throw light on some traditional and contemporary problems in social philosophy to which we turn in the remaining chapters. To extend the discussion of the strategy in this way will serve two purposes: on the one hand, we can further clarify the strategy by putting it into a larger context, and, on the other hand, we are able to show how it helps to remove certain familiar stumbling blocks in ethical theory.

PART THREE

CHOICE OF PROCEDURE IMPLICIT IN CHOICE OF VALUE

CHAPTER 7

MELIORATIVE COMPARISONS

1—The Strategy Associated with Certain Classes of Value

The strategy of disjointed incrementalism copes effectively with the difficulties that frustrate the synoptic approach—difficulties that people feel continually in real life and that press for theoretical consideration, once a critical view is cast upon the synoptic conception of problem solving and the received ideals of evaluative method that derive from it. To describe the strategy in the terms that we have used so far is to confront perplexities that arise before any specific moral concepts—liberty or humanity or good faith—are adopted as standards of evaluation; or, we might better say, perplexities that arise whatever sorts of standards one means to adopt. As such, they are perplexities that fall outside the scope of ethical theory as it is usually treated. Ethical theorists, whether they are concerned with what various moral terms mean or with what values should be adopted as standards, generally give little attention to practical techniques for coping with limited information and with the multiplicity, fluidity, and conflict of values. Yet in a changing world these are difficulties that people do encounter, regardless of the character or strength of their moral beliefs.

The full significance of the strategy has not yet emerged, however; it will not emerge until we move closer to familiar ethical topics. Nor will strategy's usefulness be entirely vindicated until we have done so. The strategy would be of little use—and little used—if it did not consort fairly easily with at least some of the specific concepts of value that people in our society are likely to invoke when they evaluate policies. The argument of the preceding chapters, with its abundant references to the practice of social scientists, has constantly implied that the strategy provides an effective way of pursuing specific values—those which social scientists, in our society, are most inclined to pursue. This implication about the mutual suitability of the strategy and certain sorts of values has not yet been investigated, although we have discussed at length the advantages of the strategy as an effective way of treating and resolving difficulties caused by the mere presence of values. When the strategy is further elaborated as we are about to elaborate it, it will be seen to vindicate the very intelligibility of certain familiar values. The strategy turns out to provide a suitable means of applying those familiar values as determinate criteria of policy, and thus answers objections which have suggested that there is no suitable means of doing this.

In the course of making this point, we shall make some philosophical distinctions, drawn between sorts or classes of value concepts, but aimed at differences between procedures of judgment. These differences in procedure (unlike those that we have already distinguished and discussed in Part One) appear only after one moves far enough into the field of ethics to identify specific values and consider the logical features that typically distinguish one from the other. Different values have different requirements of procedure. The strategy, as we shall see, meets the requirements common to one broad class of values—indeed it more than meets them, since it is adapted, not only to giving them effect in easy cases, but also to extending their range of application to cases in which the requirements could not otherwise be satisfied. In the case of another broad class of values, the relationship is not so congenial—not that the strategy excludes them, or prevents them from being applied, but the procedural requirements typically associated with values of this class either make the strategy superfluous or restrict its range of operation.

The distinction to be drawn in this chapter between "meliorative" and "peremptory" values can be reached within the field of ethics quite independently of any notions about disjointed incrementalism. Essentially, that is the way in which we shall present the distinction, and we shall be concerned to match the points about procedure that emerge from the distinction with the features already attributed to the strategy. Looking forward, we may say that the distinction will be one of the main foundations of our later argument about the accommodation of the strategy, and of utilitarianism as rehabilitated by the strategy, to some of the principal theses of current ethical theory.

Looking backward, we may point out that in matching the features of the strategy against the requirements of procedure distinguished in this chapter, we are spelling out an implication about the use of the strategy already embodied in the description of the strategy given in Part One. In that Part, we abstracted from specific values to such an extent that we did not discuss or need to discuss differences between values regarding requirements of procedure. We could not, however, avoid implying that the strategy was, as regards requirements of procedure, more fully and congenially suited to some concepts of value than others.

We were committed to this implication, in fact, as soon as we explained that the strategy was margin-dependent. It discourages giving judgment on any policy before the marginal differences between that policy and alternative ones have been compared. As we shall see, this characteristic implies that the strategy consorts on points of procedure with what we call "meliorative" values, rather than with "peremptory" ones. (The implication does not run the other way: A value may qualify as "meliorative" on points of associated procedure without those procedures being incremental.) In concrete applications, people using the strategy have to take into account, in various ways, values that are not melioratively conceived, but they are not the sorts of values for which the full powers of the strategy are needed or can be disclosed. The strategy operates fully and characteristically only when it is applied to meliorative values.

2—Meliorative and Peremptory Values

We may say informally that the distinction between meliorative and peremptory values is a distinction between two views of the necessity of inspecting alternatives before passing judgment on a policy. On a meliorative approach, judgments about accepting or rejecting any policy must wait upon a comparison of that policy with alternatives to it. On a peremptory approach, certain characteristics are looked for on the basis of which a policy would be approved or disapproved taken by itself, without any attention necessarily being given to alternatives. Clearly, the margin-dependent feature of the strategy makes it meliorative rather than peremptory, for it requires that the evaluation of any given policy reflect the marginal differences between that policy and alternative ones; and these differences cannot be discovered without comparisons.

We may begin to formalize this distinction by making use of the artifice of distinguishing between "meliorative" and "peremptory" *rules*,* although we do not suppose rules to be the normal vehicles for introducing concepts of value into discussions about policy. As applied to policies, there are two general propositional forms of moral rules: "Any policy with the feature F is pre-

---

* We shall in these chapters make expository use of a number of formal artifices, that is to say, of technical notions, including (implicitly) notions about deduction and calculation; and we shall fit these notions to the real world that we mean to describe by explaining what allowances and qualifications need to be made when the implications of these notions for the practice of the strategy are considered. This use of artifice, even though it is a very primitive one, may serve to demonstrate, better than any protestations of faith, our confidence in formal methods. We argue that, in the sort of circumstances that preoccupy us in this book, it is futile to expect evaluation to proceed by deduction and calculation to comprehensive solutions of policy problems; but that should not be taken to detract from the utility of formal methods, both simple and elaborate, in making our ideas about behavior and beliefs clear.

scribed" and "Any policy with the feature G is prohibited." [1] Both of these forms have the air of peremptory commands. They may excite objections, but they do not seem, on the part of their proponents, to anticipate further discussion. To satisfy these forms, it would apparently suffice, once one knew what features F or G were, to take any policy by itself and approve or disapprove it after inspecting its features. Suppose, however, that the feature in question is one that a policy cannot have considered apart from other policies. Suppose the feature (F in a given rule) is one of being more conducive to achieving certain specifiable results than alternative policies would be. In this case, at least the first form of rules becomes distinctly less peremptory, for whether or not a policy is to be prescribed now becomes a question that requires discussion and comparison with alternatives.

Rules that call for discussion of better or worse alternatives we call "meliorative." We formally define a meliorative rule as one that has the first form and in which some phrase of the following form takes the place of F: "of being most suitable for promoting V," V standing for some desired property of a human group or of its institutions. A peremptory rule is one that either has the first general form without any phrase of the kind just mentioned being substituted for F or one that has the second form. [2]

Taken separately from the moral *rules* in which they may figure, the aspects of policy that attract men or repel them still represent *themes* of discussion, candidates for various formulas of application and possibly for formulas that are far from being rule-like. Indeed, we have argued that such themes are most often encountered outside rule-like formulas; their appearance in rules is a special case. Nevertheless, we may, on the basis of the distinction we have just drawn between sorts of rule, draw a further distinction between sorts of theme. Meliorative themes are those aspects of policy that are designated by substitutions for V. They become, in our usage, "features of policy" when they are introduced by the standard formula, "of being most suitable for promoting . . ." Peremptory themes are features of policy designated by substitutions for F, where these do not involve introducing a further property "V"; or features of policy designated by substitutions, in the second general form of rule, for G. For example, "Any policy with the feature of being most conducive to the health of children in the community is prescribed" is a meliorative rule; "the health of children" or "the health of children in the community" is a meliorative theme. "Any policy with the feature of jeopardizing private contracts is prohibited" is a peremptory rule; "jeopardy to private contracts" is a peremptory theme.

(It should be noted that the class of meliorative themes and the class of peremptory themes may very well overlap. Some themes, even some that are prominent in one class or the other, may figure in both; in how many cases this is true we need not say. We suppose, however, that themes differ in the frequency and prominence with which they are used to suggest or formulate something approximating peremptory rules. For this reason, the themes that would most suitably represent either class, being prominent in that class rather than the other, would differ. When we *contrast* "peremptory themes" with "meliorative themes," accordingly, we mean themes that belong to the peremptory class; themes that are being used with an effect on evaluative comparisons like that which a peremptory rule would have; classes of themes that may therefore be suitably represented by themes that are chiefly used with such an effect.)

A meliorative rule, by its very form, indicates that whether or not it prescribes a given policy is not to be prejudged on the basis of some feature that adheres to the policy by itself, apart from comparison with other policies. One must inspect the actual variation in V that exists in a set of alternative policies. Whatever V is, and whatever policies happen to belong to the set, each policy can be ranked as being effective to some degree in promoting V, as effectively damaging or obstructing it, or as having no effect on it. Whether or not a given policy is to be chosen under the assumed meliorative rule depends on whether or not it ranks first in the set; but its ranking depends on the set. Compared with some alternatives, it may rank at the bottom; compared with others, it may have only an equal effect on V.

A peremptory rule takes quite a different tack. The criterion that it specifies is not a variable, like being more or less conducive to V, which every possible policy has to some degree (no effect on V counting as zero, with favorable policies ranking above, and unfavorable policies below). It is a feature that a policy either fully has or is entirely without; we may say it is a variable of the special kind treated in Boolean algebra, which has only two possible values. For example, "Any policy that has the feature of legalizing birth control is prohibited" is a peremptory rule, and a policy either has the feature of legalizing birth control or it does not. Presumably, it could be discovered to have this feature independently of any assumptions about the particular policies being proposed as alternatives to it. Comparison with other policies is not logically essential, as it is in the case of meliorative rules, to discovering whether the rule determines the choice or rejection of a given policy.

It is true that, in some circumstances, peremptory rules may confront us with borderline cases. Many people would be inclined to subscribe to the peremptory rule, "Any policy with the feature of being divinely inspired is prescribed," or to the peremptory rule, "Any policy with the feature of being dictated by natural law is prescribed." But it may be difficult to say of a given policy whether or not it is divinely inspired or dictated by natural law. Likewise, to take a humbler example, it may be difficult to say of a given policy whether it jeopardizes private contracts or not. These difficulties, however, do not make the rules in question meliorative. Once a policy is assigned to a designated class, it is either automatically qualified for adoption or automatically disqualified, whereas, under a meliorative rule, no degree of the variable feature automatically qualifies or automatically disqualifies it. Borderline cases under peremptory rules are analogous to borderline cases under meliorative rules, in which the evidence does not suffice to establish the comparative ranking of given policies; but the analogy does not threaten the distinction.

There are also borderline cases of another sort. People may formulate rules without making it clear whether the rules are to be understood as meliorative or peremptory; they may not even be clear about the distinction themselves. They may say that they want to see policies adopted that enlarge opportunities for Negroes to acquire suburban housing. This looks like an approximation to a meliorative rule. It may turn out, however, that the people proposing it mean to oppose any policy that would allow house-owners or real-estate agents the least discretion in denying Negroes the chance of buying houses that they had the money to pay for, and this looks like advocating a peremptory rule. Again, people may announce that they are utterly opposed to the government's running a deficit, which seems like a peremptory position. Nevertheless, it may turn out that, either because they do not realistically expect to be able to stop the government from running a deficit or because they are aware of the damage that stopping it from doing so might do to other objectives of policy, they are ready to settle for reducing the deficit as much as possible—and this looks like a meliorative position.

Such cases should remind us of the fluidity of evaluation and of the dangers of assuming that evaluation proceeds by fixed rules. If concepts of value are ambiguous and unstable even in attempts to formulate rules, how much more likely they are to be so when even that form of precision is not attempted! Indeed, we suppose that they generally are very ambiguous and unstable, except when they are invoked under some such combination of restraining procedures as is represented by the strategy of disjointed incrementalism, which achieves a useful degree of precision without formulating rules.

3—Open-Mindedness as Implied by the Meliorative Concern of the Strategy

People who take a meliorative position on policy issues are by no means always more tolerant and generous human beings than those who take a peremptory position; and although we have used the term "meliorative," we have not defined it to include only those things that are generally agreed to be beneficial. Varying as to specific values with persons, it may include things that most people would think it quite perverse to consider as benefits. For all that we have said so far—or shall say in the rest of this part of this book—peremptory rules, too, may be perverse and arbitrary in various ways. But they may also be attractive and inspiring, and, as our later discussion will show, it is difficult to imagine how any serious and conscientious person can escape taking a peremptory stand on some subjects, in some circumstances.

Nevertheless, there is a sense in which, without strictly implying anything about the character or temperament of the people who take these different approaches to evaluation, we can say that the meliorative approach is more "open-minded"—more adaptable to circumstances—than the peremptory approach. The notion that is involved has already been touched upon in our initial comments on the distinction between meliorative and peremptory rules. It is important enough to deserve extended illustration, which we shall now proceed to furnish, continuing in our discussion to make use of the expository artifice by which disputes over policy are described as conflicts between moral rules.

A policy dispute illustrating the difference between meliorative and peremptory positions. The school board of a certain town must consider whether to spend $800 to initiate a school dental program. The outlay would suffice for a dental survey of 500 of the 1600 children in the town's schools. The results of this survey would be used to determine whether or not to continue and extend the program in future years.

Some members of the board are quite sure from the outset that the schools have no business with the school children's teeth. These, they say, are the responsibility of the parents. The question of a dental survey is to be settled by considering *whether or not it is part of the function of the school system to conduct dental surveys;* and it is quite clear to them that it is not. They are thus invoking a peremptory rule, which might be expressed, "Any policy that falls outside the function of the school system is to be rejected."

Other members of the board have various arguments in favor of the dental survey. They say, for one thing, that the function of the school system is to educate children and that the dental survey could be related very closely to instruction in hygiene. They argue, in the second place, that the school system is already engaged in activities that everyone accepts as important and useful but which many would regard as incidental to the main function of the schools: for instance, athletics and driver training. Continuing this line of argument, they point out that many other school systems accept dental inspection as part of their function; that their own school system supports a program of medical examination; and that, in the past, their own system has run a successful dental program, which was abandoned only because local dentists no longer had the time to co-operate.

The board members who favor the dental survey have still a third line of argument. They ask, "What are the alternatives?" Suppose that, of the 500 children surveyed, 300 are found to need dental treatment. The parents of these 300 children will be notified that the children should be taken to dentists. Suppose that 200 of the 300 would either be taken to the dentist anyway or will not be taken, in spite of their parents' being notified. One might then estimate that 100 children will receive treatment as a result of the survey. No other agency in town is prepared to carry out a dental inspection. Therefore, the alternative to conducting the inspection in the schools is 100 children going without dental treatment. If the survey were to inspire further ones or the institution of a regular program for examining all the children, an even greater number would be at stake.

Finally, these members agree with their opponents that the main business of the schools is to give instruction in certain basic academic subjects. They claim, however, that this point should be applied to the dental survey in a different perspective. It should prompt the question, "Would the survey interfere with instruction in the basic academic subjects?" It is clear, they add, that there would be no such interference. The time required for the program from each child participating would be brief and could be taken from time already allotted to instruction in hygiene or from physical education periods.

Consider the ways in which the advocates of the survey have confronted the peremptory rule offered by their opponents. They have claimed first that, even if they accept the rule and its implicit definition of function, it does not apply against the dental survey; which implies that their opponents have made a mistake in applying their own definition of function. Next, the advocates of the survey have challenged their opponents on the definition of function. They have argued in effect that observation of school practice indicates that "the function of the school system" could reasonably be defined broadly enough to include the dental survey, even if it is not assimilated to instruction. Thus they imply that their opponents have made a mistake in applying their rule, by using too narrow a definition of function. (Of course, if they are wise, they avoid *saying* that their opponents have made a mistake.)

Their third line of argument is a more radical one, for it breaks with the opponents' peremptory rule entirely. The advocates of the survey suggest that the policy to be adopted should be determined on a *meliorative* basis. The meliorative theme that they invoke may be designated as "the health of the school children," or their "dental health." We may regard them as using a *meliorative rule* that might be expressed as "Any policy that is most conducive to promoting the school children's health is prescribed," although, as we shall see in a moment, attributing any rule to them artificially formalizes the dispute to some degree.

What they say at the end about not interfering with the main business of the schools indicates that the advocates of the survey recognize possible dangers in distracting the schools from their main business. Indeed, the advocates of the survey may be prepared to admit that, at least indirectly (by setting a precedent), every noninstructional activity has a cost in distraction. Unlike the opponents of the survey, however, they want to weigh this cost against the advantages of the survey. They are willing to trade one value against another in margin-dependent comparisons.

This willingness does not mean, however, that they are infinitely elastic in such matters. There are limits to their willingness to trade. They may be said to have indicated that they subscribe to a peremptory rule about the function of the school system, a rule, moreover, that they share with the opponents of the survey: that any policy that interferes with the function of instruction in the basic academic subjects is prohibited.[3] If we include under the heading of "perspective" all the factors, conscious or unconscious, that lead people to investigate certain alternative policies and to ignore or refuse to consider others even as possible alternatives, then the rule just outlined may be said to be one of the factors defining the perspective. The rule is one of the elements defining the *perspective* with which the advocates of the dental survey approach the evaluation of possible policies for the school system. Within the scope of this rule, however, the advocates are ready to consider a wider range of possible policies than their opponents are. They do not follow their opponents in narrowing their perspective by a further peremptory rule.

Investigating alternatives vs. investigating exceptions. The difference just illustrated is a difference, not necessarily in emotions, but in the strategy of evaluation. The opponents of the survey can make a perfectly intelligible and consistent application of their narrower rule if, without considering the alternatives, they reject a given policy that violates it. With a meliorative rule, however, like the one invoked by the advocates within their defined perspective, *it makes no sense to give an answer to the question,* "Is this given policy right or wrong?" until alternatives have been identified and *investigated.* The proper answer to such a question, for people taking a meliorative approach, is always the counterquestion raised by the champions of the dental survey—"What are the alternatives?" For with a change in alternatives, the final answer is liable to radical change: A policy that ranks at the top in one set of alternatives may rank at the bottom in another. But a policy that is prescribed or prohibited by a peremptory rule is prescribed or prohibited regardless of alternatives.[4]

It is true that some peremptory rules would be understood, by those who propose them, as having exceptions and would be waived if the *only* alternatives to breaking the rules would contravene still more fundamental conceptions of good and evil: For example, a rule against taking human life, as nonpacifists understand it. Where the exceptions prevail, a policy prima facie favored or disfavored by a peremptory rule will be prohibited or prescribed after comparison with the given alternatives.

The difference in "open-mindedness" and adaptation to circumstances remains real and significant, nevertheless. Although conclusions from peremptory rules are subject to revision, the necessity of revision must be shown by the persons challenging the conclusion. They must show that one of a number of precedented exceptions applies, or they must establish a new exception, which is much more difficult even when they rely on precedented lines of argument.[5] For example, they must show that human lives will be taken only in self-defense or in the course of legitimate military operations.

But such a demonstration is frequently not possible. Some peremptory rules have no acknowledged exceptions, and some of these could not acquire any without changes in their sense.[6] The acknowledged exceptions frequently do not occur in cases where the rules are relevant. (Would they otherwise be called "exceptions"?) It is frequently not possible to establish new exceptions. (If this were not the case, the rule would be reduced to insignificance.) Even where relevant exceptions could be shown, therefore, the general tendency of peremptory rules is to encourage answers first, without regard to alternatives, and accept revision only afterwards, throwing the burden of proof upon those who claim an exception.*

Because of this difference in attention to alternative policies, there is a sense in which, even if people were limited to invoking rules as means of introducing values into discussion, invoking

---

* One can always restore the force of the "open-mindedness" distinction by reformulating a peremptory rule to include mention of the acknowledged exceptions. For example, "Any policy which involves the taking of human life except in self-defense or in the course of military operations against a national enemy is prohibited."

meliorative rules rather than peremptory ones would facilitate the adaptation of evaluation and choice to changes in circumstances, to changes, that is, in the sets of alternatives, in spite of the fact that any one meliorative rule might be applied so rigidly as to bring discussion to a standstill. Suppose that two groups of participants in a policy dispute agree on the perspective in which they view the issue and therefore on the set of policies that they are willing to consider, at least to the extent of investigating them. If, in the course of investigation, one group invokes a peremptory rule that is operative within the range of this set of policies, so that it either prescribes one of the policies proposed in that range or prohibits at least one of them, then it is excluding from further consideration one or more policies that the other party, which we shall assume depends on meliorative rules within the given range, is still willing to consider on a comparative basis.[7] Whether or not the meliorative party will press for adoption of such a policy depends entirely on the set of alternatives. The meliorative rule gives them more logical room, so far as it goes, for being flexible. If people using peremptory rules are, on certain occasions, ready to consider a greater number of possible policies than people using meliorative rules, it is because the latter are also using peremptory rules that define a narrower perspective than that defined by the peremptory rules held by the first set of people.[8]

4—Themes Rather Than Rules: Thematic Flexibility

An approach to evaluation that depended on meliorative rules would be more flexible in coping with the multiplicity, fluidity, and conflict of values than one that depended on peremptory rules. Other things being equal (that is to say, mainly, initial perspectives being equal), people using one sort of rule would be ready to consider a greater number of alternative policies than people using the other sort, and this readiness would increase opportunities for reconciliation, compromise, and agreement. In the actual course of prosecuting its meliorative and margin-dependent comparisons, the strategy manifests even greater flexibility, for the strategy is more flexible than any method of evaluation that depends on the use of rules. The strategy does not use meliorative rules so much as meliorative themes.[9] (Here, as predicted, we begin to relax and qualify the expository device of talking about rules. We are back to the subject of thematic flexibility, which was discussed in Part One.)

Analysts and evaluators using the strategy of disjointed incrementalism do not, we suppose, normally commit themselves to any one fixed rule or system of fixed rules for ranking the alternatives they undertake to compare within a given perspective. They try out ideas and sometimes go a long way in developing them, and they settle on policies—but they dispense with rules. Neither in the strategy nor in ordinary practice generally are rules the normal vehicles for introducing meliorative themes into discussion or for applying them to decisions about policy. (They are often not the vehicles for introducing or applying peremptory themes, either; to the degree that they are not, peremptory approaches, too, acquire a degree of flexibility.) It is perhaps tempting to suppose that, however irregularly they may be introduced initially, the concepts of value given serious attention in a dispute will be put into rules before the dispute is over. How else can the dispute be settled? But disputes are often settled without invoking rules or marshalling deductions. They are settled by settling—for now—on a policy and leaving many other things unsettled, including the general relationships among the many themes that may have been discussed and a number of specific topics of policy that are left for later attention, if they are to be given attention at all.

The freedom that thematic flexibility confers—and that we have ascribed to the strategy—can be illustrated by pursuing the school dental dispute still further. If the meliorative party in that dispute took an explicit stand on a rule—for example, a rule prescribing that the policy that did most for health was to be chosen—they would be denying themselves room to maneuver. To be sure, the denial would not be total. Faced with objections arising perhaps from past abuses in health programs—or at least in dental programs—or connected with the prospect that the school budget as a whole might be disapproved by the citizens if expenditures for a dental survey were included, the meliorative party can admit that such considerations call for exceptions to the rule they have advanced. They cannot, of course, admit that the exception applies in the present case without abandoning their advocacy both of the rule and of the dental survey. But they can argue that the abuses of past programs can be avoided both in the contemplated survey and in any permanent program that might be adopted after the survey. They can also argue that if the idea of the survey is fully explained to the citizens, there will be no adverse effect on the school budget as a whole. They can reinforce both lines of argument by revising the survey proposal, if that will help to meet objections without abandoning the essential features of the survey; even the most rigidly stated rule leaves them some freedom of this kind, to be exercised on the proposals rather than on the rule itself.

If the rule about promoting health does not attract support, however, the meliorative party cannot easily change to another one and start all over again with a different theme. They can perhaps move within the theme of health to a subtopic that may have more chance of eliciting support than the general theme. People who object to the schools', or any part of the government's, taking on general responsibilities for health may be willing to use public funds to promote the health of children. In modifying their rule so that it specifies "the health of children," the meliorative party is only making explicit what is at issue in the given case anyway—and they have reached the end of their rope. They cannot hope to gain anything more by moving to a narrower and less important theme of the children's *dental* health; they can preserve a certain consistency with their initial rule if they modify it to make explicit what would generally be regarded as crucial subthemes, but they can go no further. Few people would consider that the children's dental health was a more crucial topic than the children's health in general or even the most crucial division of the general theme.

If they do not advocate a rule, and with it a general formula for solving the dispute, the meliorative party can move much more easily away from the theme of health to whatever other themes might have a better chance of eliciting support. Suppose, without formulating a rule, they begin simply by trying out the themes of "health" and "the health of the children." They may say, for example, "It seems to us that health is a good thing to use public funds for." If it is objected that "Health is something for people to take care of outside of government," they may counter with the question, "But isn't it different with children's health?" (Of course, there are many other forms of words that they might have used to introduce these themes without using the forms of rules.)

The opposing side may deny that children's health is a different case, and, of course, they may prove to be utterly intransigent no matter what consideration is raised in favor of the dental survey. The meliorative party has not, however, prevented itself from raising further considerations if there is any chance that other considerations may succeed (and how can anyone be sure they will not succeed until they have been tried?). Since they have never committed themselves to insisting that the dispute should be resolved by a rule concerning health, they can move easily to quite different themes. They may move on, for example, to claiming that dental health is a special problem: People have to be trained to make regular visits to the dentist and without regular visits, teeth are liable to deteriorate beyond hope of repair. Thus, the meliorative party may claim, bad dental hygiene is something that cannot be remedied without education. If children are not trained in good dental hygiene, their teeth will suffer, and they will grow up to perpetuate neglect in the next generation.

Arguing on these lines, the meliorative party may be regarded as having shifted its ground away from health per se to the notion of evils that can be remedied only by education—and fully remedied only by reaching children while they are still at school. From this point, they may move on to develop a general conception of education that would include precautions regarding health as well as standard academic subjects. Or they might develop the theme of equalizing opportunities, between families where the parents are alert to the importance of dental health and families where the parents are not. They might point out that the public schools, by their very existence, help to compensate for variations in parental concern and enlightenment—and ask why this compensatory function should not be extended to dental health.

Having marshalled these arguments—or, rather, gone through them from one to another—the meliorative party can shift the point for applying them, and can thereby hit upon new themes. They may argue that, since the immediate issue is whether or not there shall be a survey rather than whether there shall be a permanent program, questions about the permanent program should be suspended until the extent of the problem is discovered. (The opposition may not like to be in the position of suppressing facts, even facts that they are not inclined to act upon.) It could also be urged that the survey would at least publicize the problem among parents and townspeople, even if no further program were undertaken.

All these ways of connecting the dental survey with different themes also help to put the proposal of undertaking one in different lights. As it happens, public concern about health and dental health is a necessary condition for any of them to be effective; in the nature of the case, the theme of health cannot be discarded because the very policy at issue is a policy about health. (There are all sorts of policy disputes in which none of the proposed policies introduces a meliorative or peremptory theme in the very act of being proposed—for example, a dispute about whether a city council shall have one or two chambers [10]—but the present dispute does happen to be one in which this occurs.) Although it cannot be disregarded, the theme of health may nevertheless be shaped and stressed in many different ways. Working without rules through the series of themes described above, the meliorative party might well have ended up subordinating the theme of health to one of the other themes. For example, the compensatory and remedial services of the schools, applied in this case to dental health, may turn out to be the most persuasive theme. Working with themes rather than rules, the meliorative party is free to shift and change over the whole field of possible themes surrounding the subject of the dental survey; working with rules, it would forfeit a variety of persuasive arguments.

The freedom of maneuver gained (or rather retained) by working with themes rather than rules has been described as a freedom of maneuver against other disputants, but the freedom involved is not merely an asset in debate—it is a freedom of discovery as well as of maneuver. Shifting and changing from one theme to another, the meliorative party discovers ways of looking at the proposed policy that would perhaps not have occurred to its members if they had confined themselves to insisting on a particular policy's connection with a certain rule. It would be a pity if scruples about sincerity operated against making such discoveries. In fact, they need not. The shifts and changes of the meliorative party do not imply insincerity at any stage. They do not desert rules merely because the rules turn out to be embarrassments; they may relinquish themes, they have never claimed to do more than call for considering them; they may not disclose at once the full variety of themes that occur to them, but that is not necessarily insincere. In fact, they probably could not say, before the dispute had run its full course, what themes would in the end seem most important to them. After all, they usually can learn something from the opposition.

Of course, while working with themes, people belonging to the meliorative party have all the dimensions of flexibility that they would have if they did work with rules—freedom to revise the proposal that they support; freedom to deny that the objections of the opposition apply to the present case, freedom to exploit the ambiguity latent in their initial presentation of a theme. But working with themes gives them the freedom of maneuver and discovery just described. And it gives them as one aspect of this freedom, the further advantage of ambiguity that comes from being able to shift a theme in the direction of a variety of rules—without being committed to any of them. Moving from the theme of health to concentration on a broad conception of education as providing precautionary training for life, and the subsequent movement to the theme of compensating for variations in parents and households might be regarded as so many tentative gestures toward different rules, in each of which the theme of health would be differently shaped and featured. Working with themes, however, the meliorative party need not alight on any of these rules; to do so would restrict its further movement.

The strategy of disjointed incrementalism displays generally, in all sorts of disputes, the congenial connection between meliorative values and thematic flexibility that the meliorative party could exploit in the school dental dispute. The supposition that the meliorative concern of the strategy manifests itself in themes rather than in rules reflects, as we have already indicated in Part One, several of the leading features of the strategy. (That supposition may, indeed, be said to sum up the effect of those features of the strategy that differentiate it from the rational-deductive ideal in particular.) The tactic of evaluating incremental departures does not exactly imply that rules are dispensed with, but it is a tactic to which themes are better suited than rules because themes are more easily adapted to particular novelties in the increments proposed, while rules normally embody generalizing tendencies and a tendency to rely on explicit precedents. The mutual adjustment of ends and means implies a degree of flexibility in specifying ends that is hardly compatible with working by rules; and, in general, the reconstructive approach of the strategy implies the same thing.

The multi-personal aspects of the strategy show how much more fully this flexibility may be exploited than any individual analyst, however imaginative, could be expected to exploit it—although we suppose that, under the strategy, individual evaluators deliberately restrict their efforts in various ways. It should not be assumed that all the advantages of flexibility that we have described and illustrated above can ordinarily be realized by single evaluators. The shifts and changes hypothesized in our example would very likely in practice not be movements in which every member, even of a given party (supposing there were more than one member), took part. We suppose that by restricting their efforts in characteristic ways, the several members of a given party could pursue separate topics—the shifts of theme by the "party" aggregate the shifts taken in a fragmented social process.

The encouragement that a meliorative approach gives to considering a greater number of alternatives is frequently realized only in the aggregate; individual evaluators using the strategy may confine their attention to single alternatives. Even here, however, the meliorative concern makes a difference—the single alternative that an individual analyst considers may be one that others would have ruled out of consideration peremptorily. If he is working with themes rather than with rules, he is that much more able to accommodate his results to those of other people, who have considered different alternatives and different themes. (In the school dental dispute, we supposed that the difference between the whole meliorative party, on the one side, and the whole peremptory party, on the other, was that the meliorative party was willing to consider a given departure from the status quo—a single alternative to it—on a comparative basis, while the peremptory party was not.)

Finally, the ambiguity and flexibility with which analysts and evaluators using the strategy operate, even in the aggregate, should not be exaggerated or misconceived as a tendency to leave everything unsettled. The strategy begins with ambiguity and avoids restrictive sacrifices of it, but it has its own way of removing ambiguity and its own way of driving toward determinate evaluations and determinate choices. It requires, for example, that proposed policies be interpreted as serial extensions or modifications of existing policies, and this requirement fixes a definite basis of comparison. It also requires that the proposed policies be shown to remedy specific defects of existing policies, and thus makes a demand for concrete information, marshalled in a particular way.

CHAPTER 8

THE PROBLEM OF
DISTRIBUTION

1—Distributive Themes

Among meliorative themes, distributive themes may be distinguished from nondistributive themes. The strategy and people using the strategy, we shall say, are concerned with distributive themes rather than with nondistributive ones. In saying this much, however, we are moving outside the implications of Part One. We are adding by stipulation a feature that was not contained in the set of features attributed to the strategy in Part One. This feature—its distributive concern—differs from the other features in being less a general aspect of strategy relevant to the whole field of policy choices than a specialized choice of a theater of operations. Adding it is not an arbitrary move, for it will simplify references to the strategy in the last part of the book, where we shall be concerned with the implications for ethics of the strategy applied to distributive themes. Furthermore, the distributive feature belongs with the other features for the same reasons that the latter were grouped together: Whether or not they are logically connected, they occur together in practice and as we have demonstrated, they are mutually reinforcing. In the distributive feature, as in the others, the strategy is adapted to the circumstances of our society and politics and represents actual practice on the part of social scientists and other evaluators.

Given the ways in which people in our society are moved to favor or disfavor policies, meliorative concerns lead the analysts who adopt the strategy to consider policies as in varying degrees promoting or hindering health, educational opportunities, the provision of housing, personal income, recreational pleasures; or, more generally, the welfare, happiness, peace, or cultural advancement of the community; and a host of other variables. All of the themes just mentioned are meliorative. They have a further feature, which distinguishes them from other meliorative themes: Taken as properties of groups or institutions, they happen to be derivative from properties of individual persons—the members of the group—or of their individual circumstances. A group of human beings cannot be called healthy unless its members or most of them are individually healthy; the group cannot be said to enjoy increased educational opportunities unless at least some members have educational opportunities that they did not have before; the group cannot have a higher average personal income unless at least some individual members have increased their incomes. Properties of groups or institutions that derive in this way from properties of individual persons are what we call distributive properties.[1] They enter policy discussions as distributive themes.

Nondistributive themes include increasing the size of a group and the size of its dominions; maintaining the institutions prescribed by God's plan or Nature's plan for ideal government; preserving the identity of a nation; and, of course, all manner of themes that seldom figure in meliorative comparisons, although they may often appear in peremptory judgments. Where these themes refer to properties of groups, those properties do not derive from properties of the people who belong to the groups. Very often, no attempt is made to translate the values redounding to the group under such headings into values received by individual members. When such translation is attempted, the themes verge on becoming distributive ones; and the pressure for translation is evidence of pressure for considering distributive themes.

Distributive themes are a subclass of meliorative themes. Saying this implies that an essential part of their role in policy discussions is to call for comparative judgments about alternative policies. To be concerned with distributive themes, therefore, is to be concerned with the extent to which certain advantages or misfortunes are or would be parcelled out to a greater or lesser number of people, for comparative judgments that make use of distributive properties entail numerical comparisons of distribution. Concern about how these advantages and misfortunes are or would be distributed under various policies is one thing, however; deciding which pattern of distribution is best is another. Advocating one pattern of distribution rather than another generally involves taking a stand upon deserts—given that advantages or misfortunes are distributed in a certain way, do the people to whom they are parcelled out deserve them? It also involves complex adjustments among different themes. The best pattern of distribution is the one that provides the most favorable distribution of the most important values. But people disagree about which values are most important. Indeed, all the difficulties of evaluation with which we have claimed the strategy copes arise in trying to decide which patterns of distribution are better and which are worse. The question is not one that can be settled once and for all; generally speaking, answers have to be negotiated *ad hoc* by the use of the strategy or similar techniques.

The distributive concern of which we are speaking at the moment does not embrace the whole question of best patterns, but only its factual beginnings. It is a concern that may be shared by people who have very different ideas about which patterns of distribution are best, as well as by people who have not made up their minds about patterns. All these people may be concerned to know whether or not a particular policy would make the group as a whole better off in respect to health than another policy would, or better off in respect to education, or better off in respect to housing.

In our society, it is difficult to imagine people's not sharing a concern with such facts, in spite of differences among them in further ideas about patterns of distribution. Given the empirical traditions and individualistic social theories characteristic of our society, it is difficult to imagine any policy dispute that, if it goes on long enough, will not sooner or later be connected with distributive themes. Sooner or later, a meliorative party will arise (among other parties, perhaps, that have been meliorative but not, hitherto, distributive) that advocates settling the dispute by distributive considerations of one kind or another or by a combination of such considerations. There is ordinarily no need to wait for such a party to introduce distributive considerations. Policies that are politically controversial within a given human group usually affect subgroups of that group differently in respect to meliorative values. Some members believe that they are being injured while others are receiving benefits or at least being spared most of the injury. Perhaps they believe that the benefits coming to them are smaller and less frequent than the benefits to other subgroups. In a society that permits the free formation of interest groups, these people will make their objections felt in the interest-group process, whether or not they have a distributive formula for ending the dispute.

From this point of view, the much-discussed group-basis of politics can be seen to consist very largely of a complex of organizations mobilizing force and clamor behind various distributive themes. Interest groups are formed to press meliorative claims for certain policies or to oppose meliorative claims for others. In each case, their principal motive is likely to be the benefits of one kind or another that they believe they themselves will gain or be denied. These expectations, of course, are often not their principal argument; it often seems wiser to dilate instead upon the benefits and injuries to be distributed to other people. Nevertheless, whether or not the themes are frankly stated and emphasized, a strongly motivated concern with distributive themes is at work in the dispute.

People evaluating policies in our society are therefore likely to find distributive considerations inescapable if they are dealing with policies that are at all controversial within the society. Even if they do not favor settling a particular issue by distributive considerations, they are likely to confront people who do favor such a settlement. Moreover, distributive considerations arise in the path of other approaches. Some interest groups are formed to advocate peremptory rules. Even in these cases, distributive themes appear, at least in a secondary and indirect way. Whether or not they take a peremptory approach themselves, participants in a dispute may feel that it is desirable to minimize any cause others might have to feel affronted or aggrieved—being denied a polite hearing, for example. They may also feel that, as much as possible, others should be given a chance to have their own way in policy. Both these attitudes embody meliorative and distributive themes. Injuries a peremptory interest group might allege it had suffered if it failed, like the benefits it would enjoy if it succeeded, can be accommodated under them.

We have argued, however, that people using the strategy are taking a meliorative approach. The likelihood that they will have to deal with distributive considerations is then doubled. The distributive themes that they consider will be directly related to the policies being evaluated rather than incidentally arising from the procedures of evaluation and choice. In such cases, distributive considerations are likely to end up as the most important, unless the policies are noncontroversial within the society. In the latter case, distributive considerations will most often be relevant but dormant.*

2—Variations in the Distributive Concern of the Strategy

The degree to which the meliorative approach is manifested as concern with distributive themes is very variable, even under the

* The position taken in this paragraph leaves open the possibility that distributive considerations may get primary attention on a peremptory approach as well. The possibility is frequently realized, for directly related themes, by people arguing that a certain distribution of benefits and injuries is *unjust* and that the policy under which the distribution occurs should therefore be eliminated. It is realized, for indirectly related (procedural) themes, when people argue that some persons have been *unjustly* denied a hearing or the right to vote and that a policy is invalid because it was invalidly chosen. Let it be recalled that we are not saying these are unenlightened arguments.

strategy, which tends toward giving them explicit and primary attention. The variation is visible in the examples that we have discussed. In the school dental dispute, the meliorative party (once it revealed itself as such) was clearly giving primary attention to distributive considerations. To revert to an earlier example, analysts weighing the advantages and disadvantages of inflation in terms of its effects on employment are clearly preoccupied with a distributive consideration—the extent of employment, which reduces to a concern with individual persons being employed rather than unemployed.

Hyneman's evaluation of the possibilities of controlling the bureaucracy has a less obvious connection with distributive themes. Hyneman is chiefly preoccupied with various forms for dividing control between the President and Congress, and therefore with properties of institutions that cannot be reduced in any simple way to properties of individual members of the society. Nevertheless, the whole point of controlling the bureaucracy, in his view, is to promote "respect for the individual." Controlling the bureaucracy would make no difference to this, if it did not make a difference to the benefits and injuries received by individual members of the society.

The connection between Rostow and Millikan's argument for a plan of foreign aid and domestic distributive themes appears to be remotest of all. Of course, such a connection can be demonstrated. Such a program would almost inevitably have incidental effects on various citizens of the United States, with some benefiting more than others; it is not likely to be, in every respect, an indivisible public good. But would it not be more sensible, on the evidence of their discussion, to consider them as being occupied with nondistributive themes rather than with distributive ones? They consider, for example, that a more effective foreign aid program would improve our national security, and the theme of national security, while meliorative, cannot, it might be argued, be reduced in any simple way to properties of individual persons, since it involves preserving the identity of the nation and its institutions.

While it might be argued that Rostow and Millikan are mainly concerned with nondistributive themes, it does not seem unrealistic to attribute to them an active concern with distributive themes sufficient to satisfy the minimum demands that we made in constructing the extended definition of the strategy. The main reason why this concern does not become more explicit is surely that, throughout the greater part of their argument, Rostow and Millikan simply assume that everyone in American society is going to benefit to some extent from effective use of United States funds abroad. Where they do recognize differences in the domestic distribution of benefits and injuries and try to meet objections on this account, they are explicitly concerned with distributive themes. In any case, a distributive concern must be assigned to the presuppositions of their analysis: Surely their evaluation and advocacy of any foreign aid program would be much more hesitant if they believed that it would personally injure most, or even a good part, of the American people.

If we choose to make a concern with themes that are distributive as well as meliorative a feature of the strategy, it seems most sensible to require as a minimum only that such concern should be present as a potentiality. It also seems sensible to recognize that even when it is actively present, consideration of distributive themes will often be mixed with considerations of another sort. In stipulating a potentiality, however, we stipulate more than the mere logical possibility of a concern with distributive themes developing. We postulate that, as discussion about a given policy is prolonged and becomes more controversial, analysts using the strategy in our society will gravitate toward giving explicit and primary attention to distributive themes, even if they have not previously done so. We assume, moreover, that this tendency is accompanied by certain beliefs and attitudes that are characteristic of our society. We assume that it is an open question for analysts using the strategy (though perhaps not a question that they will of their own accord choose to pursue) whether any particular institution leads to greater distributive benefits of given kinds than other institutions. We suppose that those using the strategy regard distributive evidence as capable of providing good reasons for changing institutions and policies, even familiar and long established ones.

Such an attitude, of course, reflects our tradition of political theory, which (witness the Preamble to the Constitution) leads members of our society to regard government, indeed every form of social organization, as instruments for promoting the welfare of the persons who maintain them. There are other traditions in which, if distributive themes appear at all, they are subordinate to other sorts of theme. For example, Plato's and Hegel's models for the ideally well-ordered state provide standards for political endeavor that are meliorative but not distributive. Adopting such standards, one would rank policies by asking whether they led to nearer or farther approximations of the model set up as an ideal.

We remark again that we are treating a concern with distributive themes as considerably less specialized than a concern with any one view of deserts or of what is traditionally known as "distributive justice." [2] It also stops short in another way of favoring any definite pattern of distribution. Deciding upon a pattern for distributing one sort of benefit presupposes negotiation and adjustment regarding other sorts of benefit. People who share a concern for information about distribution may take very different lines in the course of such negotiation and adjustment.

To say that people who use the strategy concern themselves with distributive themes does not, therefore, imply that they are bound to end up advocating certain patterns of distribution as ideal. If they reach the point of advocating patterns, they will in all probability advocate different ones.

We remark, further, that adding the distributive feature to the strategy does not commit us to assuming that all differences among the patterns advocated by analysts and evaluators who use the strategy will fall within the bounds of utilitarianism. The values traditionally championed by utilitarianism have been meliorative and distributive. Specifying that the strategy is concerned with those values that are distributive as well as meliorative makes it easy therefore to connect the strategy with utilitarianism, as we shall do in the next part of the book. But the class of values that are both meliorative and distributive is not identical with the class of values championed by utilitarians. It includes, in fact, the direct contraries of utilitarian values—pain as well as pleasure, unhappiness as well as happiness, privation as well as decent comfort. Our discussion throughout this chapter is neutral as between these pairs of contraries, and hence it preserves a high degree of neutrality for the strategy. We are still concerned with logical and epistemological issues rather than with ethical ones.

In the next section of this chapter, it is true, we are going to describe what may be regarded as conclusive tests for rating different policies in respect to distributive efficacy. They are tests, however, only as to the facts. They can show whether or not a given policy provides a group with a greater or lesser degree of a particular distributive property than another policy would. The tests require examination of the distribution within the group of the related property attributed to persons. They do not, however, settle questions about distributive justice or about the choice of values. One does not need to take a stand regarding deserts or make utilitarian values paramount to use these tests, even though the acknowledged uses for them are limited in certain ways that correspond to considerations of distributive justice. The basic form of these tests has an origin and uses entirely outside ethics.

3—Conclusive Tests for Distributive Themes: The Census Notion

Under the strategy, evaluators express their concern with meliorative themes without necessarily, or even usually, formulating rules to embody the themes. Likewise, they express concern with distributive themes without formalizing their procedures to the point of exhibiting rigorous deductive arguments. Very often, in fact, their concern with distributive themes is indirect. As we have seen, they may be preoccupied with considerations that presuppose and can be reduced to distributive themes but do not require such reduction for immediate purposes of discussion. Even when policy discussions have been forced to take direct cognizance of distributive themes, evaluators do not insist on pressing evidence about the distributive effects of different policies to the point of casting the evidence in conclusive form. Their treatment of themes may be granted the advantage of flexibility. On the other hand, it must be recognized that they have little choice. The flux of evaluation is so great as to compel this adaptation.

The conclusive form of distributive tests is rarely realized, even by evaluators directly concerned with distributive themes, for exactly the same reasons that evaluation in general is prevented from being as neat, regular, and conclusive as the synoptic approach requires. If people commonly agreed on single themes, perhaps conclusive evidence would often be arranged for. Then policy disputes could be solved by rigorous deduction in each case from the evidence about the theme in question. (Even so, one would have to assume that there was no disagreement about questions of deserts.)

In fact, there are generally so many distributive themes to consider, so much conflict among them, and so much fluidity, both within the field of distributive themes and in the whole field of themes calling for attention, that debate rarely rests long enough with any one theme to investigate it conclusively. Even individual evaluators, acting in the spirit of strategy and choosing one theme and a limited number of policies for concentrated investigation, generally have too little time or money to gather conclusive evidence. They therefore make do with probabilities and approximations. They lump people together in subgroups, ignoring the different impact a policy may have on individual persons within the subgroups. They concentrate on subgroups that especially interest them for theoretical or other reasons, and they discuss only the distributive effects on these subgroups.

In offering to talk about conclusive tests for distributive themes, therefore, we are offering to talk about a model for presenting evidence rather than the usual form for presenting it. The model is concerned at any one time with a single distributive theme. The usual form of evidence, even when the evidence is confined to a single theme, is at best only an approximation of the model—and the process of evaluation, especially as reflected in the use of the strategy, seldom rests on a single theme.

The model assists in explaining the logic of distributive considerations. That is our main reason for introducing it. Yet it is not merely a device for exposition. The conclusive form of a distributive test lies behind every distributive theme mentioned in the comparison of policies, in the sense that it is part of the meaning of such themes, as people ordinarily think of them, that the results of such a test would supersede contrary results reached by previous speculations or guesses or partial tests. In evaluation, people turn from one distributive theme to another, but as regards each theme their arguments presuppose that the quality of their evidence depends on its degree of approximation to the conclusive form of results. Without reverting to synoptic assumptions about what is possible in evaluation, therefore, we may claim that the general form of conclusive tests helps shape the reasoning even of people who do not go beyond partial tests—including, for the most part, most of the time, people using the strategy.

The census notion. The general form of a conclusive distributive test is that of a *census*—a comparative census when what is to be tested is whether one group of people exemplifies a given distributive property to a higher degree than another group, a prospective census when what is to be compared is the state of a given group with respect to a distributive theme under one policy with its predicted state under another.* The notion is not recondite. It is implicit, as regards social policy, in Roosevelt's famous reference to "one third of a nation, ill-clothed, ill-housed, and ill-fed"; in the use of statistics about mortality rates for different social classes to support arguments like those Tawney makes in his book on *Equality;* in the endeavors of interest-group leaders to show that most of the population will be hurt by policies that hurt their groups. Census-like evidence is, in fact, one of the most common ingredients of policy debate.

Let us imagine that the flux of evaluation has so much abated at a certain time and place that a policy dispute has come to turn on the single question of which of two policies will do most for the health of the population—and that someone has taken the trouble of finding out what consequences for the health of indi-

---

* A prospective census, just as the felicific calculus was a prospective calculus. If happiness is the given distributive theme, we offer a felicific census in the place of the felicific calculus.

vidual citizens can be expected from each policy. He presents his findings in the following form:

	Policy A	Policy B
Robust	20	30
Middling	40	50
Feeble	40	20

(The figures may be regarded as representing the number of individuals in a population of 100 whose condition of health will fall into the indicated categories; as representing the number of individuals in those categories discovered in a statistically reliable random sample of 100 people drawn from a larger population; or as percentages of the total population.)

This comparative arrangement of census figures clearly implies that Policy B is more conducive to the health of the population than Policy A. Those participants who have been arguing for Policy A on the basis of general signs that it would be more efficiently administered or more likely to elicit the enthusiasm of physicians, and therefore would probably do more for health than Policy B, have now been effectively silenced—unless they find some way of challenging the figures. It is absurd, according to the conventions of ordinary language for making comparative judgments about groups, to go on arguing that Policy B will not make the population healthier than Policy A, in the face of census figures showing that Policy B will make in proportion more people robust and fewer people feeble—substantially more and less—than Policy A.

There is nothing especially high-minded or ethical about the notion of a census, nor—although it does lead to counting one person's condition for no more and no less than any other's—is it a product of egalitarian ideology. The same rule of interpretation holds for all comparative judgments that assign (derivative) properties to groups of people or things on the basis ultimately of (original) properties of the members of these groups—whatever these groups and their members may be and regardless of whether we are talking about different groups or the same group at different times. If we were investigating the freshness of two lots of fish and obtained the figures given above—so that in one lot of fish, there were twenty fresh and forty spoiled, while forty were in-between, and in the other lot, the figures were thirty, twenty, and fifty respectively—then it would follow that the second lot of fish was fresher than the first lot; similarly for the ripeness of a shipment of bananas before and after two weeks in the warehouse, categorized (say) as "overripe," "unripe," and "ripe." Egalitarian politics does not enter into such questions. Of course, egalitarians may be especially insistent that considerations that lead to such tests should be paramount in policy-making.

A census requires interpersonal comparisons (of a kind constantly made in everyday life), but it does not require a comparison of utilities or an interpersonal calculus of any sort, that is to say, any method of assigning numerical scores or measurements to the persons surveyed, or to their properties. It neither presupposes such a calculus nor does it exclude the possibility of one. Without a means of measuring health, we can still classify people by observation as robust or feeble or neither. In comparing the effects of two different policies, we can match classifications and cancel like against like, one robust man against another, one feeble person against another feeble person, until we are left, in our example, with a set of people (ten robust, ten middling) *all of whom* would be healthier under Policy B than *any* of the set of people left under Policy A (twenty people in feeble condition). Such remainders are characteristic of the cases in which a comparative census gives a determinate result. None of these procedures requires a means of measurement (beyond the ordinal scale involved in the classifications), much less a means of measurement that permits quantitative comparisons of different people's health. All that the procedures imply regarding any possible system of measurement is that the numbers assigned by the system preserve the ordinal features of the property in question: For example, the ordering of "robust" above "middling" and "middling" above "feeble." Such a system of measurement would conform to the results of a census (and hence to the ordinary language conventions for comparative judgments of this kind). We need not take a position one way or another as to whether such a system would be successful in doing more than this.

The sort of favor that a census confers on a policy is, of course, limited to showing that in respect to a given distributive theme, the policy does more for the community surveyed, taken as a whole, with questions about deserts put aside, than the alternative policies with which it has been compared. This is very limited favor, especially in view of the fact that many stages of negotiation, adjustment, and reconstruction may lie ahead before any policy is adopted. The given theme may or may not play an important part in the last stages before choice; almost surely, it will not play a solo part.

A census will not always accord even this limited sort of favor to one policy as against another. Sometimes no difference will be found between the effects of two policies: Policy B may produce the same numbers of robust, middling, and feeble people as Policy A. So far as consequences for health go, the two policies would then be on a par; there would be nothing to choose between them because the population would be just as healthy with one policy as with the other.

Mixed changes. There is another obvious way in which a comparative census may be inconclusive, and in this case people might hesitate to say even that the two policies were equally effective. Suppose that a third policy for promoting health has been proposed, Policy C, and that a comparison between B and C gives the following figures:

	Policy B	Policy C
Robust	30	40
Middling	50	30
Feeble	20	30

Policy C produces more robust people than Policy B—but it also produces more feeble people. We are debarred from saying either that B will make the population healthier than C or that C will make it healthier than B. If, instead of having only two or three policies to investigate, we have a considerable number, quite a few of them may show mixed results like these, as compared with other policies.

Nevertheless, evidence like that provided by a census would be of use in selecting a policy. It would at least enable us to reduce the set of alternatives that had to be considered further by excluding from the set any policy that was determinately disfavored as against one or another of the other policies proposed (though the excluded policies may return for consideration when attention shifts to distributive themes other than health). There is even a way of breaking the deadlock reached within the set. Imitating the freedom people exercise in actual practice, an analyst might take another census, using only two categories, "healthy" and "unhealthy," from which the following results, which are consistent with the figures previously given, may appear:

	Policy B	Policy C
Healthy	70	60
Unhealthy	30	40

These results clearly favor saying that B will make the population healthier than C. In fact, with a two-place census, cases of mixed changes will never be encountered (though par cases may be).

Analysts who use the strategy are quite as free to push their investigations in the direction of two-place censuses as in the direction of three-place ones, and they are free to shift from one line of investigation to another, as seems most effective in the circumstances. There may, of course, be no question of shifting. In a case like the present one, the evidence may have been marshalled in the shape of a two-place census from the beginning. Using or approximating a two-place census does have the disadvantage of increasing the chances of arbitrary classifications. The "middling" category in the three-place census has no independent implications about the merits of the policies; the important points of comparison are the comparative increase in the number of robust people or the decrease in the number of feeble ones, although the middling people had to be counted to keep the proportions straight. Borderline subjects would be assigned to the "middling" category, so that only clearly robust and clearly feeble people would be counted as "robust" and "feeble." With a two-place census, one would get determinate results by squeezing the borderline subjects one way or the other. The results are therefore likely to be more useful, but less reliable.

On the other hand, the single line of a two-place census is already drawn for many meliorative themes. For example, if one wanted to see how far a certain public provision for maternal welfare extended, it would be natural to consider only two categories of mothers, those whose welfare was provided for and those to whom the provisions did not extend. In the case of other themes —for example, health—there does not seem to be any clear tendency in ordinary language to prefer either a two-place or a three-place census to the other. Moreover, the adoption of a two-place census in the case of health accords with the remedial interests displayed in the general strategy that we are describing. People whose perspective agrees with that imposed by the strategy are frequently most interested in how many people will be left below a certain *minimum* standard in respect to a meliorative variable, if various policies are adopted. A two-place census might serve this interest perfectly satisfactorily.[3]

Change of persons. There is another sort of indeterminacy to which both two-place and three-place censuses are formally liable —the indeterminacy that results not from mixed changes but from what we may call "change of persons." Suppose that, in the comparative census first given in illustration, where Policy B had 30 robust against 20 with Policy A, 50 middling against 40, and 20 feeble against 40, Policy A was the present policy and that continuing it would only mean maintaining the present condition of the population. Would a change to Policy B benefit the community? There is a sense in which it clearly might, at least in the eyes of those who were ready to heed the meliorative theme of health. The thirty people made robust under Policy B might consist of the twenty people robust under the present dispensation, together with 10 who are now middling or feeble in health; the fifty people who would be middling under B may now be either middling or feeble; and the twenty people who would be feeble under B may all be feeble now, under Policy A.

But this is not the only possibility. The figures are not inconsistent with some people deteriorating in health after a change to B. In fact, it is possible that all the people who are robust under A may fall into the feeble category under B. Policy B could still perhaps be said to make the population as a whole healthier than Policy A, but it would certainly be very misleading (because of the implications for choice of policy) to say so, without commenting on the adverse changes that would accompany Policy B. If the figures mean what we are currently assuming they could mean, there is a clear case of victimizing some people in order to benefit others, and this result would deter many people (including many of those who use the strategy we are describing) from accepting the census results as evidence favoring B.* An adverse change of persons might also accompany a change from Policy C, in our illustration of a two-place census, to Policy B, and it would be an equal deterrent to ranking B above C in respect to the distributive theme considered.

Redesigning and compensation. The indeterminacy resulting from change of persons can be remedied, too, but in practice—in that part of practice where the strategy of disjointed incrementalism most fully realizes its advantages in flexibility—it is remedied by modifying policy proposals rather than by changing the form of the census. Normally, people are not slow to protest when a

* Their use of the expression, "This policy would make the population healthier than that policy," and associated expressions is thus affected by their moral beliefs, in particular by certain notions of justice. Even without an adverse change of persons, census results prima facie favoring one policy over another might provoke challenges on grounds of justice. Suppose that Policy B makes ten people robust in addition to the twenty robust people under Policy A and raises twenty to a middling condition who would remain feeble if A were continued. But suppose that all those whose condition would be improved in this way belong to one of two highly visible races or social classes and that the condition of people belonging to the other race or class, which is generally worse off to begin with, is left unchanged. Again, there would, we think, be considerable hesitation to agree that the census showed Policy B would make the population healthier than Policy A (even though people might be perfectly ready to say this if they could attach the proper qualifications). If people kept facts about health and the moral values that they assign to health more strictly distinguished, their usage would be clearer and less hesitant. But in fact they do not.

policy looks like worsening their condition, and in our society, policy-makers normally spend a lot of time trying to satisfy such complaints. If Policy B looks good in other respects, policy-makers and analysts, especially those whose thinking accords with the strategy, will be inclined to stick with it, to see whether it cannot be modified to meet the protests of people for whom it would mean adverse changes in condition.

Redesigning for this purpose may take several forms. The policy may be redesigned so that the adverse changes are eliminated, or compensating features may be added to the policy to balance losses of one kind with gains of another. Sometimes these two sorts of provision come to the same thing. When, for example, a loss of income from one source is compensated for by a gain of income from another, the effect of redesigning is to eliminate adverse changes in respect to income. Sometimes, however, adverse changes are allowed to stand, even when they really hurt. In those cases, losses in respect to one distributive theme may be compensated for by gains in respect to a wholly different one, including gains that will not be enjoyed until some time later.

Even in the last type of case, "compensation" does not necessarily mean giving to those who lose or who are threatened with losing the subjective utility of their present position, though when there is a question of having to square certain people or "buy them off," their preferences and subjective utility cannot be ignored, either practically or often as a matter of justice. People may, after all, prefer their ancestral homes to any amount of money that the highway department will pay them, but if they are paid the going prices for their homes, it will generally be thought that they have been adequately compensated. In those cases where compensating features added by redesigning have the effect of eliminating adverse changes, the issue is not what people prefer but the dangers of personal loss—whether or not people who would otherwise be victimized, in respect to health or educational opportunities, for example, will be maintained in at least their present condition. Consider a project of colonization or resettlement: The people to be moved must be able to provide themselves with food, clothing, shelter, and medicines to take the place of those they receive under present policy, although the sorts of food, clothing, shelter, and medicine may all be new to them.

There can, of course, be no a priori guarantee that policies can be redesigned to include compensations of either sort—either the monetary compensations of the former cases or the compensations in kind of the latter.* Yet the necessity of arranging for compensation of one sort or the other is one of the basic reasons for demanding redesigning. (The strategy of disjointed incrementalism, with its major provisions for redesigning, is adapted to such a necessity being a frequent circumstance.) The notion of compensation is also intimately associated in practice with the use, or approximate use, of the census notion.

One can easily see why. An individual evaluator may limit himself to considering a small number of policies at any given stage of debate—possibly, if he uses the strategy, to a single policy. Participants in a policy dispute are not, however, limited to considering the set of proposals with which debate begins. Individual participants may in fact enter with new proposals at any stage. People using the strategy—people generally—are typically continually occupied with suggestions for modifying and redesigning the proposals already made, as well as with proposals sufficiently different to be considered new ones.

They use, or approximate the use of, comparative censuses in order to locate possible objections to policies, and then they seek to forestall these objections by redesigning policies to meet them. Because redesigning with a view to compensation is so frequently undertaken, those who use the strategy typically demand census information that, in some respects, goes beyond the summary figures in our illustrative tables. They want to know how specific groups and individuals will be affected, which means they want some way of estimating the breakdown figures for each of these groups. At each stage of designing or redesigning policy proposals,

---

* Nor, to be sure, will compensation always be insisted on. Differences of race or social class may have been associated with long-standing privileges and a history of exploitation. The worsened condition of some people, under a policy favoring the majority, may be felt to be merely the effect of removing unjust privileges or merely punishment for past injustices.

there will be a resort first to the census idea and second to proposals about compensating features.

It is not only the opportunity for redesigning policies that makes compensation a constant companion of the census idea. The remedial orientation of the strategy is bound to make the topic of compensation prominent. For when policy proposals originate as ways of compensating for the adverse effects of previous policies, it is certainly not to be expected that people will be indifferent to the compensations that may be required by their own remedies. Indeed, those who use the incremental strategy are constantly trying to maintain the benefits of existing policies while eliminating the disadvantages. Compensation is therefore intimately linked with both the remedial and the incremental features of the strategy.

N-place complications. Ordinary language and practice do not rigidly specify that the census for any given topic shall have two places rather than three or three rather than two. In their approximations to the census-notion, people shift from one number of categories to the other, as circumstances (available evidence, resources for collecting further evidence, costs of waiting, the caution of clients) seem to require. It is possible, furthermore, that circumstances may make a census with more than three places appropriate. A three-place census about health might mask the fact that the favored policy raises the people that it would make robust only barely above the middling standard, while it reduces the people that would be feeble under it to a condition nearly moribund. A six-place census with refined categories might vindicate a suspicion of this kind. If it did, it would reverse the implications of the three-place census.[4] Shifting from one number of categories to another is one of the opportunities that ordinary language offers for revising and correcting dubious or unhelpful results. It is an opportunity that is manifested, if not fully exercised, in common approximations to the use of the census notion in evaluation: for example, whenever an analyst, pointing to a group of people who stand to suffer destitution from a certain policy, breaks away from previous considerations limited to the fact that under various pol-

icies certain groups stand to gain or lose marginal amounts of consumers' goods.

We do not mean that the appropriate number of categories
cannot be fairly readily settled upon in particular circumstances.
The number will vary partly with the meliorative theme investigated. A census of welfare provisions, as we have already remarked, would be likely to have two places. A census of happiness
(if anyone wanted to take one) would probably require three
places, since we can clearly envisage the possibility that many people, perhaps most people, are neither happy nor unhappy. A census
of health, as we have seen, might have either three or two places,
depending perhaps on how emphatic the remedial interests of the
investigators are: If they think it urgent to bring about whatever
improvements in health are possible, they will surely consider a
two-place census sufficient. In all of these cases, categories would
be multiplied further only when the peculiarities of a given dispute demanded their multiplication; but then these same peculiarities would help establish the number of categories required.

The census as used by the strategy. The difficulties that we
have found in the census notion—its shifting form and its variable
results—arise largely from the fact that we have treated it in
abstraction from actual policy disputes, as a model or set of models, and yet have tried to give a fair account of its various applications. Even so, the rigidity of the separate tables (so many separate models) may have made more of an impression than the facts
about fluctuation between models in the set and the facts about
variable approximation in the real world to which we have alluded. It is important, therefore, to insist again that, although the
census notion operates in the real world, shaping the reasoning of
people occupied with evidence about the distributive effects of
policies, its mode of operation is fluid and flexible. In this respect,
evaluators using the strategy of disjointed incrementalism are on
the same footing as regards the census notion as are other people
who are guided by it. People using the strategy do not, typically,
pursue evidence regarding any single distributive theme to the
point of marshalling comprehensive evidence in the form of census

results. They do not even, typically, commit themselves to forms of evidence far enough to commit themselves to one number of census-places rather than another. They themselves, and certainly the debate going on between them, are continually moving between forms of evidence, between different distributive themes, and between various policy proposals.

Since censuses are not usually carried out in detail, the theoretical problems that we have mentioned are to a high degree artificial ones. People do not stage debates about the number of places to be included in a census. Instead, they employ a certain number of categories in the course of making out a case for a certain policy or of elaborating objections to their opponents' arguments. The possibility of using the census notion, in conjunction with the notion of compensation, as an explicit systematic device for selecting an optimum policy, after successive modifications, is largely unexploited.

Instead—something that fits in very well with the remedial orientation of the strategy—the most frequent explicit use of the census notion is probably to rule out policies that involve gross deprivation of one kind or another. The policies that survive are typically presented as benefiting everybody or everybody in a certain group, without affecting anyone outside it adversely. This claim may be regarded as an attempt to forestall objections that a census would marshal, if its results were unfavorable to the policy.

For their part, the opponents of the proposal try to show that certain groups or classes of people will be adversely affected or denied a share of benefits. On both sides, information approximating that which a census would collect is at issue. Surveying effects on groups is a way of estimating what happens to persons, and normally some attention will be given to overlapping membership in order to expose double-counting. The census notion is at work shaping the presentation of evidence on both sides. So that it accords with familiar practices when we say that the role of the census notion in the strategy is that it implicitly orients the investigation of evidence and the inferences made from the evidence once obtained.

We do not claim that the census notion must be regarded as

an ultimate achievement of the human intellect. Obviously, taken with its received limitations, it falls very far short of being a perfected scheme for ranking policies. There are so many cases in which it gives no results that one naturally wonders whether it could not be supplanted by a subtler scheme, which would do all that the census does and yield results in other cases as well. The census notion may seem especially crude and primitive to those who are familiar with the subtle treatments of preferences and of the problem of aggregating preferences that have been developed in welfare economics during the past forty years or so. There the problem has been to develop a calculus for aggregating preferences that begs no questions about what people ought to prefer and makes no assumptions about intensities of preference and satisfaction being interpersonally comparable. This is the problem about patterns of distribution, with the question of deserts left out, except insofar as it is allowed to count in the preferences of individual consumers between social states. What help is the census notion in solving this problem?

The answer is that by itself it is very little help, though the strategy of disjointed incrementalism and the census notion together cover the whole field of the problem. (However, they divide the problem up very differently from the way in which welfare economics has divided it.) The only sense in which tests conforming to the census notion can be called conclusive is that they conclusively establish facts on the basis of which people proceed to make differing, even contradictory, judgments about the inferences to be drawn for policy. By itself, the census notion does not indicate how different distributive themes are to be combined, any more than it indicates how to dispose of the question of deserts. It is possible to claim that tests of the census sort, somehow combined, should themselves be the standards of distributive justice. In this respect, such tests are congenial to utilitarianism and to the egalitarian scruples that play a part in utilitarian doctrines. To make the tests themselves standards, however, is to make an additional move that using the census notion, with or without the strategy of disjointed incrementalism, does not commit anyone to making.

The census notion does not exactly flout the difficulties of comparing intensities of preference and satisfaction that have caused so much trouble in welfare economics. As we have already noted, its implications regarding the measurement of such factors are very limited. The fact is that the census notion is only incidentally concerned with preferences among the themes to which it may be applied. Giving people what they prefer is, as a subject for applying the census notion, just one distributive theme among many, and evidence about it can be collected without investigating intensities of preference. The census notion is concerned with the distribution of objective properties among persons, regardless of personal beliefs or preferences (unless, of course, the objective property at issue is that of having what one wants in a certain connection). What people believe or prefer is not the criterion for judging them to be physically healthy, gainfully employed, or having had eight or more years of schooling. What people believe or prefer may even be mistaken as regards their own happiness.

There is another side to the matter, however. How are the themes chosen on which census-like evidence, or approximations thereof, is pressed for? And how, once the results on different themes are in, are they combined in judgments on policy? Here the subject of preferences is not merely incidental, nor does the strategy of disjointed incrementalism treat it incidentally. The strategy operates in the choice of distributive themes; it operates in combining them; it operates in adjusting these choices and combinations to considerations of deserts (though considerations of deserts are determined partly by the various peremptory limitations that people using the strategy may choose to observe). The strategy does not, of course, produce a general solution to the problem of aggregating preferences; it does not culminate in a standard welfare function; it does not fix upon any pattern of distribution as a permanent ideal. The strategy therefore does not solve the theoretical problems of welfare economics. But it does aggregate preferences *ad hoc* in ways often sufficient to make intelligent choices of policy, and the census notion plays a useful part in its successes.

Certainly, much subtler and more elaborate thinking has gone into the problem of aggregating preferences, as posed in welfare economics, than has ever been put into generating the simple schemes of comparison in which the census notion is ordinarily manifested, so far as it is manifested at all. The difficulties about aggregating preferences that have been turned up, for example, by Arrow,[5] suggest, however, that the apparent simplification of marshalling everybody's preferences once and for all at one side of the problem, without regard to the dynamic interplay between preferences and the quest for evidence about distributive themes, is not the most effective or intelligible plan for dealing with distributive considerations. The census notion, combined with the strategy, may shine by contrast.

Second, the fact that the census notion deals with observed properties regardless of preferences enables it, in spite of its limitations, to guide evaluators to results that the Paretian criterion forestalls in the case of a preference calculus. A policy may promote health, and a system of compensation may restore people to their accustomed level of nutrition, even though the policy is not preferred by everyone who is not indifferent to it, and even if the compensation does not suit the preferences of those receiving it.[6] Thirdly, primitive as it may be, the census notion represents an important ingredient of our present procedures; and it is useful to know what our present procedures are before we try to improve on them. Fourthly, as has been predicted, we shall see in the next part of the book that procedures shaped by the census notion have at least the considerable merit of escaping the leading objections to Bentham's calculus and thus of showing how utilitarianism has been practiced even though the calculus has not.

Finally, when the census notion is combined, as it is under the strategy, with a readiness to redesign policies, it makes a more important contribution to ranking policies than may appear when it is treated in isolation from the context of debate and bargaining in which evaluation is conducted. This point is important enough to deserve amplifying in a separate section.

4—Multiple Censuses

The strategy, we have claimed, operates in combining different distributive themes, each of which would require separate census-like investigation. The notion of redesigning may be called on again, this time more broadly, to explain, in conjunction with the census notion, how these combinations are arrived at. We may, in fact, put the question about combining themes in the following way: How do evaluators cope with multiple censuses on different themes? Analysts and evaluators using the strategy, as we have pointed out, are inclined to discuss themes without formulating rules, and we have argued that the flexibility of the strategy depends on their being free to consider a number of themes, taking advantage of this freedom at least in the aggregate. We have supposed, further, that the themes that count most in their attempts to rank policies are distributive themes rather than nondistributive ones. But each distributive theme requires a different census as a conclusive test. If—as must often happen—the results of censuses on different themes tend to conflict, how can people using the strategy consistently pay attention to a number of such themes in the same dispute?

One way in which they can deal with multiple distributive themes is to dispose of some of them before any question of taking or approximating censuses arises. They may shift from one theme to another, as in the case of the school dental dispute, exploring the attractions of the themes without specifying evidence respecting distribution. Some themes may be discarded as prima facie less attractive or cogent than others. The distributive themes that survive the discussion, if more than one does survive, may not conflict among themselves. They may, in fact, be logically or causally connected in such a way that the results of the different censuses could be expected to coincide in the rankings given to proposed policies. "Health" and "the health of school children" are logically connected in this way, given that the groups to be surveyed are composed wholly of school children. "Health" and "opportunities for dental attention" are causally connected in a way that should likewise lead in most cases to a coincidence of results.

The supersession of some themes by others may, however, occur only after census-like evidence has been introduced for one set or both. Until this has happened, the conflict may not have been felt; people involved in the discussion may have been inclined to carry along all the themes introduced, so long as they all seemed to work together in favoring one or another of the policies proposed. Then something like the results of a census appears and motivates supersession. A policy that would increase the amenities of householders in a certain town may well be eliminated when it is discovered that, by discouraging industry, the policy will lead to a quarter of the population being unemployed. The theme of employment thus turns out to be more important than the theme of householders' amenities. It is, of course, from conflicts of this kind or from conflicts that turn on the prima facie attractions of different themes, that analysts discover which themes people regard as more important. Conflicts between themes, when they lead to the supersession of some themes by others, may also be regarded as leading to the supersession of some ends by others, and thus manifest at least one side of the mutual adjustment of means to ends that was designated as one of the features of the strategy.

The other side of the adjustment is manifested by redesigning policies rather than by the supersession of themes. Redesigning makes quite as important a contribution to consistency in evaluation as supersession, and it is in some ways even more characteristic of the strategy of disjointed incrementalism because it embodies the spirit and leading features of the strategy more distinctly. When a conflict appears between censuses or quasi-censuses on different themes, the inclination of strategists is to try to retain the advantages of the policies already proposed and to improve on them in the directions in which they have been disclosed to have (relative) disadvantages. The strategy encourages doing this by working incrementally to redesign one or another of the policies already in the field.

Suppose that two distributive themes have been considered,

and it is clear that one census would rank a policy A ahead of all the others proposed in respect to one theme. A census on the other theme, however, would give top ranking to policy B. Given the fragmentation of effort inherent in the strategy, it may be expected that some analysts and evaluators will concentrate on redesigning A, while others will concentrate on redesigning B. Those concerned with A, naturally, will try to remove its disadvantages respecting the second theme; those concerned with B will try to remove its disadvantages respecting the first. For example, a zoning proposal will be redesigned to give more encouragement to industry; a plan for industrial development will be redesigned to save more of the local amenities. Redesigning, under the strategy, sets the different parties in the dispute in motion toward one another.

One or the other party of evaluators may succeed in designing a policy that is superior to either A or B in respect to both themes discussed; and once this fact is recognized on all sides, that policy may be settled upon without further ado. Suppose both parties succeed in designing policies, A' and B', which are superior to the original policies on both counts. Then redesigning may continue, until a policy that is uniquely favored on both counts has been arrived at. Possibly, at some stage, the two parties will join forces in redesigning the most likely of the policies developed by separate approaches up to that point. One would expect, at any rate, that with communication between the two sides there will be some shifting back and forth of individual evaluators and increased convergence as the process continues.

For want of information or ingenuity, efforts at redesigning may not succeed in hitting upon a uniquely favored policy; for want of time, they may not be so far prolonged. Once they have arrived at A' and B', people on both sides may be ready to settle for one of them; perhaps they agree to take a vote. They may, however, have come to a stop in redesigning much earlier. The two sides may have succeeded only in increasing the advantages of both original policies respecting both themes without either side producing policies that, like A' and B', are superior to either of the original policies on both counts. In respect to one theme, A will still be best; in respect to the other, B. A as redesigned will be better still, if it has all A's advantages respecting one theme and more than A's advantages respecting the other; likewise, B as redesigned may be better than B. If at this point, redesigning stops and the several parties to the dispute fall back upon supersession to achieve consistency, a great deal may nevertheless have been gained. Specifically, a great many of the benefits to be expected from the exploratory feature of the strategy may have been gained. By postponing recourse to a choice between the conflicting themes, the advantages of the policy that is finally selected—whether it is A or B—are greater, even with respect to the theme on which it rates lower, than would otherwise have been the case.

The strategy of disjointed incrementalism does not offer or pretend to offer a general scheme for fixing the precedence of different distributive themes or of the censuses connected with them. The interplay of the census-notion with redesigning and supersession shows how the strategy achieves consistency notwithstanding—and, even better than consistency, improved policies.

5—Logical Reconstructions

The usual alternative supplied in the history of philosophy for rational-deductive thinking is intuition, which is commonly made a mystery, liable without remedy to all the difficulties of personal caprice and idiosyncrasy. This is not the alternative that the strategy supplies. Instead, it supplies a social process, flexible indeed, especially in the aggregate, but a process nevertheless in which the participants may each be as self-consciously logical, as articulate, and as exacting about evidence, within the limits of the tasks each assumes, as anyone could reasonably desire. The census notion shows how exacting people using the strategy may be about one sort of evidence at least, and it should help to remove suspicions that the strategy achieves flexibility only at the cost of refusing to be definite about any points of information.

The strategy makes logical use of information. This can be

seen, not only in the provisions for achieving consistency in the use of the census notion that we have just discussed, but also more generally. Analysts and evaluators using the strategy do not, to be sure, pretend to a general system under which policy choices of all sorts may be reached by deduction alone; they even, we have argued, avoid formulating rules for settling the particular controversies in which they happen for the moment to be engaged. Yet what they do undertake to do is done, allowing for human fallibility, logically.

What each evaluator seeks to do under the strategy, we suppose, is to combine his information in an *ad hoc construction* of directed thought, which in the end indicates favor for one policy rather than another. This construction may be taken to be *a case for that policy*, a case which the evaluator arrives at, while accepting the limiting features of the strategy as practiced by any single analyst and exploiting the opportunities it affords for concrete adaptations to the details of particular circumstances. If many of the logical connections within this construction remain implicit, even hidden, we may nevertheless assume that with due care for limiting inferences to those warranted by the information, the connections will be basically sound. For example, analysts using the strategy will discriminate, if they are careful, between solid information and information that is only probable in various degrees and will weight their results accordingly. Some analysts may not, of course, be careful; the strategy does not guarantee that they will be. By limiting each analyst's task, however, the strategy does increase his chances of doing each part of it thoroughly.

If the case that the analyst or evaluator works up for a certain policy is consistent, then it could be reconstructed—retrospectively—in the form of a logical system. Even then, the claims for its relevance would still be *ad hoc* rather than general. The implicit logical connections would thus be brought to light, and as an incident of doing this, the systems for weighting information and different evaluative themes would be exposed. A retrospective system could also be constructed from the combined results of many participating evaluators, that would take into account the negotiations, decisions, and voting procedures that led to the combined results. Perhaps such a construction is ultimately the only way of fully appreciating the significance of all the moves made under the strategy in regard to a particular issue or set of issues. It may also be the only way of finally vindicating the consistency that the strategy displays when applied in particular circumstances. There is, however, all the difference in the world—as we have pointed out many times—between supposing that such exercises in reconstruction can be carried through after the event and supposing that they provide models that can usefully direct evaluative activities beforehand.

PART FOUR

THE REHABILITATION OF UTILITARIANISM

CHAPTER 9

UTILITARIANISM
REHABILITATED ON
MORAL GROUNDS

1—Our Purpose in Treating Ethical Theory

In the course of describing the strategy of disjointed incrementalism, we have simultaneously been elaborating the hypothesis that the strategy is commonly practiced by social scientists and other participants in policy disputes. How far people in our society and in others actually do make use of the strategy is a subject for empirical investigation, and such empirical investigations would no doubt lead to corrections and refinements in our picture of the strategy.

We cannot, however, pursue those investigations here. Instead, we propose to investigate further the ethical significance of the strategy To be sure, insofar as philosophical theories offer descriptions of moral discourse that converge with our description of the strategy on points vital to the latter, the theories tend to corroborate the hypothesis that the strategy is in common use. This tendency is empirical corroboration of a sort, since it involves references to observations that others have made of the same phenomena. But our chief aim in discussing ethical theory is to amplify our rationale for the strategy.

First, the strategy is found in practice to remedy many of the intellectual difficulties of evaluation. We have already said a good deal on this point, but the story is not yet complete. Second, the strategy is philosophically illuminating, in the sense that a number of outstanding problems of ethical theory can be solved by referring to the use of strategy. This point is very closely related to the first. Third, the strategy accords so well with common moral beliefs as to escape, we think, any unmanageable moral objections. Some of the reasons for thinking this have already figured implicitly in our argument, for we have been demonstrating by example that meliorative and distributive considerations have important roles in moral argument. The strategy does have a field of application in ethics. The question that remains is, How big a field?

There is a further reason for exploring the mutual implications of the strategy and ethical theory. If social scientists (and other people) look upon their normal practices in evaluation and decision with uneasiness, chagrin, and possibly even something like despair, it is, we have argued, mainly because they look on those practices in the false light shed by unsuitable ideals of evaluative method. But their uneasiness has another source in the disasters that have in their eyes befallen ethical theory in this century—on the one hand, the collapse of utilitarianism; on the other, the rise of emotivism. The alternatives to following synoptic ideals of method in the application of concepts of value have seemed arbitrary and irrational. Dismay about these alternatives has been aggravated by the apparent breakdown of reason in supplying the concepts of value for which application is sought. Indeed, perhaps the beginning of the uneasiness, though not its major cause, lies there: It was perhaps only when social scientists despaired of being supplied with rationally defensible values that they retreated to the position in which we find them—disavowing any professional concern with the origin or content of values, but insisting on synoptic ideals as the *sine qua non* of rational application.

The preceding chapters have exposed the delusions on which this insistence is founded. There are, as we have shown, alternatives to the synoptic approach that in normal circumstances of evaluation and decision are more rational, since they are better adapted to making effective use of information in such circumstances. To make this point, it sufficed to produce an example of such an alternative, which we have done by describing the combination of techniques that are embodied in the strategy of disjointed incrementalism. Thus we have endeavored to block off the main cause of the current malaise about evaluation.

Now that all the features of the strategy have been described, we find ourselves in a position to do something about damming up the other source of uneasiness. The reports of disaster in ethical theory have been much exaggerated, and at least in one quarter—the utilitarian—traditional theory can be rehabilitated by embracing the strategy.

Emotivism has not swept away the rational structure of serious moral discourse, nor has it made all traditional ethical theories obsolete, insofar as they have attempted to describe the basis and logic of that structure. Utilitarianism has not collapsed beyond repair, but it does need rehabilitating. Certain parts of the procedures classically associated with it have not, at least not yet, been fully developed or freed from objection. But at least in cases where the evidence of utility is not controversial, the basic conceptions of utilitarianism and its general theory of the nature of moral judgments substantially survive the concessions that must be granted the emotive and imperative theories of ethics. They survive more easily with the assistance of the strategy. The strategy, furthermore, makes utilitarianism a helpful doctrine in cases where ambiguous evidence about utility has to be resolved.

Why should we focus on utilitarianism to the exclusion of other provinces of traditional ethical theory? We do so because utilitarianism, at least in the English-speaking world, is the school toward which most social scientists are inclined, if they are inclined toward any. There are historical reasons for this inclination: Important branches of social science, among them economics and sociology, grew out of utilitarian preoccupations. There is also a natural convergence in preoccupations between utilitarianism and social science. Utilitarianism, after all, insists more strongly than any other ethical theory on forcing moral judgments to the test of facts—the facts of social science.

In any case, the other schools of traditional ethical theory will not be excluded from consideration. We shall define utilitarianism so sweepingly as to minimize the differences between it and rival schools. We shall in effect draw on the other schools for objections and the disposition of these objections will determine what shape utilitarianism will take within our definition. In the course of trying to fix this shape or character, we shall be grappling with some of the leading problems in the whole field of ethical theory, though we shall have neither the time nor the occasion to treat them fully here.

Utilitarianism, like other ethical theories, undertakes to identify and explicate the criteria for intelligible moral judgments. Having identified these criteria, it has also endeavored to provide procedures for applying them to disputed cases. Utilitarian authors have differed in the weight that they have given to these two undertakings. Hume, confining himself [1] to treating what he considered to be established judgments (that such and such traits are virtues and such others vices), was preoccupied with the first; Bentham relying—too confidently—on his idea of the felicific calculus,[2] with the second. For our purposes, however, their theories belong to the same family, and we shall say, very sweepingly, that *any* theory belongs to the utilitarian family if, first, it allows meliorative and distributive considerations a decisive role in confirming or disconfirming all moral judgments that are subject to dispute; and if, second, it supposes that, among these meliorative and distributive considerations, social welfare and group happiness justify supporting an action or policy, while their opposites do not.[3]

Given these last two features of utilitarianism, it is evident that several features of the strategy of disjointed incrementalism make it easy to associate the strategy with utilitarianism. It will be recalled, however, that even with respect to its distributive feature, the strategy does not commit its users to favoring distributive themes that are positively associated with social welfare and group happiness. Far from presupposing that such themes must be decisive in confirming or disconfirming moral judgments, our description of the strategy implies only that, if its procedures are used, there must be some policy choices (whether or not they are important and no matter how many other kinds of question must be settled first in determining perspectives) that turn on meliorative and distributive considerations—and these might be either those championed by utilitarianism or their contraries. Those are the logical grounds for saying that the description of the strategy has been neutral between ethical theories.

It will continue to be neutral. Yet there is no use denying that those using the strategy would, like other people, typically choose to promote those meliorative and distributive values that are values approved by utilitarians rather than those that are not. They are likely, at least to this extent, to be utilitarians *de facto* even though they may not formally subscribe to any ethical theory. The project of rehabilitating utilitarianism will thus throw further light on the practice of the strategy and on the remedies it affords for intellectual difficulties relevant to that practice. If the strategy helps also to clear away moral difficulties that have been raised against utilitarianism, its performance can hardly be a matter of complete indifference to its practitioners, given their *de facto* attitudes. Its performance both in respect to general intellectual and to specifically moral difficulties is bound to be illuminating even to those who profess to have no philosophical interests.

2—Utilitarianism vs. Emotivism

The strategy and utilitarianism have different relations to emotivism, and since emotivism has something to say about the whole field of ethical theory, these relations are the first topic that needs to be considered.

By itself, the strategy of disjointed incrementalism has nothing to say about what forms of words shall count as intelligible moral judgments. They may be forms of words expressing peremptory or meliorative themes of any imaginable kind: familiar or unfamiliar, popular or unpopular, civilized or uncivilized. If they express meliorative and distributive themes, these may conceivably be—not those comfortable themes that utilitarians favor—but contrautilitarian themes like pain, degradation, unhappiness. Such themes might not attract many true enthusiasts outside the ranks of the insane, but that does not disqualify them from consorting with the strategy. Both in description and in practice, the strategy is compatible with the existence of a variety of such judgments large enough to include, beside those invoking or repudiating any given theme of evaluation, those that invoke or repudiate its contrary. Every possible variation of emotion and temperament can be allowed for among the sources of such judgments.

Utilitarianism, with or without the strategy, cannot be so easily reconciled with this variety. If one claims for utilitarianism that it explicates the whole of moral discourse—the logical conditions governing the utterance of all meaningful moral judgments whatever—then one is denying that some forms of words can express moral judgments at all. They must be held to misuse moral locutions to the point of becoming mere gestures at judgments, not themselves moral judgments at all but some form of nonsense. If one retreats (not very far) to the position that utilitarianism explicates, not the whole of moral discourse but at least the system of tests or criteria that judgments must pass when subjected to sustained moral argument, then one must hold that though the judgments that fail these tests (by invoking, for example, contrautilitarian values) may be intelligible, they are false or invalid. They would, moreover, be so *obviously* false that inquiries into the evidence which they allude to could neither save nor ruin them. A judgment that a given policy is good because it will promote pain and misery would, on this account, be so obviously invalid that the question of vindicating it by *evidence* as to pain and misery would not arise.

Even if the broader claim for utilitarianism were made good, it would not, of course, prevent people from making mistakes in moral judgment. People might believe that utilitarian considerations favored a certain action or policy, but believe this mistakenly. People might, furthermore, act in defiance of utilitarian considerations, whether or not they knew that they were doing so. Ethical theory cannot make bad actions impossible. Yet there are attractions in the broader claim that might lead a champion of utilitarian theory to make it, opening up a larger role for the strategy to play when joined with utilitarianism than we shall in fact ascribe to it in the forthcoming discussion. If the broader claim were made good, the danger of anyone's crediting purported moral judgments for which no reasons at all or only contrautilitarian reasons could be offered would be minimized. Such judgments would not make sufficient sense to be classified as moral judgments. They would not even be mistaken moves in moral debate—they would not be moves at all. The only judgments that people debating from a moral point of view would—or logically could—entertain would be those that (whether true or false) were put forward on the assumption (or with the pretense) of being able to pass utilitarian tests.

There are ways of making the broad claim plausible and perhaps no way of refuting it conclusively. If a man says of a controversial policy, "It's a good policy; in fact, it's the one that we ought to follow," and then explains, "I mean only that it attracts me and I want you to support it, too," he does raise doubts about his comprehension of the terms of discussion. (Suppose an issue has been made about people who would be victimized by the policy.) These doubts might well incite the comment, "He doesn't understand the use of 'good' and 'ought'—he thinks they are merely used to express one's own personal tastes." (The comment applies especially forcibly to the use of "ought.") It is hard to believe that an objection of this kind is not well taken, and if it were allowed full scope, it would rule out of moral discourse an enormous number of vexatious judgments—all those that frankly depend on nothing more than personal tastes. This would be a big step toward establishing the broad claim.

There are impressive reasons for refraining entirely from taking this step, however: It offers at least as many disadvantages as advantages for utilitarianism. To begin with, ordinary language seems to offer another recourse against idiosyncratic judgments that dispenses with the charge of misuse and yet works quite as effectively. One might concede that the man who meant only that the policy attracted him and that he wanted others to support it, too, was using moral terms in a comprehensible way, but condemn his judgment as a frivolous one, so far from being an attempt at truth (given the speaker's explanation) as to be unworthy of further attention. In the second place, it seems that even though the charge of misuse might be justified, the misuses are not such as to make the speaker's judgment unintelligible. On the contrary, even before he gave his explanation, those who heard him understood that he was expressing favor for a certain policy and seeking favor for it from other people. His judgment continues to be intelligible even when we learn that it is deliberately idiosyncratic.

One of the principal theses that may be attributed to the *emotive theory* of ethics—or, rather, to the combined emotive and imperative theory that is the actual doctrine of leading emotive theorists—applies at this point.[4] The thesis is that moral locutions are intelligibly used in accordance with the present conventions of ordinary language, if they are used only emotively or imperatively—that is, to do no more than express emotions and convey prescriptions.

The strength of this thesis is at least threefold. In the first place, it seems possible for people to be affected favorably or unfavorably by any describable feature of policy whatever and likewise possible for them to prescribe or prohibit any such feature. In the second place, people are in fact known to have favored and disfavored a great variety of such features, including some that are contraries of others—among them, both utilitarian and contrautilitarian features. In the third place, it seems that moral terms like "good" or "ought" have been used often enough over this whole range to be comprehensible when used anywhere within it (even though some of these uses might still be stigmatized as misuses).

In the face of emotivism, the part of prudence for an advocate of utilitarianism seems to be to concede its truth as regards the facts of usage and to acknowledge that nakedly emotive and imperative uses fall within current conventions for the use of moral terms. One runs a risk otherwise of underestimating the variety of possible moral positions. The point that there are further criteria for *weighing* moral judgments, criteria that the nakedly emotive and imperative uses do not fulfill, is not prejudiced by the concession. Indeed, it can be made more neatly. One distinguishes between the characteristics that all moral judgments have in common and the criteria for selecting *valid* ones by resorting to some reasonably full account of such criteria—for example, the one given by Hume, which is a standard ingredient of utilitarian doctrine. Since many people—especially many social scientists—accept the emotive theory, it is important to show that even if the theory does accurately define the field of moral judgments, it does not offer the whole story about the field.[5] It is equally important, of course, to give the emotive theory its due.

The narrower position, that utilitarianism explicates the criteria governing true moral judgments (and attempts at these), is in fact the most that utilitarian authors have seriously argued for, and it is only utilitarianism so conceived that we propose to discuss further in connection with the strategy.

The strength of this position depends on whether one can find some sort of firm apparatus of criteria at work in typical moral arguments. Utilitarian authors have claimed that one can, and that considerations falling under the head of "utility" play an essential part—though not the sole part—among these criteria. One may, of course, endorse any moral judgment whatever by saying that it is true or valid (as emotive theorists have pointed out)[6] but, according to utilitarian authors, the only plausible way of defending such claims is to show that the judgment in question conforms to a combination of criteria that rule out idle, capricious, and subjective judgments. Hume's explication of these criteria may be taken—so far as it goes, which is not far enough to provide a definite procedure for cases in which utility is controversial—as representative of utilitarian doctrine. Hume assumes that many judgments about human traits do satisfy the criteria—for example, that the disposition to practice justice is a virtue and that infidelity to promises is a vice. Taking these truisms to typify valid moral judgments, he finds that they all fulfill the criteria, first, of being disinterested, and, second, of being consistent (both among themselves, for any one speaker and for all speakers together, and in application to diverse cases, making adjustments for differences in times and places). But they are also moving. They express and arouse sentiments—inclinations toward action—and they would not be moral judgments if they did not. They can be all three—moving yet disinterested and consistent as well—because of the particular sort of sentiment or emotion that they are by convention attached to, namely, the sentiment of humanity, which, other things being equal, leads men to favor those traits (or actions or policies) that are *useful* to the people affected by them, that is to say, conducive to human happiness and welfare. To make a considered moral judgment favoring a certain trait (or action or policy), then, is to imply that the trait (or action or policy) is useful in this way. Since utility is a matter of fact, it can and must be investigated as such. It demands and encourages judgments that are consistent and free from personal bias.

Judgments that fail to meet the criteria described by Hume are subject to attack on points that almost everyone who takes part in moral discourse (e.g., in evaluating social policies) regards as very grave indeed. What more formidable retort to a moral judgment can there be than to show that it is inconsistent with other judgments accepted by the speaker; that it is self-interested; and that it recommends a policy that would actually harm more people than it would help? The strength of the utilitarian claim to have explicated the common criteria of true or valid moral judgments lies in this connection with observed ways of establishing and discrediting moral judgments.

3—Enlightened Peremptory Objections

There are some moral judgments, however, that seem to have force independent of utilitarian considerations and that seem capable of withstanding utilitarian criticism in cases of conflict. The stratagem of renouncing any attempt to accommodate them will not work so convincingly as it did with nakedly emotive or nakedly imperative judgments, nor can they easily be discredited —in fact, no serious theorist has tried. The most that can be said is that they can be more easily accommodated by utilitarianism when it is combined with the strategy of disjointed incremental-ism than when it is not so combined.

The judgments in question are all peremptory ones. (Objec-tions to utilitarianism on the basis of meliorative considerations that are negatively associated with social welfare and happiness may be regarded as foredoomed. We may assume that utilitarians have chosen the right sort of meliorative considerations, the only such considerations that play acceptable parts in ethics.) Among them are peremptory rules such as these: that one should keep promises, even when the consequences of doing so in a par-ticular instance would be less happy than the consequences of breaking them; that however superior any person's capacity for happiness it would not be right to make the rest of the community miserable in order to make him happy; that one should not de-liberately sacrifice the lives of some members of the community (that is, by telling them off by name and sending them to certain death) in order to make gratuitous contributions to the happiness of other members; that the products of individual members of the community should not be taken from them without compensa-tion, when these have been produced on their own time with re-sources that either belong to them or were hitherto free for the taking; that people should not be incarcerated or executed for crimes they have not committed; that people should not be con-victed of crimes and punished on the basis of *ex post facto* legisla-tion. Subscription to such rules almost suffices by itself to qualify a person as morally enlightened. A literal application of utilitarian-ism might nevertheless conflict with them. Some of them are at the root of long-standing objections to utilitarianism.*

The conflict, or apparent conflict, between these rules and

* Sydney Smith, writing tongue in cheek to a lady who had published a discourse on education: "Education has many honest enemies; and many honestly doubt and demur, who do not speak out for fear of being assas-sinated by Benthamites, who might think it, upon the whole, more useful that such men should die than live." Nowell C. Smith, ed., *The Letters of Sydney Smith*, Vol. II (Oxford: The Clarendon Press, 1953), p. 632.

utilitarianism taken as a theory of valid moral judgments has been aggravated by Bentham's recommendation, far more insistent than any statement of Hume's, that the greatest happiness principle be steadily and systematically invoked to settle all moral questions—and by the association between utilitarianism and Bentham's felicific calculus. The felicific calculus, it will be recalled, presumes that the utility of an action (or policy) can be reduced to the "value of a lot of pleasure or pain." The value of the lot is to be measured by first taking each pleasure and pain that the action will produce and considering, for each person affected, its intensity, duration, certainty or uncertainty, propinquity or remoteness, fecundity, and purity, and then considering the number of persons to whom it extends. The plus measurements of the pleasures in the lot and the minus measurements of the pains are combined to reach an algebraic sum or "balance," "which, if on the side of *pleasure*, will give the general good *tendency* of the act, with respect to the total number or community of individuals concerned; if on the side of pain, the general *evil tendency*, with respect to the same community." [7] Thus in principle, every policy in any set of alternative policies can be ranked vis-à-vis all the rest according to the score that the calculus assigns to its consequences.

The calculus, seeking to make the notion of utility perfectly definite, gives concrete shape to the possible conflicts with enlightened peremptory rules. However much one may deplore the fact, it is quite possible that almost everybody in a given community would feel happier if a certain man's products were seized. In such a case, the calculus may give an overwhelming score for seizure and against heeding any peremptory rule raised in objection. The calculus takes no precautions to make sure that men's scruples affect their feelings or that their scruples prevail in any particular instance. (As we shall see in a moment, the strategy of disjointed incrementalism observes a number of such precautions, and this in itself favors substituting it for the calculus.)

To give them the benefit of a reasonable doubt, it is possible that the proponents of the calculus deserve to have imputed to them certain presuppositions about its use in providing a criterion for policy. For example, one might impute to them the presuppositions that no member of the group surveyed is to be eliminated as a means of increasing the magnitude of average or total happiness and that no member's condition is to be worsened as a means of doing this. The instruction to increase the average or total happiness may be compared with an instruction to a physical therapist to increase the fitness of a group of patients. If one wishes to insist on the point that the happiness of different people is liable (much more than their fitness) to be mutually dependent, one may consider the instruction, addressed after a coal mine disaster to some employee on the surface, to try calming the anxious waiting wives. No one would expect that a sane therapist needed to be told that he was not to shoot the weakest patients or make some of them instruments of exercise—say, punching bags—for the others. If he had time and facilities, he would be expected to do something to help every patient. It would be an equally absurd misinterpretation of instructions for the assistant superintendent of the mine to drop the more agitated wives down the mine shaft, or for him to ridicule the anxiety of one wife, making her hysterical as a means perhaps of shocking and shaming the others into silence. By analogy, it may seem only reasonable to impute generalized presuppositions of the same kind to proponents of the felicific calculus. If this is done, some of the most important objections arising from enlightened peremptory rules will be satisfied.[8]

There is more than analogy to go on, however. On any interpretation, Bentham's *phrase*, "the greatest happiness of the greatest number," leaves out of account the presuppositions mentioned, even if his overall doctrine does not. But the phrase does at least indicate that he did not contemplate sacrificing the happiness of most members of the community to the happiness of a few, no matter how superior the capacities of the few for happiness might be. His leading disciple, John Stuart Mill, held that the object of the greatest happiness principle was to produce happy lives; and he declared that morality itself, conforming to the greatest happiness principle, ought to consist of "the rules and precepts for human conduct, by the observance of which an existence . . . exempt as far as possible from pain, and as rich as possible in enjoyments . . . might be, to the greatest extent possible, secured to all mankind." [9] It is difficult to believe that this position is, in intention, indifferent to questions about invidious sacrifices of any person's life or happiness.

Nevertheless, the required presuppositions are not made explicit, and utilitarianism is commonly taken as ignoring them. It is supposed that, according to utilitarianism, the average or total happiness of the group is to be increased, regardless of how many or how few people are made happy, some perhaps at the expense of making others unhappy and regardless even of the continued presence or absence of certain members. In his elaboration of the felicific calculus, Edgeworth frankly declares that, if some members of the community have greater capacities for happiness than others, they should be specially favored, although he does not seem to contemplate sacrificing the very lives of the less capable.[10] That possibility and the possibility of eliminating people on other grounds equally shocking, may be said to figure in the common interpretation of utilitarianism, however, because common objections depend on them: For example, the objection that utilitarianism might sanction "punishing" anybody by any form of punishment, if it was calculated that the community as a whole would gain by it.

If the calculus is to be used this way—and the calculus itself, whatever people may have meant in proposing it, does not preclude obtaining and acting upon such results—the objections about invidious sacrifice apply with full force. Furthermore, Bentham's intention that the principle of utility should supply the need for an interpersonal moral standard attractive to every member of the community is frustrated. It is frustrated not merely because the people who would be called upon to make the sacrifices may not be self-sacrificing enough to do so willingly. People who would benefit from the sacrifices may be sufficiently altruistic to dislike accepting them.

4—Overcoming Peremptory Objections in Alliance with Strategy

Utilitarianism can avoid these difficulties and a number of others by abandoning the felicific calculus and allying itself, at least for the present, with the strategy of disjointed incrementalism. The strategy resorts to the census notion when it has occasion to press home the question of how different policies will affect a given group of people, and pressed this way, the question clearly presupposes that the membership of the group surveyed is not to be diminished to make the comparison more favorable for any policy. How could it make the comparison more favorable? It would not be the same comparison: not different fates for the same group, but different groups. Furthermore, if a policy is shown by a census to involve diminishing the membership of the group, this is, even on a meliorative basis, a count against the policy. The dead or banished are clearly going to be among those deprived of medical care or opportunities for education or recreation within the community.[11]

Some invidious shifts of benefits and injuries would be detected and ruled out by the straightforward application of the census notion: when, for example, the condition of a few is improved, but the condition of so many others is worsened that a comparative census discovers that more people would be badly off, and fewer well off, under a proposed policy than under the present one. Other questionable sacrifices will be confronted by the reluctance, which appears in the ordinary use of the census notion, to draw favorable conclusions from results associated with mixed changes (more people becoming well off, but more becoming badly off, too) or with changes of persons (some persons now well off becoming badly off).[12] The census notion already incorporates in practice some provisions for fair and equal treatment that the felicific calculus, as it is usually interpreted, lacks. What is more, in default of any practical calculus, the census notion is a practical way of achieving equality and justice in these respects.

It does not go all the way in assuring that the whole list of enlightened peremptory rules given earlier—or an extended list of equally enlightened rules—will be heeded, but neither does it obstruct the fulfillment of those rules. By itself, a comparative census on the subject, say, of nutrition, might favor a policy of appropriating products created privately by members of the community, or of imprisoning people who were not guilty of any crime, or at any rate, of doing anything that was reckoned a crime at the time they did it (they might be less happy in prison, but just as well fed). But there is no need to take this census, or any other on a single theme, by itself—there are other censuses to take, on other meliorative themes. There are, furthermore, opportunities at any stage to make discoveries or to bring home points that have peremptory connections, and nothing that we have said bars people using the strategy from heeding such points. We have not supposed that they take an intransigent stand on any meliorative theme or rule or on the results of taking or approximating a census on one topic alone.

Peremptory rules defining perspective. The general position of peremptory rules vis-à-vis utilitarianism combined with the strategy is one that we have already discussed in connection with the strategy alone: Such rules may be called on to help define the *perspective* in which policy problems are approached and within which the strategy—or utilitarianism-with-the-strategy—operates. (The moral precautions that we have associated with the census notion itself, which have peremptory characteristics, may also be assigned a place here.) Policies that run counter to peremptory prohibitions will be ruled out of discussion, regardless of any meliorative case that may be built up for them by the operation of the strategy. Policies that, alone of the suggested alternatives, are favored by a peremptory prescription (like that of keeping promises) will be adopted without further ado. People who use the strategy can have no complaints about this procedure unless they happen to reject the peremptory themes that the rest of the community finds decisive. They themselves, we may presume, are attached to peremptory themes of their own. This attachment is a normal characteristic of human beings. Perhaps it is also an indispensable device for limiting and focusing comparisons as the strategy requires, although we have supposed that other factors have a part in determining perspectives—habit and tradition, for example, and the scope of received social science, all of which limit investigations and comparisons for other than moral reasons.

We may add that the strategy helps to save utilitarianism from many conflicts with peremptory rules by insisting on a remedial orientation. Part of the sting in the rules cited lies in the supposition that utilitarianism, operating without any peremptory limits to perspective, would violate these rules in order to achieve purely gratuitous benefits—to increase, for example, the happiness of people who were already happy.* The prospect of starving some members of the community or sending them into battle merely to make some other members more comfortable is, most people would think, morally horrifying. The situation, however, changes appreciably if we suppose that the sacrifices are forced —if some people, as yet unselected, are going to have to make them anyway. If it is a question of sacrificing the lives of some members in order to preserve the lives of a greater number (or of the women and the children in their care) or a question of sacrificing them to preserve the identity and the free institutions of the community—then the peremptory rule against wantonly sacrificing human lives does not apply. These are just the cases in which exceptions to formulated rules appear, and the conclusions reached by the strategy, about which policies make the best of a bad business, may fall in with the exceptions.

When it is allied with the strategy of disjointed incrementalism, utilitarianism thus anticipates some peremptory moral judgments that have in the past been made objections to it. It may more or less readily accommodate others, if they are conceded to figure in defining the perspectives within which utilitarian values are to be heeded and the strategy applied. This accommodation within perspectives does not, however, signify that the relation of utilitarianism-with-the-strategy to peremptory judgments is a purely passive one—that utilitarianism and the strategy are, as

---

* Consider the old chestnut about torturing an innocent child to make the rest of mankind happy forever. It does not suffice (though it is important) to say that the choice has not arisen.

it were, allowed on the scene only after wholly autonomous arrangements have been made by peremptory judgments. On the contrary, the pressure of circumstances—the normal circumstances in societies like ours for evaluating and deciding upon social policies—constantly converts peremptory rules into meliorative and distributive considerations. Evaluative themes that are introduced under peremptory auspices constantly call for treatment by techniques like those of the strategy and thus begin to resemble utilitarian values, if they do not actually merge with them.

Consider, for example, peremptory rules about justice. Some fundamental aspects of the notion of justice may be expressed, following John Rawls, as a combination of two principles:

"First, each person participating in a [social] practice, or affected by it, has an equal right to the most extensive liberty compatible with a like liberty for all; and second, inequalities are arbitrary unless it is reasonable to expect that they will work out for everyone's advantage, and provided the positions and offices to which they attach, or from which they may be gained, are open to all." [13]

Peremptory demands may be made for the observance of these principles, but, in the first place, observing them is not likely to be an "all or nothing" matter. So long as the principles of justice are only approximately satisfied, there will be meliorative and distributive questions about whether they are fulfilled more or less. One may very well adhere to peremptory principles of justice and to the associated requirement of mutual recognition and consideration, yet recognize that the only practical way of bringing fulfillment about is step by step. At each step, there will be census-like questions to attend to, about what proportion of the population will be accorded the liberty and equality required by the principles under one policy rather than another. Very likely, there will be mixed effects on different liberties and on different aspects of equality in different respects to consider, which would be suitably dealt with by tentative *ad hoc* priorities. The use that there might be for the strategy during these successive approximations toward fulfilling the principles of justice is obvious.

It may be remarked, in the second place, that as soon as one turns from the formal side of the conception of justice to its concrete applications, meliorative and distributive considerations mass for attention. By "inequalities," for example, Rawls intends us to understand such things as "differences in the benefits and burdens attached to [offices and positions] either directly or indirectly, such as prestige and wealth, or liability to taxation and compulsory services." [14] The distribution of such differences among a group of people is, of course, a subject that requires census-like investigation. Balancing differences in one respect against differences in another and determining which combination most nearly works out to everyone's advantage are subjects that invite the use of the strategy.

Far from conflicting with the concept of justice, the strategy already incorporates some of the features required by Rawls's principles. The census notion calls for counting everyone's fate equally, and the inconclusiveness of the census notion in cases of mixed changes and changes of persons arises from perception of the injustice that these might involve. It is, among other things, to satisfy the same scruples that alternatives are redesigned to include compensation. The strategy does not guarantee that everyone's interests will be consulted. By affording many views an opportunity to be expressed and negotiated, however, it does go some way toward seeing that no one is victimized. It can be made to go all the way, by accepting the appropriate restrictions in perspective.

There is a deeper sense in which the strategy accords with the conception of justice mentioned. Like the utilitarian family of theories, the strategy seeks to embody an attractive interpersonal orientation for evaluative procedures. For Hume, the consideration of utility represents a solution to a certain problem—namely, to find what standard for moral judgments gives consistent, disinterested results and still is moving. For Bentham, the principle of utility supplies the need for a standard that can be consistently recommended to all who have an interest in any policy-question by a person "addressing himself to the community." It is not unreasonable to interpret both writers as making the claim that utility is a consideration that people accept because it agrees with their conception of what a moral criterion for policy should be, while conceding that certain leading features of this conception are defined by something like the two principles of justice mentioned above. This conception, in other words, may be regarded as implicit in the notion of "disinterestedness" and in the search for an attractive *inter*personal standard.[15]

Utilitarianism, utilitarianism with the strategy better than utilitarianism with the calculus, thus supplies the demand constituted by the principles of justice. It may supply moral demands based on other peremptory rules as well. Traditionally, however, the philosophical ambitions of utilitarians have not stopped there. Besides anticipating some peremptory rules and accommodating others within their own presuppositions, utilitarian authors have endeavored to show that important peremptory rules or judgments can be derived from utilitarian principles in which they are not embodied or presupposed, if one takes these principles in conjunction with observed facts about utility. The more success achieved on these lines, of course—the more peremptory rules that can be derived in this way, instead of having to be accepted from exogenous origins—the more powerful and interesting utilitarian doctrine becomes. A considerable amount of success of this kind has been achieved.

Hume, for example, employing a conception of justice rather narrowly associated with assignments of property, recognizes that justice may require in particular instances that property be taken from poor men and given to rich ones; that "a man of merit, of a beneficent disposition" may be required to restore "a great fortune to a miser or a seditious bigot"; that "the labor of the industrious" may have to be bestowed on "the dissolute." [16] Yet the rule that justice must be observed may be defended on utilitarian grounds. Although in individual cases, there may be greater utility in retaining another's property than in restoring it or in breaking a promise rather than keeping it, the community is held to benefit in the long run from maintaining the rule in all these cases, refusing to let each of them be settled independently on their meliorative and distributive merits.

It is not merely the harm that would be done if these departures were publicly known that argues against them. It is an important feature of this and other peremptory rules that they *preclude* meliorative variations in individual cases; otherwise the rules would lose that stability on which members of the community rely and which is one of their chief advantages. More exactly, one should perhaps say that at least those meliorative variations must be precluded that are not passed on and accepted by impartial judges. People must not make meliorative variations that are not vindicated by public procedures for modifying the rules, and one presumes that in the interest of stability many or most such variations, even if otherwise well-founded, cannot be publicly vindicated.

This sort of argument opens up a wide field to the program of deriving peremptory rules—or, rather, to cases for adopting such rules as matters of social policy—on utilitarian grounds.[17] How much of the field can the program exploit successfully? We shall not attempt to say, pending the collection of further evidence, but we may ask, How good is the evidence collected so far? Hume assumes too easily that inflexible observance of a rule of justice will in the long run confer greater benefits than the community would gain from observing it part of the time and departing from it on occasion. In general, how can it be shown that any peremptory rule is more beneficial than some quite different rule, and what is even harder to show, more useful than incrementally different alternatives (some of which might allow for vexed cases as exceptions)? Here the need for intelligible and practical procedures for collecting and marshalling evidence becomes inescapable. Here, to perform such services the felicific calculus is most urgently called for, but the felicific calculus is not ready to perform them. The strategy of disjointed incrementalism is, in ways both morally convincing and philosophically illuminating.

CHAPTER 10

THE STRATEGY AS A PRACTICAL SUBSTITUTE FOR THE CALCULUS

In the last chapter, the combination of utilitarianism with the strategy of disjointed incrementalism showed itself capable of dealing with objections that do not involve the question of intelligible procedures. They were objections that could be launched against utilitarianism even if the felicific calculus were perfectly practical. The advantage of introducing the strategy was not that it substituted intelligible procedures for unintelligible ones, but that it accommodated certain moral objections which the calculus did not.

The program of reconciling utilitarianism with enlightened peremptory judgments cannot rest there. It is now time to call into question the intelligibility of the felicific calculus. Bentham's suggestion, realized or not, has never gone out of fashion. Ethical theorists and economists—the two classes of people who have worried most about the problem—have always conceived that the problem of making utilitarianism perfectly definite and intelligible was the problem of carrying out Bentham's suggestion of a calculus. Attempts to carry it out continue in our own day. In matters of controversy, utilitarian considerations seldom fall wholly on the side of one policy and against every other with which it is compared. If one is to obtain definite results for utilitarian considerations in such controversies—if he is to show, for example, that observations of utility vindicate some peremptory rules but not others that at first sight seem as useful—then either the felicific calculus must be made practical or some other set of procedures must be found. We suggest the strategy of disjointed incrementalism.

1—The Questionable Feasibility of the Calculus

Some of the traditional objections to the calculus notion touch upon its feasibility. The most immediate and most familiar are, first, that Bentham's calculus can hardly be a calculus of happiness, for neither the happiness of a person nor the happiness of a society can be defined as a sum of pleasures and pains; and, second, that there is no way of obtaining sums of pleasures and pains anyhow or at least no way of measuring them to produce the interpersonal sums that Bentham requires.

These objections are a little unimaginative and perhaps not quite to the point.[1] Bentham's sketch of the felicific calculus is so primitive that it seems most sensible to regard it as intended to be something less than an adequate set of specifications for the procedure whose necessity Bentham perceives. (He does not even bother to explain whether the algebraic sum of pleasures and pains for the community is to be conceived as a simple additive property—like the weight of a collection of boxes—or as merely an arithmetical step toward specifying an average—like the total temperature of a group of fever patients. We saw in the last chapter how significant the difference between these two views might be morally.) On the one hand, the sketch might be considered as simply an expository device for enumerating the sorts of considerations customarily involved in weighing the advantages and disadvantages of policies. On the other hand, we might conceive of it as a proposal that pleasures and pains be identified and measured in such a way that happiness *can* be equated, without distortion with sums of pleasures and pains.

If the latter interpretation is adopted—the one offering a proposal that a certain scheme of measurement be invented— then if the proposal could be carried out, it would dispose at once of both the objections mentioned: that happiness is not a sum of pleasures and pains and that there is no way of calculating interpersonal sums of pleasures and pains. It would dispose of a third objection besides—namely, that not all pleasures are on the same footing with regard to happiness, some of them counting for more toward our being able to say that a man was happy than others—the pleasures of friendship, for example, more than the pleasures of push-pin.[2] For suppose "counting for more" means, because of the meaning of "happiness," logically counting for more: This would be allowed for in the weights given to various pleasures in the calculus. For example, the maximum value assigned the pleasure of push-pin, continued for a certain time, might be stipulated as smaller than the maximum value (or, possibly, smaller even than the minimum value) assigned the pleasure of friendship, enjoyed for the same time. Suppose, on the other hand, "counting for more" means counting for more, as a matter of fact, in the case of people who have enjoyed them as well as other pleasures. Then if this is a true impression of what in fact makes people most happy, the calculus, assuming that it is properly set up, will confirm it. Calculations from observation will show that people who enjoy the higher pleasures have, other things being equal, a higher happiness score than people who do not.

But is it possible to invent such a scheme of measurement? We think that it would be rash to say that it is not, even for so elusive a concept as happiness. There have been continuing ef- forts, some of them very sophisticated in conception, to work out an interpersonal calculus for happiness or for related concepts like satisfaction or "strength of preference."[3] Possible or not, however, an entirely convincing design for the felicific calculus has not yet emerged from these efforts.

In the absence of a calculus, how are policies to be evaluated? The comprehensive ambitions and the practical uselessness of Bentham's calculus are typical of the synoptic approach to evaluating policies. Indeed, the calculus may be regarded as a classical illustration both of a welfare function and a rational-deductive system (since it can be interpreted either way). We assert that the strategy of disjointed incrementalism is a means of doing what the calculus as yet gives us no means of doing; it is an effective technique, though not invariably a successful one, for arriving at determinate meliorative evaluations of policies. It is a technique, moreover, that is in use, and, taken together with the census notion, it explains how men have been able to make sensible applications of meliorative values to questions of policy these many years, since time immemorial in fact, while we have been waiting for a calculus like Bentham's.

The strategy of disjointed incrementalism escapes these objections to the calculus, and it escapes them, not by resting its case on a mere proposal, as Bentham may be said to have done, but on a technique whose intelligibility can be demonstrated from familiar successful practice. The sort of utilitarianism that recognition of the strategy rehabilitates is a utilitarianism of themes and procedures that can be discovered among the existing features of moral discourse and needs only to be described to make sense.

The strategy provides, in the census notion, distributive tests that are not compromised, though they deal with meliorative values, by the difficulties of measuring or summing up pleasures and pains. Although, as we have seen, these tests do not always give determinate answers favoring one policy over another, the range within which they can be expected to supply determinate answers can be greatly extended by using the concepts of compensation and redesigning.

The strategy does involve interpersonal comparisons. However, while it could be adapted to the use of measurements for pleasures and pains and sums of these to determine happiness and unhappiness—so that it does not require rejecting a calculus of the sort Bentham proposed out of hand—it does not, given its present arrangements, require measurements of "subjective utility." It does not require measurements of the intensity with which one person prefers one given policy to another as against the intensity with which another person prefers it, of one person's satisfaction with a certain policy as against another person's dissatisfaction.[4] (It does not even require any system, beyond ordering, for measuring such things *intra*personally.) On the contrary, the censuses on which it relies presuppose simply that ordinary intelligent persons can *classify* the people whom they observe. They do not have to say of anyone, "His satisfactions are twice as intense as this other man's dissatisfactions"; they need only say, "He is satisfied; this other man is dissatisfied."

The strategy allows for a variety of personal tastes and envisages the mutual accommodation of persons and groups with different tastes through free discussion. The list of meliorative themes is not fixed either as to the number of possible items or as to the priority with which the items are to be treated. By allowing for a range of possible tests—censuses on different topics—the strategy meets in part the objection about different pleasures having higher or lower places in happiness. Part of the point of this objection is to call attention to the multiplicity of meliorative themes and to the necessity of accommodating them consistently. As we saw in the previous chapter, the strategy responds to this need in two ways: by redesigning policies so that, as far as possible, they satisfy multiple demands, and by supersession. Supersession in effect establishes an order of priority among different values. Under the strategy, however, the order of priority adopted in a given dispute is determined, if it has to be determined at all, *ad hoc* (and probably not in ways that are easily isolated from the ways in which the dispute as a whole converges on a solution). Often the question of priority can be entirely evaded by redesigning. Within the limits of their opportunities, people using the strategy will seek, for political reasons, to redesign policy alternatives so that *all* the values that have been invoked in discussion favor the policies that are finally advocated. It is perfectly possible in practice to find the various compensating features needed, regardless of the difficulties of formulating a general solution to the problem of combining values.

The question whether all meliorative values can be reduced to one—for example, pleasure—is thus left open. Certainly the strategy does not pretend to prescribe that the order or priority be determined by such a reduction. The strategy thus escapes the most penetrating part of the objection about higher and lower pleasures, which is that such a distinction must be drawn, since some pleasures are clearly more valuable than others, but that it must be drawn on some other basis than Bentham's principle of utility, which cannot be the ultimate standard because it treats all pleasures equally.[5]

2—The Problem of Consequences

Utilitarianism would by no means have come to the end of its troubles if the felicific calculus were rescued from the difficulties of measuring pleasure and pain and of defining happiness on the basis of such measurements. Difficulties quite as formidable would remain. Utilitarianism requires that persons evaluating policies consider the consequences of those policies as they affect happiness. But how can that be done? May not the policies each have infinitely many consequences? Then not all of them could be considered, but on what principle shall those be selected that are to be considered?

It is true that there are not literally an infinite number of consequences of any action. One cannot go on counting consequences to infinity because consequences cannot be counted at all. There is no principle of identity to tell us when we are dealing with two consequences or with one consequence described in two different ways; or whether we should count only general consequences and not partial aspects of them. (Consider, for example, the statements, "It was a consequence of the mill's closing that a number of men lost their jobs;" "It was a consequence of the mill's closing that unemployment figures in the town surpassed the worst figures of the Thirties;" "It was a consequence of the mill's closing that John Weaver lost his job." Have we two consequences here, or one, or three?)

Dismissing literal infinity, however, does not help very much, for it seems that we are confronted with something very like it anyway, in respect to time, in the first place, and, more generally, in respect to multiple formulation. One event is a consequence of another; it, in turn, has later consequences of its own; and so on ad infinitum. Yet there is no criterion in ordinary language for judging events not to be consequences because they are too remote in time. If the chain reaches them, it is possible to hold that they are consequences of the earliest event in the chain.[6]

In general, the *formulas* attributing consequences to a given action seem liable to indefinite multiplication, and there is considerable incentive for multiplication, as we would expect, in the multiplicity of values that we have so much stressed in discussing the strategy of disjointed incrementalism. Even if we disregard the possibilities of variation opened up by such statements as "It was a consequence of the mill's closing that the number of unemployed in the town was greater than the number of people who, according to the *World Almanac*, have attempted to climb Mt. Everest," there are indefinitely many possible statements that do touch our sense of relevance. Consider the consequences of the mill's closing and, in turn, of unemployment for home life, for the school system, for the town budget, and the wider and wider ramifications of these. Ordinary language does not seem to supply a rule entitling a person who is going to act on the basis of consequences to disregard formulas multiplied in any direction: It may be just this item or just that general summary that brings out a decisive moral consideration. One might always cut off the account just at the point in time or in breadth of investigation at which overwhelmingly injurious consequences began emerging.

The embarrassment of being unable to obtain complete and accurate accounts of consequences afflicts the synoptic approach to evaluation with particular intensity. The solutions deduced from a rational-deductive system or calculated for a social welfare function will be untrustworthy, by the very assumptions of those methods, if they are not comprehensive solutions, as will the solutions that might be sought for with a Benthamite calculus. How can they be comprehensive? On the other hand, it is no good (given the synoptic approach) suggesting that one can make do with reasonably reliable approximations. No approximations can be relied on to take into account every crucial factor; the solution may fail to be comprehensive not only on minor points but on the very points that lead to disaster. For the synoptic approach to work, there must at least be a criterion for judging an account of consequences sufficient even though incomplete. There is no such criterion, however, and stipulating one would, at the very least, have the effect of assuming that moral concepts (and thus the specifiable kinds of consequences that have to be looked for) are fixed in number and content. In general, such a stipulation would simply have the effect of giving arbitrary sanction to an arbitrary limitation, but this is bankruptcy for the synoptic approach, which seeks to be not arbitrary but complete.

One way of saving the synoptic approach from the embarrassment of consequences would be to ignore themes of value that require consequences to be considered. That would be preposterous, for it would mean omitting to consider health, happiness, welfare, cultural progress—even the future performance of duties and the future respect for rights. Another way would be to allow that consequences are to be considered but to assume, first, that all the consequences whose consideration may be demanded can be inferred from the theories of social science that happen to be on hand; second, that the time at which the world or at least human history will come to an end is known; and third, that there is (at least in the mind of anyone adopting the synoptic approach to evaluation) a complete system of values that will not change, so that some consequences that seem tolerable now will not turn out to be intolerable in the future. These assumptions are equally fantastic.

Clearly, there are two things that have to be done in answer to the objection about consequences. First, it must be shown that utilitarianism can be associated with reasonably specific ways of selecting the consequences that are to be considered in evaluating actions and policies. Second, it must be shown that utilitarianism deals as prudently as possible with the inevitable fact that some important consequences may be overlooked (partly because not all the consequences will have been formulated). The felicific calculus is of no help to utilitarianism in either connection. The strategy of disjointed incrementalism provides as much help as, in the nature of things, can be hoped for.

Disjointed incrementalism copes at its best as effectively as can reasonably be demanded, with the various parts of the problem of consequences. It does not do so by relying on intuitions.[7] Instead, it encourages an exchange of complaints and expectations among many different participants, limitation of debate to topics on which the community is likely to possess a concentration of information, and observance of the limits within which existing social institutions are prepared to alleviate results unfortunate but unforeseen.

Philosophical demands for the analysis of a general claim about consequences like the statement, "The consequences of P will be better than the consequences of Q," may be dismissed when they reach the point of demanding a complete list of the statements of fact entailed by the claim. One does not have to provide such a list in order to vindicate the meaningfulness of the claim. Ordinary statements of fact cannot themselves pass such a test, among other reasons because we cannot say in advance of novel circumstances just how we are going to extend the only partially definite conventions for using the expressions of our language. Yet such statements are commonly made and commonly understood, proved, contested, and disproved without leaving any genuine doubts about their truth or falsity. Similarly, even though general claims about consequences are one degree less definite than ordinary statements of fact, because their meaning varies with the values invoked and incorporated, they have a perfectly significant use. The claim that P will have better consequences than Q is understood to be logically corrigible, although its truth is in fact often quite certain.

How is it settled what values shall be invoked? We have been saying that it is settled very largely *ad hoc*, that is to say, the operations and counter-operations of various parties in the actual context of discussion will determine which of the values recognized by society will be brought into play. This claim, although it invites further investigation, is not a mere evasion of the issue. It is a misconception of the problem to suppose that it is practical or possible or desirable to schedule in advance, once and for all, the order of values that shall be considered in evaluating consequences.

It is equally a misconception to suppose that when someone ignores various facts about prospective policies, he is always guilty of suppressing evidence, like someone who refuses to look at items of information that are offered him as liable to upset his conclusions. A judge and jury, who must decide the fate of a prisoner yet refuse to look at certain items of evidence which are plausibly claimed to fall within the bounds of receivable evidence as to his part in the crime, create a scandal. The general situation of people evaluating alternative policies, including people practicing the strategy, is quite different. There, as our previous discussion indicates, information can be disregarded without creating a scandal about suppression. What is relevant, in that general situation, is not known, then disregarded. What is relevant to the evaluator's problem is determined by his conception of the problem, and, in deciding upon that conception, the evaluator decides to disregard certain types of information. We may note that in deciding to attack the problem in a certain incremental perspective, an analyst using the strategy is making a claim about relevance that he expects to have assessed against other claims linked with other conceptions of the problem. Use of the strategy does not imply that the analyst ignores information, including information about consequences, that is known to be relevant to accomplishing his chosen task—only that he defines his task so as to leave out some information that will have to be dealt with in the course of other tasks.

Efficient use of information. The predictions on which the strategy relies for tracing consequences are thus *ceteris paribus* predictions of the ordinary kind, subject to ordinary kinds of failure. By favoring limited, incremental departures in policy, the strategy does, however, improve the chances that the predictions will be reliable. The changes contemplated under the strategy are not only relatively less drastic; they also take place within a range of moves for which the community as a whole possesses a concentration of information. Those using the strategy endeavor to preserve the known benefits of present policies while eliminating the known disadvantages. Because the discussion is focused in this way, the advantages and disadvantages of all the alternatives brought up can be considered more systematically, so far as it is worthwhile to investigate any of them. The discussion will thus have something like a defined agenda. Whatever information is mobilized will run less risk of being lost from sight because of wild fluctuations in the terms of discussion, a point that no one will undervalue who has ever sat in a committee.

Partisanship and fragmentation. The advantage of this kind of focusing is doubled in the social dimension. If there is a problem of assembling information even for an individual investigator, the problem is considerably larger when one turns to coordinating the information communicated by a number of disputing parties. The strategy raises the need for co-ordination to special prominence, because it depends on fragmentation and division of labor in evaluation. To discover how the community will be affected by the alternative policies proposed, it holds, in effect, multiple hearings beforehand. It arranges for each group alert enough to make its interest felt to evaluate the advantages and disadvantages of the various policies from its own point of view. Instead of discouraging partisanship, for fear that it will distort the information presented, it welcomes it, because partisanship for one's own group's interest is a dependable motivation for investigating consequences with some zeal. It is surely also better to have prospective benefits and injuries (especially injuries) exaggerated than never to hear of them at all (an important consideration in evaluating the strategy and one that accords with its remedial orientation).

It is, of course, one of the tasks of mutual discussion to compare and correct these partisan pictures, though it will not usually be felt necessary to correct them beyond the point at which a reasonably harmonious decision on policy becomes possible. Biased though they may be, however, they provide the community with information about those hazards and benefits of policy which the different groups belonging to the community most fear and most desire (allowing that there are some fears and desires that it would be impolitic for a group to disclose). The expectations with which different groups greet policy proposals are not, of course, always well founded. Nor do every group's expectations get a hearing. Some groups are not well enough organized or well enough led to make themselves heard—a familiar and important defect of the interest-group process. However, at least those fears and desires about consequences that are expressed must be confronted if the community is to be satisfied that the consequences of the various policies proposed have been sufficiently considered.

Institutional insurance against oversights. Part of the problem about consequences is to be sure they are discussed extensively but not aimlessly. The strategy makes considerable headway against this part of the problem, as we have just shown. But how does the strategy affect the more disturbing, central part of the problem, that accounts of consequences are bound to be incomplete? The people who have been disturbed by the problem of consequences have, after all, not meant to deny that some accounts of consequences are more extensive and relevant than others. What has troubled them is the thought that even the best of such accounts is incomplete and may leave out very damaging consequences. They might say that the strategy of disjointed incrementalism does not, any more than other practical techniques for evaluating consequences, free policy-makers and their advisers from being liable in the future to the reproach, "You did not consider all the consequences," uttered in painful circumstances.

We must acknowledge that the strategy does not remove this liability. It is beyond human power to remove it. Does the strategy then do nothing to mitigate fears about innumerable undetected future consequences? No one can tell what reefs and breakers lie ahead or where the icebergs are that may be drifting in the fog. The voyage into future seas must continue, but how can anyone pretend to set a safe course?

Much of ethical theory concentrates attention on the responsibility of single moral agents in a way that invites intense fears about overlooked consequences. The institutional environment in which any given agent acts is left unspecified; at most, it figures among the passive data of his problems. He is considered as acting upon his environment. Possibly it responds to his actions, but it does not participate in making decisions. He is all alone so far as his decisions are concerned. There is no way in which he can parcel out parts of his problem-solving task to the agents and institutions surrounding him. Moreover, his task is not only lonely— it is fateful in the highest degree. Each agent acts irrevocably, once for all. Each in acting assumes responsibility for the whole of the future so far as it will be affected by his present action.

If any abatement in the agent's responsibility is allowed (as it would be allowed by Moore but not by certain existentialist philosophers), it is only on the grounds that his knowledge of the future is limited—not because his responsibility can in any way be shared or postponed. Every agent, however, has a duty to inform himself about consequences, and if what he ought to do is nothing less than act in the way calculated to have the best possible consequences, can he be satisfied to act on incomplete knowledge? It seems, if the agent's situation is treated in these terms, that he must try to cover all the possibilities beforehand.

The fears generated by this view can be avoided by recognizing it for what it is—a fantasy induced by excessive abstraction. Agents in the real world do not assume responsibility for the whole of the future. It would not be ethical perfection for them to assume such responsibility—it would be madness. Nor do agents in the real world usually act irrevocably. Why should they be supposed to forget, in ordinary moral situations, that they will have future chances of intervening, which they may watch for and use? Even if each agent were sailing entirely by himself, he could place some reliance on his capacity to steer away from dangers when he came upon them. The fact that he could not prove any course was a safe one does not stand in the way of his sailing prudently and changing course when necessary.

It is of crucial importance, however, to recognize that he is not sailing by himself. He does not have to do all the work of navigation. He is not even the only man at the tiller. The most important fact about responsibility in the real world is that it is defined and limited by a man's social role. There are institutions surrounding him that may be called upon to assist him in dealing with unexpected and untoward consequences. The over-all task of anticipating and dealing with consequences is parcelled out among different men and different institutions. If one considers the implications of these forms of assistance being available, the moral problem about unforeseen consequences takes on an entirely different aspect. There may be no way of foreseeing all the consequences of an action or policy. There are ways of taking precautions even when they are unforeseen. What is required in the real world, instead of vain endeavors to identify and evaluate all the consequences of given actions or policies, is that precautions be taken to ensure that when unforeseen consequences do appear, they will be manageable ones. (Needless to say, this does not mean that extensive and varied efforts to foresee consequences should not be made. To do so forms part of the precautions, though not the whole of them.)

This requirement is one that people have a practical chance of meeting. The strategy of disjointed incrementalism maximizes the chance, and thus it mitigates fears about undetected consequences. As we have said, it encourages extensive and varied discussion yet provides means of giving the discussion focus. The precautionary advantages of the strategy go beyond this, however; they cover, substantially if not perfectly, the gaps that discussion leaves untreated and unexplored. The presence and importance of the precautionary advantages of the strategy in this connection are suggested by the feature of remedial orientation. All the features of the strategy, in fact, have precautionary aspects. They combine to make maximum use of the opportunity of relying on existing social and political institutions for insurance against unforeseen disaster.

Among these institutions are the central features of popular government—periodic elections and regular sessions of the legislature, both of which guarantee periodic opportunities for reviewing policies, although they cannot guarantee that the opportunities will be used or wisely used by the people or by their representatives. Again, however, groups alert to their own interest will make themselves heard. Other institutions provide ways of suspending the operation of policies until they can be submitted for legislative review and ways, either automatic or discretionary, of relieving immediate suffering, pending the reaction of other agencies. There are courts to which injured persons can resort for redress of grievances. There are various welfare schemes for making sure that people are extricated from floods, resettled, given unemployment benefits, supplied with food and medical care. There are discretionary funds and emergency powers in the hands of executive officers with various responsibilities, and there are ways of creating temporary new agencies, public or private, to deal with crises. When a policy goes wrong, there is usually a way of remedying its most urgent disadvantages immediately. The existence of such remedies is one of the tests of an adequate political organization—indeed, of an adequate social organization of any kind.

Further light can now be cast on the significance of insisting on limited, incremental departures. Limited departures are in general better insured. They are safer because they leave so much more room, in the way of other factors that can be adjusted, for remedying unforeseen consequences. In particular, the inclination of the strategy—the virtue of incrementalism—is to shun any policies whose scope is such that if they miscarry, the evils will exceed the remedial powers of existing institutions. This inclination does not rule out innovations, even far-reaching innovations, but it does require that insurance be in force for each step.

So far as the problem of consequences stands in the way of accepting utilitarianism or, in general, of applying meliorative values of any kind to policy choices, the strategy shows how it can be cleared away. We have, it turns out, incorporated in the description of the strategy an account of the ordinary precautions that suffice to make public attention to consequences both prudent and intelligible. There is a discrepancy, perhaps, in logical refinement between these precautions and the difficulties that come to light in the philosophical elaboration of the problem of consequences, but this discrepancy does not show that the precautions are misconceived. It tends to show, rather, that the philosophical elaborations are rendered irrelevant by intelligent evasions in practice.

3—Shift of Reference Groups

There is another difficulty about finding an intelligible procedure for assessing meliorative and distributive considerations, which is partly real and partly factitious in the same ways as the problem of consequences. Again it illustrates how a synoptic approach to evaluation leads to disregarding the institutions and practices that form the circumstances of evaluation—the very circumstances on which the strategy of disjointed incrementalism relies.

The problem in question is one of identifying suitable reference groups, the consequences for which are to determine the rankings of policies. The problem arises, to be sure, only after the reference group traditionally prescribed by utilitarian authors —a group that must always include everyone who is affected by the actions or policies being compared—is found unsuitable. But unsuitable it seems to be, because steady resort to it leads to morally counter-intuitive results.

Employing the principle of utility either as the fundamental rule of a rational-deductive system or as the generating concept of a social welfare function, let us consider applying it to the question of whether or not Yale University should have a department of astronomy. If we asked whether or not the American people as a whole would be happier if Yale had a department of astronomy, it is logically possible—even plausible, in spite of the excitement about space flights—that the answer would be no. It is quite possible that most Americans would be happier if the resources used by Yale's department of astronomy were diverted to television research or used for instruction in arts and crafts, which would give great numbers of people a chance for genuine creative expression. The attempt to save the principle of utility at this point exposes the inadequacy of official utilitarian procedures. For, given the principle of utility and with it a certain meliorative theme or combination of themes, it seems that at least one of the moves required in its defense is to say that it is not the business of the whole American people what Yale does about astronomy. The next move would be to claim that, if a more suitable reference group is chosen—consisting of the faculty, students, and alumni of the university—astronomy would triumph by the principle of utility. (We may say that the "reference group" assumed by someone who sets out to evaluate a policy with a certain meliorative and distributive theme in mind consists of all those people the effects on whom he considers must be investigated as liable to favor or disfavor the policy.)

Some distinction must surely be made between suitable and unsuitable reference groups if the principle of utility is to be saved. If the principle is not to lead again and again to offensive results, gratuitously interfering with the plans of private groups, it is essential that the reference groups be suitably shifted as policy questions change. What principle is to govern the shifts? The variety of interest groups—which concretely manifests the multiplicity of values present in societies such as ours—suggests that, for any given question of policy, arguable claims can be found for many different reference groups. The possibility looms up that every policy question will then be indeterminate because different reference groups, each with an invincible claim to suitability, give contrary results on being investigated by census-like procedures. If we take Bentham's formula, "all those whose interest is in the question," [8] as implying that the suitable reference group would always be the most inclusive, this will guide us right back to results of the kind originally objected to.

Determination of suitable groups under the strategy. The rational-deductive model has brought us once again to an impasse. It impels us to seek a general principle (which in this case would be associated with the principle of utility) that will justify every choice of reference group, beginning from scratch. Is such a principle really necessary? Certainly it is not necessary to forestall capricious and indeterminate treatment of every choice, for this is not the sole alternative to having a principle in which no reference groups are taken as fixed. Again, there is a practical way out of the dilemma—and again the way out relies on institutional circumstances to minimize the number of choices that must actually be made. The way out consists in taking reference groups as given, the legacy of history, until challenged; and in refusing to put them all up for reconsideration simultaneously.

People using the strategy of disjointed incrementalism manage to fix on reference groups and to shift them according to circumstances. They conserve points of departure without necessarily being conservative in the points departed to. Their working procedure may be described by the following two-part rule: First, some injury or liability to injury must be shown for the reference group in which any shift is to be made; second, the burden of proof lies upon those who advocate a shift from the reference groups traditionally used. (We may define "injury" broadly enough to include missed opportunities.)

This rule is enforced in practice by the operation of the various features of the strategy. It conforms to the serial and incremental features of the strategy that, in the absence of challenges, the reference groups should be the ones used in the past. The remedial orientation of the strategy determines the sort of challenge that is recognized. Finally, whether or not the burden of proof has been sustained by the challengers depends, not on their having evidence that meets any advance criterion of sufficiency, but on their succeeding in convincing other participants in the dispute that the evidence of possible injury is serious enough to require a shift in reference groups.

Social pluralism and the use of information. By refusing to use any more inclusive group as a steady reference, the strategy operates to preserve the autonomy of multiple-interest groups smaller than the general population. The libertarian values usually claimed for social pluralism are thus brought into play. Quite apart from these values, social pluralism and the fragmentation of decision-making that it entails have a special advantage in the use of information, as appears from considering those cases in which the shift of reference groups would take place between one group and a larger group that wholly includes it, ultimately reaching a group as comprehensive as "society as a whole."

Inevitably, if the shift occurs in this way, toward more and more inclusive reference groups, it is accompanied by another change: The policy under consideration becomes more and more inclusive. For example,

(a) The question whether or not it conduces to the utility of Group G to adopt Policy P

may become

(b) The question whether or not it conduces to the utility of Group G′ to adopt Policy P′, under which Group G may choose (or be allowed to follow) Policy P because it conduces to the utility of G,

which at the next stage becomes

(c) The question whether or not it conduces to the utility of Group G″ to adopt Policy P″, under which group G′ may choose, on grounds of greater utility, Policy P′, under which group G may choose Policy P because it conduces to the utility of G,

and so on.

The more inclusive policy questions thus generated are inevitably more obscure than the less inclusive ones: With each additional stage, there is an added dimension of variation in possible policies. For example, the question whether or not society as a whole would benefit more from having Yale's resources channelled into arts and crafts instead of astronomy is a much more obscure question than the question put to the Yale community of whether or not astronomy should be sacrificed. All the difficulties of evaluation—the multiplicity, fluidity, and conflict of values—are aggravated by shifting to the larger reference groups.

The strategy that we have described, in its tendency to avoid grand questions and in its provision for fragmentation, makes the best of this situation. The presence of myriad quasi-autonomous groups, which is the precondition of fragmentation—of having a general social policy evaluated by many different groups, each from its own perspective—is also a precondition for effective delegation, for having policies determinately tested and chosen, part by part, by the groups with both the means and the concern to test them. If it makes sense to hold that the weights of various utilitarian considerations are to be settled *ad hoc* and therefore settled differently on different occasions, then it makes sense to hold that the power to settle them should be pluralistically distributed to match the distribution of information.

The remedies that the strategy of disjointed incrementalism offers to the difficulties of evaluation and decision-making thus not only illuminate some of the problems of ethics but also cast some light deep into political philosophy.

NOTES

1. This historical statement and the qualified reference to Aristotle above have been influenced by points made by Elizabeth Anscombe in *Intention* (Oxford: Basil Blackwell, 1957).

2. Florian Znaniecki, *The Social Role of the Man of Knowledge* (New York: Columbia University Press, 1940), p. 86.

3. Quoted in *A Survey of Contemporary Economics*, I, ed. Howard S. Ellis (Homewood, Ill.: Richard D. Irwin, Inc., 1948), p. 417 (our italics). See also Bergson's original article, "A Reformulation of Certain Aspects of Welfare Economics," *The Quarterly Journal of Economics*, LII (1937-38), 310-334. In *Foundations of Economic Analysis* (Cambridge, Mass.: Harvard University Press, 1947), Paul A. Samuelson takes over the idea in this sense of a general function whose shape is determined by specific decisions regarding ends (pp. 219 ff.).

4. In an interesting comment on welfare economics in *A Survey of Contemporary Economics*, II, ed. Bernard F. Haley (Homewood, Ill.: Richard D. Irwin, Inc., 1952), Melvin W. Reder assumes without question that the social welfare function is a manifestation of the rational-deductive ideal. Ruefully contemplating objections to the Bergsonian social welfare function and other leading notions of recent welfare economics, Reder writes, "But the wreck of *formal* welfare theory has not and ought not to prevent economists from making specific policy recommendations. Such recommendations are the proper subject matter of welfare economics, and the development of a set of axioms from which these various recommendations can be deduced is merely an instrument for facilitating the rendering of still further recommendations" (p. 35). He goes on to suggest that, regardless of the success or failure of formalization, economists can develop effective "*ad hoc* criteria" for making recommendations and that it would very likely be a good thing to use a plurality of such criteria (p. 36). These remarks are entirely in the spirit of the present book. In a footnote, Reder indicates that they are not to be taken as entirely typical of his own position, for he does not mean "to deny that a single welfare criterion (in the sense of a single set of axioms sufficient for all welfare judgments) should be

sought, but to assert that its achievement is no *sine qua non* for welfare theorizing" (p. 36).

5. Kenneth J. Arrow, *Social Choice and Individual Values* (New York: John Wiley & Sons, Inc., 1951), p. 23.

6. Jan Tinbergen, *On the Theory of Economic Policy* (Amsterdam: North Holland Publishing Company, 1952), p. 1.

7. Our conception of a method that might embrace any of a great variety of rules, ranging from those that attempt to be scrupulously fair and sensitive in response to variations in individual orderings to those that are so perverse that they entirely ignore the existence of such orderings, exactly accords with Arrow's, which makes him a suitable source of illustration. Arrow, of course, is concerned with the problem of discriminating, within the field of possible rules, between satisfactory and unsatisfactory ones. We are not—when we come, later in the book, to treat the subject of distribution, we shall not identify it with the subject of preference.

It may be useful to point out that the problem with which Arrow is concerned does not present an insuperable difficulty to adopting the radical conception of the social welfare function as a method of evaluating policies, even for those who find the anomalies discovered by Arrow great drawbacks. Arrow demonstrates that, where there are three or more alternatives, and individuals' orderings are conceived to vary every which way, *no* rule or function can be supplied that will satisfy certain apparently reasonable conditions for producing a consistent social ordering reflecting personal preferences. This is a stunning conclusion—but it is also an abstract and theoretical one, from which a practical man has a chance of recovering. One may hope that circumstances will not in fact be such that the rule or function one adopts will eventuate in any of the anomalies detected by Arrow's very general theory.

8. Many readers will be struck by the difference in character between the adaptations we try to codify in this book and the refinements of method now pursued enthusiastically under the names of operations research, activity analysis, systems analysis, and electronic computation. In an era in which these refinements are fruitfully being explored and applied, the adaptations of analytical method that we rescribe may seem backward and retrospective.

We by no means wish to set ourselves in opposition to these refinements. We are simply pursuing a quite different approach, describing as it turns out not methods by which "scientific" problem solving can be extended but methods by which, for problems that are much too complex for "scientific" problem solving, analysts can turn to strategies that appear to fall outside its range. We see no conflict between the two kinds of method or strategy, and we think that the fruitfulness of each can best be understood when contrasted with the other.

We want especially to acknowledge the significance of high-speed computation in extending the possibilities of rational calculation for policy analysis. Some problems of policy analysis that have hitherto been treated by something like the strategy described in this book can now be treated with the help of computers. So far as the sheer quantity of data and operations have obstructed realization of the rational-deductive ideal or the welfare function this obstacle has in many cases probably disappeared. The boundary between problems that can be solved by calculation and those that must be treated by a strategy of multiple adjustments has thus shifted. With the development of more and more sophisticated computer techniques, the boundary may be expected to go on shifting. We are not so rash as to predict when and where it will stop shifting.

We can say, however, that it has not yet shifted so far as to abolish the predominance of strategic techniques in policy evaluation; nor is it likely to do so in the future. To suppose otherwise is a fantasy—to misunderstand both 1) the functioning of computers and 2) the sources of difficulty in evaluation. Difficulties do not arise merely from the quantity of data or the quantity of operations. Basically, they arise from the fact that values must be co-ordinated without fixed co-ordinating principles.

Computers are marvelously flexible instruments of calculation. When they are programed in certain respects, they can develop their own programs in other respects (e.g., they can find an algorithm and then store it for future use). Everything that a computer does, however, depends on the original program it is given and on subsequent inputs. These must be selected outside its operations. How is this to be done? Selecting the original program and the sequence of inputs raises, in cases of social policymaking, all the difficulties that we cite against the rational-deductive ideal and the welfare function. The presence of computers may well inspire attempts to formulate real-world problems of social policy in ways capable of machine-solution. Some of these attempts will no doubt succeed. But whether they succeed or not depends essentially on whether the coordination of values they achieve corresponds accurately to the coordination that is socially desired. What that coordination is, however, can frequently not be discovered without resorting to a complex social process in which strategic techniques must play a large role.

This process can be simulated by computer programs. Indeed, simulation seems to us the most promising way of finding out more about it. Simulation may reveal that there are relatively simple processes at work, on the basis of which the strategic techniques that we describe could be simplified and otherwise improved. Nevertheless, in this connection, too, the social process retains its autonomy and so do the techniques employed in it. There cannot be a serious question of bringing the social process to a halt and substituting a general computer program for it. The difficulties that obstruct the coordination of values, except as coordination can be achieved *ad hoc* by multiple adjustments, are real difficulties, which rest on real complexities present in our society and in the characters of its members. The development and readjustment of those complexities will continue to require social attention so long as social intercourse continues.

9. Karl Popper, "The Poverty of Historicism," *Economica*, XI–XII, N.S. (1944–45) (published in book form, London, 1957); *The Open Society and Its Enemies* (London: George Routledge and Sons, Ltd., 1945), revised in 1952, 1957.

10. Gunnar Myrdal, *Value in Social Theory* (London: Routledge and Kegan Paul, 1958). See especially the introduction by Paul Streeten.

11. See *The American Style, Essays in Value and Performance,* ed. E. E. Morison (New York: Harper and Brothers, 1958), especially the essay by Abraham Kaplan and comments by Carl Kaysen.

Notes to Chapter 2

1. A rather generalized argument for doubting that an approximation to an ideal is desirable when the ideal itself is unattainable has been much discussed in recent years by economic theorists. Considering alternative policies that approximate the competitive ideal, R. G. Lipsey and Kelvin Lancaster, for example, have shown (in "The General Theory of Second Best," *Review of Economic Studies,* XXIV [1956–57], 11–32) that failures to meet some of the conditions of the competitive ideal undermine the desirability of meeting others. Similarly, we are arguing, *not with respect to alternative policies, but with respect to alternative ways of analyzing policies,* that failure to meet some of the conditions necessary for the rational-deductive ideal or the ideal of the welfare function calls into question the desirability of aspiring to those ideals at all.

This observation about the theory of the second best, as applied to choosing among methods for analyzing policy, is not to be confused with our later observations in the closing pages of Chapter 5 about the same theory applied to choosing among policies themselves.

2. Duncan Black, *The Theory of Committees and Elections* (Cambridge: Cambridge University Press, 1958), p. 125.

3. Economists are accustomed to represent the phenomenon of satiation of desires through the analytical device of a demand schedule or indifference schedule that postulates a stable relation between amounts of values available to the demander and intensity of desire for marginal increments of them. The dependence of one's preferred choice upon costs of achieving various alternatives is simultaneously represented. The inference of a stable structure of preference behind apparent instability and fluidity is analytically useful, especially for small repetitive choices among goods and services in which even the chooser himself begins to see a stable pattern. In public policy choices, however, the inference of a stable structure, while useful for certain analytical purposes, is not to be confused with an inference that choosers or analysts are aware of such a stability. Their choices are not so repetitive as to permit them to perceive a stable underlying structure, if indeed there is one. They are, of course, aware of their stable commitments to such vaguely described values as liberty, security, equality, or progress, but these indefinite commitments leave their more specific, politically relevant preferences quite fluid.

4. Pendleton Herring, *Politics of Democracy* (New York: Norton, 1940), especially p. 102 and ch. 18.

5. These and other shortcomings of utility theory are developed in Lindblom, "The Handling of Norms in Policy Analysis," *The Allocation of Economic Resources,* ed. Moses Abramovitz and others (Stanford: Stanford University Press, 1959).

6. R. A. Dahl, *A Preface to Democratic Theory* (Chicago: University of Chicago Press, 1956), p. 124.

Notes to Chapter 3

1. The kind of problem we are talking about when we use the term "problem solving" is, of course, the kind of problem that calls for a decision or a policy. And the kinds of decisions and policies we are talking about are, of course, those pertaining to public affairs. We normally use the terms "problem solving," "policy-making," "decision-making," and "policy analysis" synonymously. In some passages, however, we choose among them with an eye to their individual colorations, even though we do not wish to stop to draw distinctions among them. Later we shall want to draw a distinction, for the moment both unnecessary and troublesome, between "decision-making" in its usual sense and "policy-making," in which the latter term encompasses both decision-making and the course that policies take as a result of interrelations among decisions and/or in which the latter term incorporates certain political processes, in addition to analytical processes, into the determination of courses of action.

2. Jan Tinbergen, *Economic Policy: Principles and Design* (Amsterdam: North Holland Publishing Company, 1956).

3. Marshall Dimock, *A Philosophy of Administration* (New York: Harper and Bros., 1958), p. 140.

4. John Dewey, *Logic* (New York: Henry Holt, 1938), p. 172.

5. Arthur Smithies, *The Budgetary Process in the United States* (New York: McGraw-Hill, 1955), p. 16.

6. Herbert A. Simon, *Administrative Behavior* (New York: Macmillan, 1959), p. 83.

7. James G. March and Herbert A. Simon, *Organizations* (New York: John Wiley and Sons, Inc., 1958), pp. 137 ff.

8. *Ibid.*, p. 138. The distinction between risk and uncertainty is the conventional one: A decision maker faces risk "if each action leads to one of a set of specific outcomes, each outcome occurring with a known probability"; he faces uncertainty if any action among the alternatives contemplated "has as its consequence a set of possible specific outcomes, but where the probabilities of these outcomes are completely unknown or are not even meaningful" (R. D. Luce and Howard Raiffa, *Games and Decisions* [New York: John Wiley and Sons, 1957], p. 13).

9. J. S. Bruner, J. J. Goodnow, and G. A. Austin, *A Study of Thinking* (New York: John Wiley and Sons, 1956), chs. 4–5.

10. Donald M. Johnson, *The Psychology of Thought and Judgment* (New York: Harper, 1955), p. 109.

11. Charles M. Hardin, "Political Influence and Agricultural Research," *American Political Science Review*, XLI (August, 1947), pp. 668–686.

12. John Dewey, *How We Think* (Boston: D. C. Heath, 1910), p. 106.

13. Michael Polanyi, *Personal Knowledge* (Chicago: University of Chicago Press, 1958), pp. 49–50.

14. Karl Popper, *The Open Society and Its Enemies*, I (London: George Routledge and Sons, Ltd., 1945), pp. 138–144.

15. Herbert A. Simon, "A Behavioral Model of Rational Choice," *Quarterly Journal of Economics*, LXIX (February, 1955), 99–118. But see also S. Siegel, "Level of Aspiration and Decision Making," *Psychological Review*, LXIV (July, 1957), 253–262.

16. Richard C. Snyder and Glenn D. Paige, "The United States Decision to Resist Aggression in Korea: The Application of an Analytical Scheme," *Administrative Science Quarterly*, III (December, 1958), 376 ff. (our italics).

17. Martin Meyerson and Edward C. Banfield, *Politics, Planning, and the Public Interest* (New York: The Free Press of Glencoe, 1955), pp. 279–280.

18. "There exists no known algorithm which will guarantee a win or a draw in checkers, and the complete explorations of every possible path through a checker game would involve perhaps 10^{40} choices of moves, which a 3 millimicroseconds per move, would still take 10^{21} centuries to consider." A. L. Samuel, "Some Studies in Machine Learning Using the Game of Checkers," *I.B.M. Journal of Research and Development*, III (1959), 211–212, cited by S. Watanabe in *Dimensions of Mind*, ed. Sidney Hook (New York: New York University Press, 1960).

19. March and Simon, *op. cit.*, p. 138.

20. Roland N. McKean, *Efficiency in Government Through Systems Analysis* (New York: John Wiley and Sons, 1958), ch. 2.

21. Donald M. Johnson, *op. cit.*, p. 63.

22. George Humphrey, *Thinking* (London: Methuen and Co., Ltd., 1951), p. 312.

23. And sometimes the synthetic problem corresponds almost exactly to one of the "original" subproblems. That is to say, the analyst believes that the problem of some one group can be taken as the organizing and dominant problem for organizing some number of problems.

24. James W. Fesler, "National Water Resources Administration," *Law and Contemporary Social Problems*, XXII (Summer, 1957), 445.

Notes to Chapter 4

1. B. F. Skinner, *Walden Two* (New York: Macmillan, 1948).

2. Woodrow Wilson, *First Inaugural Address*, 1913, cited by John R. Moore in testimony before the Kefauver subcommittee on antitrust and monopoly, July 16, 1957.

3. A more exact statement of the conditions and the explanation of their necessity to democracy will be found in R. A. Dahl and C. E. Lindblom, *Politics, Economics and Welfare* (New York: Harper and Bros., 1953), pp. 294 ff.

4. James W. Fesler, "National Water Resources Administration," *Law and Contemporary Social Problems*, XXII (Summer, 1957), pp. 468 ff.

5. In other countries, incremental characteristics may have been less

prominent. Speaking partly from his own experience, one of the critics who helped us most with useful and penetrating comments on a draft of this book cited the change in Great Britain from a peace economy to a war economy as a striking example of comprehensive plans smoothly and successfully applied. That his impressions had some foundation we do not wish to deny. Yet the testimony of other participants seems to reflect an incremental process. Professor E. A. G. Robinson, for example, writing on "The Overall Allocation of Resources," in *Lessons of the British War Economy*, ed. D. N. Chester (Cambridge: Cambridge University Press, 1951), maintains that "The development in the years 1939 to 1945 was wholly empirical. There was no . . . conscious thought in the early stages of a definite goal in the form of the perfect war economy towards which we were moving. At each stage we relied on the working of the normal incentives so far as they were practicable, and replaced them only to the extent that they appeared at a particular moment to be working badly in a particular field" (p. 35). Although Robinson considers that "the manpower survey and the manpower allocations" that were "the backbone of the central planning in the later phases of the war" (p. 52) were on the whole quite effective, he writes that manpower planning was "always done for comparatively short periods only. There was no official and agreed long-term appreciation of the manpower position two years or more ahead. The departments had to use their own judgment about the planning of extensions of capacity, in almost complete darkness as to the likelihood that a sufficient proportion of the progressively diminishing manpower resources would come their way" (pp. 54–55). Robinson goes on immediately to make the interesting comment, "While this is a valid criticism, it would not be true to say that it was a criticism often advanced during the actual course of the war. It may be that departments, irked by central control, did not wish to add yet another link to their fetters. It remains that I have no recollection of actual demands for longer-term manpower forecasts or of refusals to undertake them" (p. 55). Our argument in this book will invest this comment with a great deal of added significance.

6. Luther Gulick, *Administrative Reflections from World War II* (University, Ala.: University of Alabama Press, 1948), p. 3. The data about industrial mobilization in the United States in this and succeeding paragraphs are taken from Gulick.

7. *Ibid.*, p. 6.

8. *Ibid.*, pp. 27 ff.

9. *Ibid.*, pp. 37 ff.

Notes to Chapter 5

1. Karl Popper, *The Open Society and Its Enemies*, I (London: George Routledge and Sons, 1945), pp. 139–44 and 245n.

2. Charles S. Hyneman, *Bureaucracy in a Democracy* (New York: Harper and Bros., 1950); W. W. Rostow and Max F. Millikan, *A Proposal: Key to an Effective Foreign Policy* (New York: Harper and Bros., 1957).

Why these two books? We examined a number of samples of policy analysis, developing criteria of selection as we encountered features in one example or another that disqualified it. It might have been expected that we would choose some of the older classics of social science that are widely known among all the disciplines, but the classics tend to be theoretical or descriptive and therefore too short on policy analysis for our purposes. Similarly, journal articles are too short to permit illustrations of method that do not incur the risk of stretching an author's thinking into a larger context than that of his article itself. We came to decide that we wanted excellent pieces of policy analysis, representative of the best practices of the professions, that are not idiosyncratic and that, taken together, are representative of more than one discipline. A number of works satisfy these criteria, but in addition we, of course, had to restrict our choice to pieces of policy analysis that happened to be written in such a way that we could lift short quotations that would constitute self-contained statements or illustrations of the author's method. This last requirement considerably narrowed our alternatives.

3. As economists will recognize, this and other points pertaining to marginal adjustment of values can be stated even more formally at some cost in persuasiveness to noneconomists.

4. If the welfare function method is taken in its usual form to prescribe a ranking of all "technologically" possible states, then it achieves formally or in principle some adjustment of ends to means, even though it does not point to a practicable way of achieving that adjustment.

5. We can hardly fail to acknowledge all that John Dewey has written on the interdependence of means and ends, for example, on the impossibility of separating the postulation of values from empirical inquiry and the necessity of evaluating ends in the light of means. (See, for example, his *Logic* [New York: Henry Holt and Company, 1938], ch. 9.) If we add anything to Dewey on the interdependence of means and ends (and to others who have made similar points), it is in our attempt to show that policy analysts have achieved a sort of systematic adaptation to these interdependencies, while attending at the same time to other troublesome aspects of evaluation.

6. Economists in particular may ask at this point, if not sooner, what relation the strategy might bear to that implicit in the theory of the second best (R. G. Lipsey and Kelvin Lancaster, "The General Theory of Second Best," *Review of Economic Studies*, XXIV [1956–57], 11–32). According to that theory a policy-maker should, at least in some circumstances, no longer aspire to meet certain preconditions of a desired social state once he finds that certain other preconditions cannot be satisfied. If various features of the strategy of disjointed incrementalism are taken as normative, they prescribe, *inter alia*, moving away from known ills even if ideal states are not known; moving to "better" situations without either defining or hoping for the "best"; and moving serially along the same lines. In these and other respects, it seems that one who practices the strategy seeks a second best, or even a third or nth best, rather than striving for an ideal.

If, however, the practitioner of the strategy is seeking a second or nth best rather than an ideal, it is not for the reason noted in the theory of the second best—that some of the preconditions of best are not met, thereby calling into question the desirability of aspiring to the ideal at all. In problem situations in which the strategy is employed, the ideal usually cannot even be specified. In the eyes of one practicing the strategy, therefore, the theory of the second best is pertinent only to a very special or unusual case in which an ideal is identified.

Those economists who have discussed the theory of the second best have such a case in mind, that is, a situation in which the competitive ideal is held to be relevant for certain economic policies like tariff policies or policies toward monopoly. In circumstances in which such an ideal can indeed be contemplated as a policy target, would a practitioner of the strategy subscribe to the doctrine that, if some of the conditions of the ideal are not satisfied, the other conditions should not be sought? Our examination of the strategy suggests that often there will be a strong case for pursuing the ideal with respect to certain preconditions even if other preconditions are not met. We have seen that when policy-making is fragmented, any one independent policy-maker can be viewed as attacking his problem well or badly if his relations to other policy-makers—each in his own eyes acting independently—are taken into account. In a fragmented decision-making process, there will presumably be many circumstances in which a kind of implicit agreement to strive for certain desired conditions will serve as a useful operative rule. Any one policy analyst will sometimes do well to assume that, in the pursuit of an ideal like the competitive ideal, other policy-makers' failures to meet the conditions of the ideal are only temporary. He would not in general be wise to assume that their failures relieve him of an obligation to seek to meet those preconditions of the ideal that are related to his policy choices. This will be true, we say, in "many circumstances." We need not identify the circumstances beyond saying that they must be those characterized, *inter alia*, by an ideal that is not beyond the range of incremental choice.

In short, the policy-making implications of the theory of the second best conflict with the strategy as much as they harmonize with it.

What we have said here about the relation of the second best to choices among policies should not be confused with what we said in note 1 to Chapter 2 on the second best argument applied to the choice, not among *policies*, but among alternative *analytical methods* for choosing policies.

7. See, for example, Gustav Radbruch, *Der Geist des Englischen Rechts* (4th ed., Göttingen: Vandenhoeck and Ruprecht, 1958), p. 56.

8. *Ibid.*, p. 10. The difference between a "code system" of law and a "case system" or a system based on precedent is a commonplace among writers comparing English and continental law. See, for example, Arthur L. Goodhart, *English Contributions to the Philosophy of Law* (New York: Oxford University Press, 1949). Goodhart writes of a "basic difference between a legal system which follows a code and one based on precedent. Under the code system, which is theoretically regarded as complete, every novel case must be placed logically under some existing principle. . . . But when we turn to the common law we find that the system is not regarded as being theoretically complete, and that when a novel case—a case of first

impression—arises, then it is the duty of the judge to create the necessary principle which will govern the case" (pp. 32–33). His power to create, of course, is supposedly narrowly limited by the existing precedents most nearly applicable. In a footnote on p. 30, Goodhart joins a French jurist in defending Blackstone's efforts at synthesis against those who, from admiration of "the piecemeal case-system," carry their opposition to codification to extremes. For the same distinction between two conceptions of law, see C. K. Allen, *Law in the Making* (6th ed., Oxford: The Clarendon Press, 1958), pp. 157–158. Allen draws the distinction between "deductive" and "inductive" theories of judicial decision. He is inclined to minimize the supposed difference between them. He nevertheless takes the difference as the point of departure for a long discussion.

9. In a comment immediately following, Radbruch indicates that such an approach to the law has the same limitations as the strategy. He brings us back to the point about its unsuitability for crisis:

> Waiting for the lessons of future individual cases and developing legal thinking from case to case is possible, however, only so long as deep chasms do not appear between one case and another, and only so long as the development flows steadily in the same stream, without going through locks or over waterfalls. When disturbed social relationships press urgently for legal adjustment, general theories about the ends and means of the law must be ready to hand, as must a philosophy of law—and a policy about it. For just this reason, the rapidly changing relationships of American society have come closer to bringing about a rebirth of legal philosophy than the intellectual climate of England, which up to the Second World War was a much calmer place (pp. 53–54).

10. Cited by Radbruch, pp. 9–10 (in German, without documentation). We are indebted to Calvin Woodard for locating this passage in Macaulay's *History of England*, Vol. III (New York: Harper and Bros., 1856), p. 67.

11. Radbruch, *op. cit.*, especially pp. 36–37.

12. Radbruch, *op. cit.*, p. 39.

13. See note 8 to Chapter 1.

Notes to Chapter 6

1. Not all policies unacceptable in the near future to decision-makers belong to the nonincremental and politically irrelevant class. Fesler's proposed "apolitical" reforms of national water resource administration, for example, though unacceptable to Congress, fell within the ranges both of the incremental and the politically relevant.

2. *The Spectator*, CCIII (November 20, 1959), p. 690.

3. Martin Meyerson and Edward C. Banfield, *Politics, Planning, and the Public Interest* (New York: The Free Press of Glencoe, 1955), pp. 280 ff.

4. *Ibid.*, p. 282.

5. Note, then, that we are drawing a distinction between the advantages of serial and remedial policy analysis (coupled, of course, with serial and

remedial policy-making) and the advantages of deliberate experimentation in social reform. Our conception is that each policy step is made on its merits and not as an experiment. Popper's concept of piecemeal social engineering seems to contemplate experiments (*The Open Society and Its Enemies*, Vol. I [London: George Routledge and Sons, Ltd., 1945], p. 144) in a way that we do not.

6. Victor A. Thompson, *The Regulatory Process in OPA Rationing* (New York: Columbia University Press, 1950), p. 77.

7. It is possible to distinguish among various processes of mutual adjustment in the following way: (1) A policy-maker defers to another policy-maker, that is, finds policies that do not adversely impinge on or make demands on another; (2) a policy-maker finds ways of pursuing goals without having to achieve, as a precondition, control over or agreement with any other policy-maker, even though he impinges on another; and (3) a policy-maker controls or manipulates another policy-maker through negotiation, including bargaining, or through other means. The adjustment process, which bears a relationship to mutual adjustment among enterprises in a market and the importance of which is not wholly subsidiary to the clarification of the strategy of disjointed incrementalism, is the subject of a forthcoming book by Lindblom.

8. We do not deny that there are many ways of introducing rules for consideration without committing oneself to advocating them. In order to bring out the advantages of themes without rules, we are taking extreme cases. We would argue—although the argument needs empirical confirmation—that any way of carrying on policy disputes as disputes about rules is likely to gravitate toward an inflexible form, such as that present in extreme cases. In practice, however, there are many degrees of flexibility, depending, for example, on how tentatively rules are suggested for consideration.

Notes to Chapter 7

1. If a policy is not prescribed, it is either permitted or prohibited; if it is not prohibited, it is either permitted or prescribed. This statement exhausts the possibilities, and we do not regard a statement of the form, "Any policy that has the feature H is permitted," as a moral rule. This is to some degree arbitrary, but harmless. For obvious reasons, no one has ever proposed to formulate "rules" regarding the vast majority of permitted policies. It may be noted, further, that we are using "rule" in a sense that would include both "rules" and "principles," which are sometimes distinguished. (For example, in a very useful and penetrating article by Marcus G. Singer in *Essays in Moral Philosophy*, ed. A. I. Melden [Seattle: University of Washington Press, 1958], pp. 160-177; also in Singer's *Generalization in Ethics* [New York: Alfred A. Knopf, 1961].)

2. Considerations of symmetry suggest that there might be a third kind of moral rule, related to the second general form in the same way that meliorative rules are related to the first (while peremptory rules straddle

both forms)—"pejorative" rules, the form of which would be, "Any policy with the feature of being *least* conducive to V is prohibited." A rule of this form would serve no purpose that would not be served equally effectively or more effectively by one of the other types of rule. We shall therefore ignore pejorative rules and treat meliorative and peremptory rules as if they divided between them the field of moral rules applying to policies.

3. The concept of function is not, of course, a necessary ingredient of peremptory rules (consider the earlier illustrative rule about birth control). Moreover, people who may be perfectly willing to have their thinking *reformulated* in the language of function may not use that concept in expressing themselves originally. It is, however, a concept very frequently and familiarly used in the discussion of social institutions, which is why we have pictured both sides in the dental controversy as using it. Not only does it help define perspective and thus lighten the burden of evaluation; it also helps people form a comprehensible picture of the social world. If this way of picturing the world is carried to an extreme, of course, a conception emerges of every social institution as having a limited number of rigidly defined functions quite distinct from the functions of every other institution. Such a conception might have room only for peremptory rules, never for meliorative ones.

4. The difference may suggest to some people that those who heed peremptory rules follow "principles," while those who use meliorative rules fluctuate according to the dictates of "expediency." These familiar terms of opposition do parallel (and therefore, help to vindicate) the distinction between "peremptory" and "meliorative," but they make a perverse distribution of honors. People who follow meliorative rules may be as steadily attached to them and as disinterested in applying them as opponents who cling to peremptory rules. As we shall point out, reasonable use of peremptory rules would very often involve admitting exceptions to them.

5. These lines of argument may be meliorative or they may not. One might be able to persuade people to make exceptions by appealing to familiar analogies or by citing the opinions of some revered person in authority.

6. Singer (see footnote 1 above) treats some peremptory rules as "principles"; and he makes the fact that "principles" have no exceptions, while "rules" (in the sense of "rule" that he adopts, which is narrower than ours) are always liable to have them, a point of distinction between the two.

7. If application of the peremptory rule is challenged in these ways and the challenges are made good, then either the rule will have been rendered inoperative within its range, in which case we assert nothing about it, or the rule will remain operative with modified effect, in which case what we are asserting continues to apply.

8. The distinction between meliorative and peremptory rules roughly mirrors a distinction, originated by Professor C. D. Broad (in *Five Types of Ethical Theory* [London: Kegan Paul, 1930], pp. 162–164) and often used by contemporary philosophers, between *teleological* ethical theories, which make a consideration of consequences as the supreme test of right or wrong, and *deontological* theories, which claim there are at least some ultimate principles of obligation that disregard consequences. Broad's distinc-

tion, however, has been applied to theories about the foundations of ethics rather than to forms of moral rules. It makes use of the concept of obligation, which our exposition has dispensed with, and it turns upon whether or not decisive attention is given to consequences, whereas our distinction turns upon whether or not the question of accepting a given policy is normally decided without specifying the alternatives. We do not claim that peremptory rules involve a disregard of consequences; consequences are to be considered in arriving at an appropriate description of any policy to be judged. A sensible deontological theorist would perhaps admit that some consequences of actions would have to be incorporated into the concept of the actions themselves, before it could be discovered whether or not a moral rule applied to them. Such an admission, however, would threaten the distinction between actions and consequences on which, according to Broad, his position depends. A further reason for drawing our own distinction and using our own terms is that we do not wish to imply allegiance to any familiar "solution" of the dispute between teleological and deontological theories: for example, S. E. Toulmin's contention that the first apply to relatively sophisticated discussions of whether or not to adopt a rule or a practice incorporating rules, while the second apply to invoking rules that fall under accepted practices. (S. E. Toulmin, *The Place of Reason in Ethics* [Cambridge: Cambridge University Press, 1950], pp. 154–155.) We would rather say that both meliorative and peremptory rules are current at every level of moral discussion and that rules of the one kind are not necessarily ultimately justified by any selection of rules of the other kind, either in the opinion or in the practice of persons who use both kinds. These topics will be discussed further in later chapters.

9. Would an approach using peremptory themes rather than peremptory rules be as "open-minded" and as flexible as an approach using meliorative themes? There is always, as a matter of logic, a greater danger of restrictiveness in the case of peremptory themes, for if anything like a peremptory rule is invoked to apply them, it will be more restrictive than a meliorative rule operating over the same range of alternatives. The restrictive effect, moreover, is likely to occur even in the absence of formulated rules, for alternatives can be excluded from consideration without invoking rules. The mere suggestion that the peremptory theme of "socialized medicine" would tell against a certain policy may suffice to exclude it from consideration. On the other hand, one must recognize that the restrictive potentialities of a peremptory approach may be associated with behavior that is in fact rather flexible. The people who take peremptory stands—even stands purporting to be stands on rules—may be more easily shaken by contrary opinions and quicker to change their minds than the people who adopt meliorative approaches. This seems unlikely, but the question cannot be answered firmly without statistics.

10. It is possible that participants in such a dispute would have peremptory rules to the effect that unicameral or bicameral city councils were prescribed or prohibited. We are assuming that is not the case.

Notes to Chapter 8

1. The properties of individual persons to which distributive themes call attention may be designated as "original properties of persons"—being happy, for example, or healthy, or educated, or having access to books or to swimming facilities. (Since there is some lack of elegance in speaking of "having access to books" as a property of a person, we also speak of properties of a person's individual situation or circumstances.) Original properties of persons give rise to derivative properties of groups. In contrast to these properties are original properties of groups—for example, being numerous, being hierarchically organized, having written laws—with which there may be connected "derivative properties of person"—such as belonging to a populous nation, belonging to a hierarchically organized society, belonging to a society that has written laws. There are tricks involved in making this distinction exact and explicit. We could say that attributing original properties to one person does not imply the existence of other persons; to attribute derivative properties to a person implies that other people exist and that the person in question belongs as do the others to the same organized society (or at least to the same set of people, the membership of which is assumed to be relatively stable). But this way of making the distinction goes too far for our purposes. Although it allows for properties, like being able to speak a language, that can only be acquired through social training *in the past*, it does not include among original properties of persons various relations to subgroups of a given society: Having educational opportunities, for example, if it means anything more than having access to books, involves having teachers and fellow-students. Therefore, we define the difference between original properties of persons and derivative properties by assuming an organized society, and specifying as original properties of persons those that a person may have regardless (logically) of the continued existence of S or of any organized society larger than S; such properties may require the continued existence of groups smaller than S, which would be included in S if S continued to exist.

2. Aristotle holds that distributive justice requires distributing honors and money and other such things, both desired and divisible, proportionately to the merits of the citizens receiving them; but he deliberately leaves open the question of what shall be considered merits, recognizing that, with different conceptions of merit, different patterns of distribution will be prescribed. Aristotle, *Nicomachean Ethics*, Book V, chs. 2 and 3.

3. Another way of serving it would be to augment the rule for interpreting a three-place census. Suppose, in a *three-place* census, Policy B would, as above, make thirty people robust, fifty middling, and twenty feeble, while Policy C would make forty people robust, ten middling, and fifty feeble. Or suppose that C would make sixty people robust, ten middling, and thirty feeble. There would then be a much stronger inclination among people with remedial interests to draw a conclusion favorable to B in the first case than there would be in the second, though the inclination would

exist in both cases. In both cases, however, the inclination goes beyond general conventions for comparative judgments about groups. In the case of fish and bananas, all these results would be indeterminate for judgments about groups as a whole.

4. Suppose the original census had shown:

	Policy A	Policy B
Robust	20	30
Middling	40	50
Feeble	40	20

Consistent with these results a six-place census might show:

	Policy A	Policy B
Very Robust	15	5
Robust	5	5
Healthy	40	40
Under-par	30	30
Feeble	5	5
Very Feeble	5	15

On the one hand, this liability to reversal by more refined evidence is simply a characteristic that census results share with all empirical information. On the other hand, there are limits in practice to the multiplication and refinement of categories. The categories used in a census must be intelligible in themselves, so that the census-takers—those who might actually try to classify every member of the population or sample—can apply them. They must also correspond to the policy-makers' notion of what differences in health, for example, are important enough to require heeding. People know very well how to distinguish between robust persons and feeble ones, but when we speak of "robust" versus "very robust" persons, we are already moving beyond the crude distinctions that are in steady use in ordinary language. Producing an acceptable *ad hoc* distinction between "eminently robust," "very robust," and "fairly robust" would be still more problematical, and the problem would be one that the challenger, not the people who took their stand on fewer categories, would have to solve. The logical possibility of multiplying categories and reversing results does not, therefore, seriously undermine the census idea in practice. It must be borne in mind, furthermore, that when reversed results are obtained, the policy-makers are not bound to choose between the original proposals only. In a case like the one above, they might redesign a policy so that it dealt separately with the "robust," "middling," and "feeble" groups of the first census, incorporating the successful features of different policies as they applied to each group. In effect, they would be proceeding according to a battery of two-place censuses carried out separately for the three separate groups identified in the original three-place census. Starting with this base, they would seek to improve it—incrementally—in every department.

5. See Chapters 1 and 2 above.

6. Compare the possibility, which is considered now and then in the writings of economists (for example, in recent unpublished work by Owen Aldis), of escaping the limitations of the Paretian criterion by identifying

the strength of preference with the strength of primary drives or wants like hunger. A social policy that made a difference as regards preferences so conceived would make a corresponding difference in terms of a census.

Notes to Chapter 9

1. In his *Treatise of Human Nature*, Book III (1740) and his *Inquiry Concerning the Principles of Morals* (1752), works that can hold their own in insight and penetration with any subsequent works in ethics, certainly any in English.

2. In his *Introduction to the Principles of Morals and Legislation* (1789) and in other works.

3. This definition is (deliberately) sweeping in at least three different respects. (a) It disregards the difference between interpreting utilitarianism as a *descriptive* ethical theory, which undertakes to explain what criteria people actually do use in making moral judgments, and interpreting it as a *normative* theory, which undertakes to set forth the criteria that people *ought* to use, even if they were required to change their habits, including their habits of language. We shall treat utilitarianism as if it aimed to be *both* descriptive and normative and as if its proponents would retreat from claims to describe all or part of the field of received moral discourses only under extreme pressure.

(b) The definition does not embody the thesis of Bentham and his followers—that the sole concern of morals with actions and policies is the greatest happiness of the people affected by those actions and policies—nor does it include the subsidiary Benthamite thesis that happiness may be interpreted as an algebraic sum of pleasures and pains. Many people would regard these two theses as distinguishing marks of utilitarianism. Hume, however, does not propound either thesis. He gives a plural list of values, of which happiness may be representative, but which are not necessarily entirely reducible to it: "the happiness of mankind, the order of society, the harmony of families, [and] the mutual support of friends" (*Inquiry*, Sec. II, Part II). Hume gives no indication that he considers even this list exhaustive.

Cf. G. E. Moore's argument against utilitarianism taken as embodying the Benthamite theses, which is to the effect that besides pleasure, love and knowledge, indeed, "an *immense variety* of different things," are intrinsically good (*Ethics* [London: Home University Library, 1912], pp. 247–248). But Moore himself is as much a utilitarian as a critic of utilitarianism. He is commonly reckoned among the proponents of "ideal" utilitarianism, holding as he does that "the total consequences of right actions must always be as good, intrinsically, as any which it was *possible* for the agent to produce under the circumstances" (*op. cit.*, p. 227). For "ideal," one might simply put "pluralistic."

(c) The definition clearly offers the utilitarian family of theories extraordinarily generous room for overcoming moral objections. Suppose some objections cannot be turned aside. Can they not be incorporated into a set of moral judgments recognized as not subject to dispute and made presuppositions of a utilitarian theory? Given some reasonably comprehensive selection of meliorative and distributive considerations positively associated with social welfare and group happiness, it seems plausible to suppose that a utilitarian theory might succeed in covering the whole field of intelligible or valid moral judgments left outside the set recognized as beyond dispute and hence acknowledged as presuppositions. If the set of presuppositions was very large and rich in content, the resulting theory would not be very powerful; it would still be utilitarianism by our definition.

4. See A. J. Ayer, *Language, Truth and Logic* (2nd ed. [London: Victor Gollancz, 1946]) and C. L. Stevenson, *Ethics and Language* (1944). The emotive theory, although it may be represented as a modern elaboration of Hume's basic thesis that there is an indispensable connection between moral judgments and emotions, does not attempt, like Hume's doctrine, to inquire into the *sort* of emotion that consorts with the various logical features demanded of valid moral judgments (see below, p. 212). Stevenson, for one, is very careful to state that it goes only far enough to make some general points about moral discourse that are logically preliminary to analyzing in detail the criteria that people invoke for moral judgments. The theory calls attention to certain dimensions of meaning in moral expression, neglect of which has led to philosophical confusions—the "noncognitive" dimensions that express emotion and convey prescriptions. Logical positivists (as well as a great many other philosophers who would not call themselves by this name) generally follow the emotive theory in according these dimensions great importance, but at least from this point on they have no official ethical theory. Some positivists (early Ayer and early Carnap) have been inclined to call all moral judgments strictly meaningless; others (e.g., Schlick) have gone on to develop a form of classical hedonism. Development on Humean lines is another possibility—we think the most judicious one.

5. Nor is it the end of the story. The theory may seem to be required for the ultimate value judgments upon which we may conceive all others to rest—for must they not be postulated and laid down without any show of proof? This is to assume that there is already a unique axiomatic system implicit in received moral discourse. It is true that no arguments can be given *within the same system* for value judgments that are taken as axiomatic for the system. But received moral discourse is no more an axiomatic system than is ordinary language generally and we are not bound to select any particular moral values as axiomatic. We can, in ordinary language, give reasons of sorts to justify any of them, and we can choose to treat any of them either as axiom or theorem. It remains to be seen whether the values invoked in received moral discourse can all be comprehended within any axiom system. It would be most surprising, if it could be axiomatized at all, that it could be axiomatized in only one way. Logic itself (e.g., the propositional calculus) is susceptible of many different axiom systems.

6. Cf. Stevenson, *op. cit.*, ch. 7.

7. Bentham, *Principles*, ch. IV, par. V, § 6.

8. The presuppositions mentioned have to be qualified to allow for punishing criminals, and further attention to peremptory rules (for example,

to the prohibition of *ex post facto* legislation) might well be required in defining what sorts of actions were to be regarded as criminal. (In the last chapter of the *Principles,* Bentham disavows *ex post facto* laws, because, he says, the punishments they might prescribe would be inefficacious.)

9. John Stuart Mill, *Utilitarianism,* ch. 2.

10. F. Y. Edgeworth, *Mathematical Psychics* (London: C. K. Paul, 1881).

11. In comparing the condition of a given population at two different times, one must of course allow for births and deaths and for immigration and emigration, the rates of which are affected to some extent by the policies of the community. But if the very policy that is being considered has the consequence of eliminating some members of the group by death or banishment (forced emigration), it cannot be claimed that it ameliorates the condition of the same population; the policy throws open the question of the identity of the population as normal continual changes do not. With a policy of forced emigration, if the emigrants are traced and their fate taken into account in the census, then the comparison is of course valid in the normal way; but only then.

12. See our discussion of the census notion in Chapter 8.

13. John Rawls, "Justice as Fairness," *Philosophical Review,* LXVII (April, 1958), 164–194.

14. Rawls, *op. cit.,* p. 167.

15. In Bentham's case, if he is interpreted this way, the most common interpretation of the felicific calculus must be abandoned in favor of one that parallels the census notion, with stipulations against mixed changes and changes of persons.

16. Hume, *Treatise,* Book III, Part II, Sec. II; and Part III, Sec. I.

17. The most substantial and penetrating contemporary discussion of utilitarian arguments for nonutilitarian moral rules is to be found in another article of Rawls's: "Two Concepts of Rules," *Philosophical Review,* LXIV (January, 1955), 3–32. For different views, see J. J. C. Smart, "Extreme and Restricted Utilitarianism," *Philosophical Quarterly,* VI (1956), 344–354, and *Outline of a System of Utilitarian Ethics* (Melbourne: Melbourne University Press, 1961). See also Richard B. Brandt's *Ethical Theory* (Englewood Cliffs, N.J.: Prentice-Hall, 1959), ch. 15. Smart and Brandt have not seen all the reasons for insisting that the rules be upheld without variations (even the best intentioned) decided upon by individual moral agents.

Notes to Chapter 10

1. Bentham cannot be said to have evaded them entirely. He speaks of "pain" and "pleasure" as "names of homogeneous real entities" (*Principles,* ch. VI, footnote to par. VI), distinguished from causes of pain and pleasure, which he considers to be "various fictitious entities." It is by no means clear what he means by this distinction, but it suggests some sort of phenomenological priority for pain and pleasure, which would put them on the same footing as (say) heat and light and noise. If this suggestion is

taken up, there is no recourse for Bentham against the objections mentioned, so far as the calculus goes, nor against the objection that men do *not* take pleasures as their goal (but at most situations with which pleasures are associated), so far as his general assumptions about motivation are concerned.

2. John Stuart Mill accepted this objection (see again, *Utilitarianism*, Ch. 2) and has been much criticized on this account for inconsistency with his professions of utilitarianism. Accepting the objection does not, however, entail abandoning utilitarianism or even the felicific calculus. It entails only recognizing that the reduction of happiness to pleasure is more complicated than Bentham imagined.

3. More work, it is true, has gone into calculi whose units are not interpersonal but professedly hold good only for individuals observed singly. A number of theories and experiments on this line have been inspired by Von Neumann and Morgenstern's suggestion that subjective utilities can be measured by considering how the consumer evaluates various chances of receiving different goods. These theories may be sampled in R. D. Luce and H. Raiffa, *Games and Decisions* (New York: John Wiley and Sons, 1957), and in D. Davidson, P. Suppes, and S. Siegel, *Decision Making* (Stanford, Cal.: Stanford University Press, 1956). The possibility of finding an interpersonal basis for such measurements—that is to say, one that would permit observers not only to calculate quantities for an individual subject but also to add results from different subjects and calculate averages—does not seem to have been entirely precluded, even by the newly discovered difficulties about variations in "subjective" probability. On the other hand, no wholly convincing way of obtaining units for interpersonal comparisons has been discovered, although such attempts as those of Robert McNaughton ("A Metrical Concept of Happiness," *Philosophy and Phenomenological Research*, XIV (December, 1953), 172–183; Goodman and Markowitz (discussed by Luce and Raiffa, *op. cit.*, pp. 345–348); Hickman and Kuhn, *Individuals, Groups and Economic Behavior* (New York: Dryden Press, 1956), pp. 155–179; and Owen Aldis (in work as yet unpublished) suggest that the pursuit is not hopeless.

4. See Chapter 8.

5. Another way of meeting the objection is to restate the felicific calculus (as we suggested above) as a proposal for identifying and weighing pleasures, so that their effect on happiness is preserved; the distinction between higher and lower pleasures would then be incorporated in the calculus.

6. H. L. A. Hart and A. M. Honoré, in *Causation in the Law* (Oxford: The Clarendon Press, 1959), pp. 64 ff., describe certain restrictions that commonly govern the ascription of consequences to given actions, e.g., consequences will not be traced back beyond certain sorts of intervening actions or coincidences. If one man drops a match, but the ensuing fire would have gone out if a second man had not fanned it back into life, then subsequent damage would be a consequence of the second man's action, but not of the first's. Restrictions of this kind do not dispose of the problem of consequences, however. It does not follow, from the application of the restrictions, that only a manageably small number of consequences will be left to evaluate. Moreover, the restrictions cited by Hart and Honoré can

be applied only retrospectively. They are no actual help to agents or policy-makers trying to evaluate actions and policies beforehand. One cannot assume, beforehand, that the chain of consequences is going to be broken by an intervening action on someone else's part or by a coincidence. It is true that the sort of *jeu d'esprit* that people sometimes play with historical consequences—like tracing the discovery of America under Spanish aus-pices to the attractions that Cleopatra displayed to Caesar and Antony—gives results that would not be amusing if they were not felt to be far-fetched. They would not be amusing, however, if they were senseless re-sults. None of the concepts employed is used inconsistently or incoherently; they are pushed too far, but they have not been pushed over any exact boundary.

7. Consider the following statement by a philosopher of some renown: "We have at least constantly to take consequences into account, even if the utilitarian is not right in saying that, for deciding what we ought to do, the good and evil consequences *alone* matter. . . . However the way to evaluate the consequences of an action does not lie through any quasi-mathematical calculus. . . . All we can do is consider all the appreciable advantages and disadvantages of which we can think in regard to each of the alternative actions between which we choose, and having done this see what the total impression is on our mind, taking into account also the de-gree of probability of attaining the results we desire and the risk of any unintended evils. . . . Having thought as far as possible of all importantly relevant considerations, we then see in what state of mind we are put by our whole process of thinking, i.e., how we are impressed by the influence of all those considerations taken together." (A. C. Ewing, *Ethics* [London: English Universities Press, 1953], pp. 70–71.) Notice that Ewing sees the task as one that we are each responsible for performing ourselves. If we could each work out a complete account of consequences, we should each do so. Since we cannot, we must pile up as many facts as we can and assess them intuitively.

8. Bentham, *op. cit.*, Chap. I, first footnote. Bentham means, of course, all those who are liable to be affected, pleasantly or otherwise, not merely those who are aware of the question and curious about it. Hume speaks similarly of "the interest of those who are served by the character of action approved of" (*Inquiry*, Sec. V, part I).

INDEX